M000281327

Sustainable Residential Development

Sustainable Residential Development

Planning and Design for Green Neighborhoods

Avi Friedman

New York Chicago San Francisco
Lisbon London Madrid Mexico City
Milan New Delhi San Juan
Seoul Singapore Sydney Toronto

The McGraw·Hill Companies

Library of Congress Cataloging-in-Publication Data

Friedman, Avi, 1952-
  Sustainable residential development : planning and design for green
neighborhoods / Avi Friedman.
      p. cm.
  ISBN 0-07-147961-9 (alk. paper)
  1. Ecological houses--Design and construction. 2. Sustainable
engineering. 3. Planned communities. I. Title.
TH4860.F68 2007
307--dc22

                              2007020264

McGraw-Hill books are available at special quantity discounts to use as premiums and sales promo-
tions, or for use in corporate training programs. For more information, please write to the Director
of Special Sales, Professional Publishing, McGraw-Hill, Two Penn Plaza, New York, NY 10121-2298.
Or contact your local bookstore.

Sustainable Residential Development: Planning and Design for Green Neighborhoods

Copyright © 2007 by The McGraw-Hill Companies. All rights reserved. Printed in the United
States of America. Except as permitted under the Copyright Act of 1976, no part of this publication
may be reproduced or distributed in any form or by any means, or stored in a database or retrieval
system, without the prior written permission of publisher.

1234567890 QPD QPD 01987

ISBN-13:   978-0-07-147961-5
ISBN-10:   0-07-147961-9

Sponsoring Editor   Cary Sullivan   **Production Supervisor**   George Anderson
Project Editor   Janet Walden   **Composition**   Tolman Creek Design
Copy Editor   Lisa Theobald   **Art Director, Cover**   Jeff Weeks
Proofreader   Francesca Ferrie   **Cover Designer**   Jeff Weeks
Indexer   Claire Splan

 This book was printed on recycled, acid-free paper containing 10% post-consumer waste.

Information has been obtained by McGraw-Hill from sources believed to be reliable. However, because of the
possibility of human or mechanical error by our sources, McGraw-Hill, or others, McGraw-Hill does not guarantee the accuracy, adequacy, or completeness of any information and is not responsible for any errors or omis-
sions or the results obtained from the use of such information.

To Sorel, Paloma, and Ben

About the Author

Avi Friedman received his Bachelor of Architecture degree from the Technion-Israel Institute of Technology, his Master of Architecture degree from McGill University, and his Ph.D. from the Université de Montréal. He is the Director of the Affordable Homes Program at the McGill University School of Architecture, where he is a professor.

Dr. Friedman has written extensively on subjects ranging from sustainable construction practices to urban planning. He is the author of the books *The Grow Home*; *Planning the New Suburbia: Flexibility by Design*; *The Adaptable House: Designing Homes for Change*; *Peeking Through the Keyhole: The Evolution of North American Homes* (with David Krawitz); *Room for Thought: Rethinking Home and Community Design*; and *Homes Within Reach: A Guide to the Planning, Design, and Construction of Affordable Homes and Communities*.

Dr. Friedman has designed the *Grow Home*, a narrow-front rowhouse that was built in various countries, and the *Next Home*, a model for sustainable design and construction. His design work and projects have been covered extensively on television shows such as ABC's *Good Morning America*, *Dream Builders*, and Stewart Brand's *How Buildings Learn* (BBC); in magazines such as *Popular Science, Architecture,* and *Home*; and in newspapers, including the *New York Times, Los Angeles Times,* and the *Times of London*. He has spoken at many meetings of development authorities, homebuilders, architects, planners, and in universities. He has received numerous awards for his research, design, and teaching, including the American Institute of Architects Education Honors, the Association of Collegiate Schools of Architecture Creative Achievement Award, the Progressive Architecture Research Award, the Manning Award for Technological Innovation, and the United Nations World Habitat Award.

Contents

Preface

Global warming, depletion of non-renewable natural resources, and urban sprawl have become global challenges. Decades of poor planning, inconsiderate building practices, and overconsumption of goods have done little to reverse course in the residential environment. This book is about the steps that need to be taken to alter that course.

The term *subdivision* suits most suburban developments. Land is partitioned with disregard to the site's natural features, wide roads are paved, and oversized residences with huge garages and big expanses of picture windows are constructed. Identical homes attract households of similar demographic background and means, robbing the place of relationships that sprout when people of different age groups and incomes mix. The common sense that led the development of neighborhoods in earlier centuries has been abandoned.

The thrust of this book is to reintroduce common sense to the design of neighborhoods. The principles of community that are proposed in this book are the outcome of my examination of environmental, social, and economic concerns during residential neighborhood planning and after occupancy. The approach in this book is a stark deviation from that of contemporary developers, who initiate processes in which a few aspects, be they stylistic or monetary, are the focus. Residents' needs and the area's natural conditions are often ignored, while the initiating party's financial objectives are the focus of these developments. Affordability, proximity to open spaces, and privacy still hold great promise and attraction, yet these considerations must be reconfigured to align with other concerns brought about by the twenty-first century.

Principles of *sustainable development* represent a better approach. Sustaining present needs, while considering the needs of future generations, is the focus of this book, which offers discussions of these principles and presents projects that demonstrate them. The scope of sustainability includes a variety of manifestations. Both the conception processes and, once built, the life span of the communities and homes are important considerations. Each chapter deals with one stage in the process, from selecting a site while conserving its natural conditions, to siting a development, planning for a denser community, designing "green" homes, rehabilitating neighborhoods and dwellings when they age, and finally implementing it all. The text walks the reader through historical roots, planning and design principles, and a project in which the thought process, its application, and its outcome are described.

Chapter 1 offers fundamental terms, recalls the contemporary genesis and interpretation of sustainability, adds an expanded definition and formulates principles to evaluate the merit of sustainable communities, reviews the role of key stakeholders, and provides a sketch of a sustainable place. Learning from the past is essential to charting a road to the future, and Chapter 2 is devoted to the historical evolution of the neighborhood and the rise of suburbia. Chapter 3 discusses items that need to be considered in residential project site selection. The relationships between nature and society are traced, principles are listed, and a detailed project with an integrated approach to sustainable design is described.

The need to offer a response to the many negative consequences of rampant urban sprawl led to my writing Chapter 4 on denser neighborhoods. When proper planning strategies are adopted, even dense communities can maintain many of the attributes that draw people to suburbia. This chapter reviews the evolution of high-density living, outlines planning and design principles, and demonstrates their implementation.

Chapter 5 discusses dwellings whose design and mode of operation make careful use of resources. Past roots of such settlements and homes are traced, and design and construction principles are outlined. The later part of the chapter offers an in-depth look at a community that integrated a number of sustainable planning and design principles.

Planning for and regarding the renewal of a community as a large recycling and retooling project, while respecting urban and architectural heritage, is the subject of Chapter 6. Neighborhoods and homes are built onto history, and life-cycle approaches must accompany their planning process. When a neighborhood's physical and social standing decline, extra efforts are required to place them back on good footing. Heritage conservation is discussed, guidelines are laid out, and the rehabilitation of a neighborhood and its renewal along sustainable principles is described. Finally, Chapter 7 offers considerations for implementing sustainability. It lists general criteria for acceptance of innovation, describes common certification methods, and presents demonstration projects.

If I were to illustrate the thrust of my own professional work, it would likely be a row of homes standing tall next to each other. Over the years, in collaboration with others, I have studied, designed, thought out, and advocated for common-sense neighborhoods and homes. The work spans from physical features that enhance the web of community relations, to the reduction of resources necessary to build and operate such places. I hope this book successfully shares the knowledge I have gathered and helps decision-makers and professionals design neighborhoods using sustainable principles.

Acknowledgments

The sources that inspired the writing of this book span many years and include a number of research and design projects. My work over the years has involved many colleagues whose names are listed here and in the Research and Project Teams section. My thanks extend to them all, with my apologies to those whose names I accidentally omitted.

The impetus to write this book began with a grant from the U.S.-based Woodcock Foundation to study sustainable residential development patterns. Special thanks are extended to Jeremy Guth and Joyce Jenkins, who initiated and facilitated the process. Martine B. Whitaker, a talented and dedicated research assistant, was another motivator. She contributed to the research and writing of the historical introduction at the outset of each chapter and some of the principles in the book's present version. She also insisted that I publish this book, and for that, many thanks.

Cary Sullivan, my editor at McGraw-Hill, embraced the book and sped up the proceedings. Project editor Janet Walden and copy editor Lisa Theobald were instrumental in turning the manuscript into a book.

A number of people participated in background research. Joanne Garton helped collect and organize and write material for the "Green Homes" chapter, and in particular the EcoVillage section, which she also photographed. Wendy Schuster helped with information on several segments, and Annette Fuher offered editorial assistance.

Jennifer Steffel collaborated on research on the genesis of cities. With David Krawitz and Qin Lin, I co-authored a paper that inspired the urban renewal chapter. Vince Cammalleri was instrumental in the Greening the Grow Home research project and cast ideas to the chapter on implementing sustainability; his contribution to technical matters is much appreciated. The work of Jim Nicell, Francois Dufaux, Joanne Green, Susan Fisher, Aud Koht, Kevin Lee, Aryan Lirange, Denis Palin, Mark Somers, Nicola Bullock, and Michelle Takoff, members of the Green Grow Home team, also inspired and contributed to the writing of the chapter on green homes. Thanks to Daniel Casey for his coordination of the West Island project and contribution to the "Features of Sustainable Community" section. Thanks to Liz Walker, Rod Lamber, and the residents of the EcoVillage at Ithaca for showing us around and providing material about their inspirational community.

Many participated in the conception and the production of the book's graphics. Fu Mingcheng, Clara Shipman, Michelle Côté, Janice Wong, Juan Mesa, Jack Goldsmith, Wendy Schuster, and Erin Shnier were involved in the project at various stages. Special thanks go to Jeff Jerome for his meticulous work, dedication, organizational skills, talent, and useful suggestions in giving the graphics their final look. Heritage Canada and the Montreal Chambre of Commerce provided grants through which their work was made possible.

Special thanks is also extended to Nyd Garavito-Bruhn. Nyd's hard work and dedication in organizing the data, editing, and preparing the book for printing is much appreciated.

I would also like to offer a vote of gratitude to the McGill School of Architecture for its support of the Affordable Homes Program, where many of the research projects took place. My colleagues, collaborators, and students were sources of inspiration.

Finally, my heartfelt thanks and appreciation to my wife, Dr. Sorel Friedman, and children, Paloma and Ben, for their love and support.

Fundamental Terms and Principles

Unsustainable is perhaps the best term that describes the lack of common sense that characterizes contemporary suburban residential development. Present consumption of natural resources at the expense of future need is the hallmark of today's development environment. Numerous definitions, interpretations, and suggested strategies and remedies exist for this unsustainable predicament. However, prior to offering a discourse and demonstration of *sustainable* planning methods, this chapter will discuss the concept of sustainability itself. It traces the roots; elaborates on terminology, components, and concepts; establishes benchmarks; and sketches the elements that make up a well-designed, sustainable community.

Looking Homeward

The causes of environmental phenomena such as global warming, depletion of natural resources, and waste generation point to several sectors. Close examination of the data shows that the residential sector follows the industrial and transportation sectors in energy consumption, for example (Office of Energy Efficiency, 2006). This data comes as no surprise, however, because since the middle of the twentieth century, the size of an average North American home has undergone constant expansion, with significant environmental ramifications.

Most low-density, low-rise homes are constructed of solid sawn lumber. Considered to be an inexpensive, renewable resource with relatively low energy requirements, wood, for example, has become the material of choice over light-gauge steel in house building. According to the Nebraska Energy Office (2006), the amount of lumber necessary to build a 1700 square foot (160 square meter) wood-frame home, including its structure and finishes, consumes 1 acre (0.4 hectares) of forest. The figure becomes even more staggering when you consider that some 2 million dwelling units are constructed each year in the United States alone. The building process is also responsible for a large amount of generated waste. Some 8000 pounds (3.6 tons) of waste is produced when a 2000 square foot (190 square meter) home is constructed, all of which is shipped to landfills.

Along with expansion in home size, energy consumption has grown. According to the U.S. Energy Information Administration (2007), energy consumption in the residential sector rose from 14,930 trillion BTUs to 21,879 trillion BTUs between 1973 and 2005. Since some 60 percent of the total energy consumed in the residential sector is used for space heating, the energy increase can be attributed to an increase in home size, the number of windows installed, and poor construction practices. It can also be attributed to a number of features that have become standard in the modern home.

Air conditioners, large energy consumers and emitters of Chlorofluorocarbon (CFC) refrigerants, are quickly becoming the norm in North American households. According to a report by Natural Resources Canada (2005), 45 percent of Canadian households made use of some sort of air conditioning unit in 2003, compared with 25 percent in 1993. Some attribute the increase to the rise of hotter than average summers, while others argue that this is just another manifestation of the rise in North American household consumption. According to the report, the average room air conditioner uses roughly the same amount of energy in one cooling season that a refrigerator uses in a year. Furthermore, central air conditioners consume in one cooling season roughly the same amount of energy as the annual consumption of a refrigerator, range, and clothes dryer combined. The same survey suggests that appliance use is also on the rise. In 2003, almost 25 percent of households owned three or more television sets, and almost 33 percent used two or more refrigerators. Furthermore, of the primary and secondary refrigerators owned by these families, 67 percent of the main units and 35 percent of the secondary units were considered large, with capacities greater than 16.4 cubic feet (0.46 cubic meters). And, finally, a large increase in ownership of personal computers was noted between 1993 and 2003.

Another natural resource whose consumption rose is potable water. The average American household consumes approximately 409 gallons (1550 liters) of water per day (Mayer et al., 1999). With the expansion of the average lot size, outdoor irrigation accounts for 20 to 50 percent of residential water use depending on climate zone. An average American household also consumes some 173 gallons (655 liters) of water per day indoors. According to the American Water Works Association (1999), the average house contains two or three toilets with an average of 12 to 13 flushes per day.

Although the depletion of freshwater resources is not considered to be an imminent threat in most areas of North America, over-consumption in the residential sector contributes to major wastewater management problems common in most municipalities. Wastewater from homes must be treated before it can be released into local bodies of water. Municipal treatment centers, however, consume large amounts of energy and are limited in the amount of wastewater that can be treated at any one time before the system is overloaded. Since many municipalities treat stormwater and sewage together, problems arise with overloaded systems: overflow is released untreated into local bodies of water, creating a *combined sewer overflow* (CSO). In fact, such situations occur with surprising frequency. New York City's combined sewer and stormwater system, for example, overloads on average once per week, each year releasing an estimated 40 billion gallons (150 billion liters) of untreated wastewater, 20 percent of which is raw sewage, into local bodies of water (Hoffman, 2006). If frivolous residential consumption of water could be diminished, the load on municipal treatment centers would be reduced, and less untreated waste would be dumped into our water sources.

Residential energy consumption does not stop indoors. With low-density planning practices, North American homes have become highly dependent on private motor vehicles. According to Schwela and Zali (1999), the number of vehicles in use increased from 53 million in 1950 to 450 million in 1994. This vicious cycle contributes to decreased use of public transportation and leads to cutbacks in services provided, in turn making public transit less safe and attractive (Low et al., 2005). The negative effect of the growing number of vehicles equals more health risks, greenhouse gas emissions, and global warming. Although the particular composition of motor vehicle exhaust varies according to the type of fuel, the primary constituents that pose health risks are present throughout. Carbon monoxide (CO), nitrogen dioxide (NO_2), ozone, photochemical oxidants, and suspended particulate matter all contribute to the deterioration of urban air quality. Nitrogen dioxide contributes to respiratory complications such as reduced efficacy of lung defenses. Carbon monoxide also hinders the transportation of oxygen from the blood into the body's tissues, requiring more blood to circulate to deliver the equivalent amount of oxygen (Schwela and Zali, 1999).

In addition to the health risks, emissions from motor vehicles also pose an imminent threat to the general environment. Between 70 and 90 percent of carbon monoxide emissions in most cities come from motor vehicles. Cars also contribute to the greenhouse effect, and in turn to climate change, through the release of carbon dioxide (CO_2), methane, and nitrous oxide (N_2O). Road transport contributes 15 to 20 percent of carbon dioxide emissions worldwide (Organization for Economic Co-operation and Development, 1995).

Despite the health and environmental risks of fuel emissions, many North Americans purchase larger cars, such as minivans and sports utility vehicles (SUVs). In the 1970s, due to the gas crisis, many families opted for higher efficiency vehicles with smaller engines, but as fuel prices stabilized in the 1990s, the popularity of larger cars increased. According to Natural Resources Canada's 2005 report on energy efficiency trends in Canada, performance levels, or horsepower, of the average car owned by Canadians increased by 32 percent, from 118 horsepower in 1990 to 156 horsepower in 2003. Had this increase in horsepower not occurred in the 13-year span, the report states that today's cars would be an estimated 33 percent more efficient than current levels. Therefore, any attempts that were made in the last decade to render automobiles more fuel efficient were offset by North Americans' growing attachment to larger vehicles.

All this information paints a grim picture of the present and a threatening view of the future. We must rethink planning and design practices for our residential environments, and we must simultaneously sustain natural resources.

Roots and Definition of Sustainability

The proliferation of the term *sustainable development* and the conditions that brought it about can be traced back to the mid-1970s. In 1972, the United Nations Conference on the Human Environment in Stockholm dealt with concerns about the fact that humanity is stretching the carrying capacity of the earth to its limits (Canada Mortgage and Housing Corporation, 2000). The meeting served as a podium for the first international discussion on the relationship between ongoing environmental damage and the future of humanity. It was recognized then that population growth in some nations and over-consumption in others could not be sustained indefinitely, and that development practices leave noticeable footprints in the form of land degradation, deforestation, air pollution, and water scarcity. The Stockholm meeting led to the establishment of a number of international organizations, such as the United Nations Environmental Program (UNEP) and the International Union for the Conservation of Nature and Natural Resources (IUCN). The actions of these organizations put in place mechanisms that disseminated findings about the deteriorating state of the environment and recommended appropriate actions.

These initiatives laid the foundation for several widely accepted views, with the main one being that the stock of *non-renewable resources* on Earth is finite (CMHC, 2000). Years later, this reflection has led to the establishment of the World Commission on Environment and Development (WCED), also referred to as the Brundtland Commission, which is probably the best-known international initiative. In a 1987 report, *Our Common Future*, the commissioners defined sustainable development as "development that meets present needs without compromising the ability of future generations to meet their own needs." This definition established a conceptual approach to development, whereby any action taken must be pursued with its future effects in mind. The commission also created a paradigm for development whose main anchors are a need for social equity, incorporation of fair distribution of resources within and among nations, and the need to resolve the conflict caused by development pressures and the environment. Over time, these three underpinning issues and the relationships among them have become the standard through which the success of all development activities is judged.

Additional views and definitions of sustainability and the harmful effects of development on the planet were voiced in the writings of several scholars and became an ideological catalyst to the environmental movement. In *Small Is Beautiful: Economics as if People Mattered*, E. F. Schumacher (1973) drew a line between the economic effects of globalization and the environment. He directed attention to the disparity between developed and developing countries. Rachel Carson's book *Silent Spring* (1962) alerted society to the irreparable environmental damage caused by the use of man-made chemicals, especially DDT.

A perspective on society's ability to gain sustainability was expressed by Charles Kibert in "The Promises and Limits of Sustainability" (1999). He questions whether today's available natural systems and resources can meet the varied demands of rich and poor societies while leaving adequate resources and better environmental quality for future generations. According to Kibert, the realm of sustainability currently relies on *reduce-reuse-recycle* strategies to educate the public that resources must be used at a replenishable rate, allowing for biodiversity. Kibert questions how attainable this goal is, as we still face technological obstacles, unfavorable human behavior, and pure laws of physics. The Second Law of Thermodynamics, he reminds us, essentially states that the fate of all systems is degradation in energy and quality.

Kibert also argues that with the adoption of sustainable principles, society will still decline but will have a "soft landing" as the population adjusts to the level of the earth's resources. He suggests that as we pit the *anthropocentric view* (the planet is here for human use) against the *Gaia view* (Earth is a living system being destroyed by humans), being sustainable means recognizing that both views are in action—that is, while humans will always ravage natural resources, we will also be clever and adaptable, and we will increase efficiency, reduce material consumption, and adopt environmentally friendly behaviors.

Kibert believes that humankind's best attempt to attain sustainability will occur in stages—first with pollution control, second by minimizing lifecycle impacts, and third by developing technologies in sync with natural systems. The effort invested in reducing operating costs of buildings must be extended to designing buildings that can ultimately be entirely reused and recycled. The future, according to Kibert, lies in our realizing how helpless humans are against the greater forces of nature; we must respect natural systems to ensure our physical, economic, and social survival.

The interconnectedness of environmental, economic, and social concerns is also addressed by Stephen Wheeler. In *Planning for Sustainability* (2004), he lists these goals as part of a holistic approach, addressing them as the "Three Es" of *environment*, *economy*, and *equity*. Historically, according to Wheeler, since the 1960s, many advocates have focused on the environmental impact of buildings. The initial definition of the environment as a wilderness issue, however, was expanded to include every element that people see as part of their "environment," from air quality in homes and the use of toxic chemicals, to international development and global climate change. As the ecocentric approach to society takes root and grows, the intrinsic value of nature is being rediscovered and debates are emerging as to the limits of disturbing natural systems for human use.

According to Wheeler, equity, the least developed of the Three Es, is fought by most policymakers who wish to concentrate wealth and power in countries selectively and within people of one country. Within cities of developed countries, tax revenues continually benefit suburbs lined with malls and office parks, leaving empty city centers with old infrastructures in need of repair. Many city zoning officials resist multifamily units or low-income housing, ensuring that only costly single-family homes are created and that residents are not troubled with any effects of NIMBYism—the "Not in my backyard" mentality.

Although, at first glance, it seems necessary to pinpoint the definition of *sustainability* for the sake of effective use of the word, it becomes clear after considering the preceding ideas that the topic is broad and vague, because, at present, so many systems, issues, and thoughts are part of the environment and need to be sustained. Our efforts cannot be focused solely on the environment without repercussions in the economic and social realms. Similarly, decisions based purely on economic initiatives will affect the environment and local or global society, and actions driven by social concerns will have both positive and negative environmental and economic impacts. While scholars differ in their opinions of the best ways to achieve sustainability in the built environment, all seem to agree that the problems facing the environment and society are imminent and must be addressed at once if we hope to disembark from our current path of fostering negative effects on the earth.

The Scope of Sustainability

Considering environmental, economic, and societal aspects as equal underpinning elements in the planning of sustainable residential development is a benchmark of this book. These concerns differ from those of common private-sector development initiatives, which tend to focus primarily on monetary return on investment. This book's sustainable approach also differs from the purely environmentalist point of view, which regards nature and natural resources as encompassing and influencing decisions in other realms. When we attempt to give equal weight to all three aspects, a well-balanced, sustainable residential community where all concerns are addressed is more likely to emerge. None of the pivotal issues should be marginalized at the expense of others (Figure 1.1).

The first concern among the three factors reflects and responds to the social needs of a community's inhabitants and their values. *Social needs* is a broad, all-compassing concept that can be explained and interpreted in a multitude of ways. The following paragraphs will attempt to link the term to and articulate it with examples from residential development. When the creation of a sustainable health-care system, for example, is an objective, ensuring that sufficient funds will be continually available is a key factor. Contribution to public health can be achieved by encouraging fitness. People with an active lifestyle, it has been shown, are less likely to suffer from cardiovascular- and diabetes-related illnesses. It is, therefore,

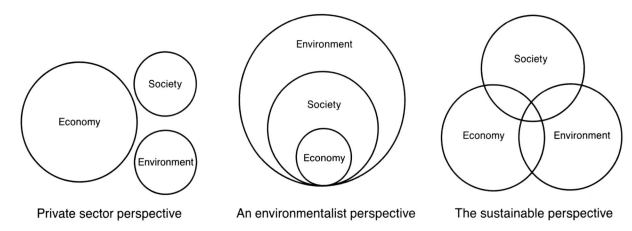

Private sector perspective   An environmentalist perspective   The sustainable perspective

Figure 1.1: Societal, economic, and environmental issues need to be considered equally in the process of developing sustainable systems.

in the best interest of society at large that neighborhoods be designed with bicycle lanes and pedestrian pathways and that residential and non-residential functions be integrated.

A similar argument can be made when considering the need to house families with modest incomes. When people rent their homes, they do not accumulate capital. They are also more likely to experience dire monetary need when they get older, as significant portions of a reduced income must be devoted to shelter. Some may become dependent on social assistance. It is, therefore, once more in the best interest of society, and community leaders in particular, to see that lower income households can be housed affordably.

Promoting vernacular culture and preserving heritage buildings also contributes to society in direct and indirect ways. Old buildings worth preserving are visible reminders of human history. People who appreciate the past contribute to the quality of buildings in the future. Converting and updating old buildings also helps reduce consumption of natural resources that may otherwise be used in the construction of new buildings.

Fostering economic sustainability is another objective with ramifications for community planning. The thrust is to avoid the transfer of costs, a result of bad present decisions, to future generations. In a privately run housing sector, such as the North American sector, planners may attempt to sustain prosperity by not imposing strict guidelines on developers who may, as a result, decide not to build at all or raise dwelling prices beyond reach of people with modest means. Building unnecessarily and excessively wide roads, for example, will have long-term economic implications. The streets will need to be resurfaced periodically, and more snow will accumulate and need to be removed in cold climate regions. When a development is privately initiated, the cost of wider roads will raise the price of each house, forcing buyers to borrow more money that they will have to repay over a longer period of time, thereby putting at risk their own financial sustainability.

Environmental sustainability relates to the ecological burden created by the construction and upkeep of a development, including its roads, open spaces, and homes. A "cradle-to-grave" cycle assessment is necessary when planning a development. It regards not only the initial effect of choice of materials, for example, but also their long-term performance and their recyclability once their use is ended. Asphalt-surfaced roads will make rainwater runoff stream to manholes. Creating a trench at the side of a road will promote the growth of rainwater flora when it is planted, thereby saving runoff. A similar approach can be taken in the construction of a house, where rainwater can be directed from roofs to holding tanks that can be used for household chores, including watering garden plants in dry periods.

The three pivotal factors critical to sustainable development can be viewed independently. Yet, when you closely examine the inner workings of residential development, designed and built on sound sustainable principles, you can see that the confluence of these three aspects is critical in its effects on the built environment; this confluence is the focus of this book (Figure 1.2). These three overlapping issues are presented here as a way by which concepts will be formed and applications illustrated. It is important that you understand the inner workings and the interrelationships of these aspects. General principles are, therefore, proposed in the following sections to help you better recognize how these relationships can take place.

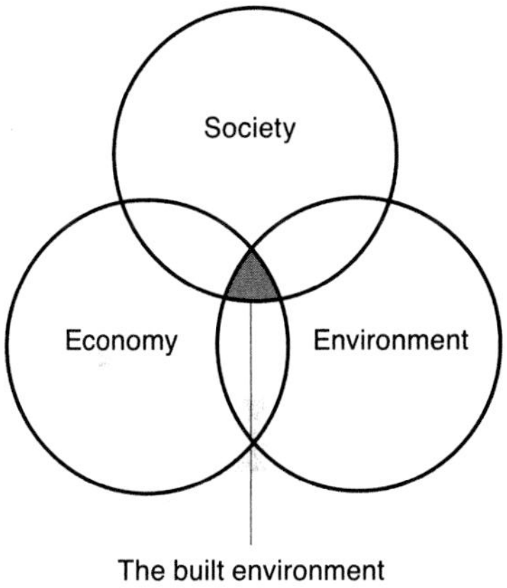

Figure 1.2: Sustainably built environments are a combination of societal, economic, and environmental considerations.

Principles of Sustainable Systems

The current systems of urban planning and dwelling design face challenges in both philosophy and form. With the turn of the twenty-first century has come the need to reconsider and reformulate traditional perceptions of urban sprawl, with its many far-reaching negative implications for society, the economy, and the environment. As we attempt to diagnose the root cause that led to poor suburban planning practices, we are led to the factors of ignorance of the inner workings of three pivotal issues: environment, economy, and society. Mainstream developments are often regarded as a *product*, rather than a *process*, in which a range of aspects are being systematically explored and manipulated. The process, the key issues, and the relationships between them are illustrated with four general principles. When followed, these principles can guide the conception of a sustainable residential community.

The Path of Least Negative Impact

Since the beginning of the twentieth century, and especially after World War II, poor development practices have left noticeable scars on our surroundings. Forested landscapes and verdant fields were cleared to make room for residential subdivisions with wide roads and lawns. Homes have swelled in size and complexity and have consumed excessive amounts of energy to keep them warm in winter and cool in summer. Such activities have had immediate and long-lasting damaging effects on both the local and global environments.

The path of least negative impact is the sustainable path that a decision-maker of any planning endeavor needs to choose—a path that will result in the smallest negative impact on the environmental, societal, and economic factors of a project. At the process's outset, impact assessments should be undertaken to ensure that decisions made during the planning stage will have limited short-term and no long-term disruptive ramifications.

A project can also have unwelcome economic ramifications. A high-priced luxury project in a neighborhood comprising low-income rental units may trigger conversion of properties into condominiums and force out residents. Poorly constructed homes may stigmatize its occupants and cost more to heat or cool. When such a project is constructed by a government authority, taxpayers will have to foot the bill throughout its lifetime.

Self-Sustaining Process

When a development is planned, minimizing the project's initial impact should be a priority. The project's lifecycle can also be viewed as a *self-sustaining process* of resources and activities. Metaphorically, you can regard the energy used in the project's conception and building as a generator of additional sources to power its existence and even contribute to the creation of additional similar projects (Figure 1.3). The self-sustaining principle is applied to each of the subcomponents that make up sustainable approaches to design that are listed in Figure 1.2.

For example, when homes are designed and constructed to include photovoltaic panels or solar collectors, energy generated through them can power the house and avoid reliance on public utilities. Similarly, when rainwater is gathered, purified, and converted into drinking water, the home will have a self-sustaining water source. If excess energy or water is produced, it can be used for communal needs. Additional stored energy, for example, can be used to power streetlights. A similar analogy can be made when a project's economic performance is studied. Successful projects will attract occupants which will lead to the rapid sale of units whose profit will be invested in initiating other projects. A self-sustaining initiative can also benefit from a proper mix of dwelling units. When a project offers homes to young families and seniors, a self-sustained social network is put in place. When needed, the young can care for their older family members who live in the same community.

Supporting Relationship

Another keystone of a sustainable project is the relationship of its pivotal parts. When a *supporting relationship* is established, attributes of one component can propel activity in another. Influence among disciplines and effects of one on the others will in turn create a supporting system. A design that seeks to leave the least environmental footprints on the site will see fewer trees cut and could become a marketing success. The project's economic outcome can benefit clients who will be attracted to the project due to its "green" image. A supporting relationship is therefore established between environmental and monetary interests (Figure 1.4).

The use of lower cost products made of recycled materials may help address environmental concerns but may also give a developer a price advantage over competitors and benefit the project financially. Building smaller homes in a denser configuration, for example, will result in a reduction of urban sprawl. It will also save on cost of land and infrastructure that, when transferred to eventual occupants, will produce affordable housing. Municipalities will benefit by ensuring a supply of housing that will help keep young, first-time homebuyers in the community, and create a much-desired social and demographic continuum.

A Lifecycle Approach

The mark of good decision-making for a sustainable system is a project's ability to sustain itself throughout its entire lifecycle. Be it through each of its compo-

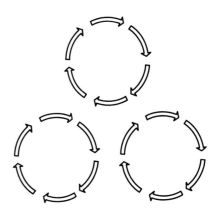

Figure 1.3: A sustainably built environment can become a self-sustaining generator of resources and activities.

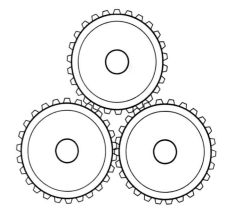

Figure 1.4: The project's three pivotal factors can propel each other, resulting in a supporting relationship.

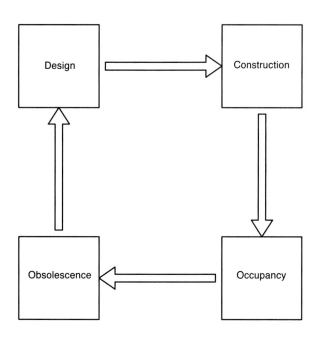

nents or their interrelationships, the conception and construction need to ensure that the original attributes of the project will be valued for years to come. If the project is well-conceived and economically successful, homeowners will be more likely to invest in maintenance and upkeep, such as replacing old windows with more energy-efficient models, which will contribute to energy savings. A well-built home will save its owner expenses on maintenance and operation in the long run. The longer the useful life of a project can be stretched, the more sustainable it is (Figure 1.5).

Figure 1.5: The thought process of a sustainable community needs to foresee the project's entire lifecycle.

A lifecycle approach sees the built environment subjected to an ongoing change and evolution. The process's elasticity and ability to adapt to various emerging circumstances are among its key attributes. A product with a finite life is less valuable than a product that can be refurbished and reused. When dwellings are designed for adaptability and can easily be modified to accommodate the needs of subsequent occupants, obsolescence and demolition are prevented. A similar view should prevail when codes and bylaws are created. They ought to provide a framework for action, yet not restrict the introduction of amendments and changes when times and circumstances require that they be introduced.

Renewable Resources

The practice of sustainable development is closely linked to the conservation of natural resources. Industrialized societies, some argue, use too many virgin resources and degrade the environment in many ways. Kibert (1999), for example, suggests that the built environment uses 40 percent of all extracted resources in most industrial countries and 30 to 40 percent of all generated energy. He argues that such practices cannot continue much longer without very serious consequences. The ability to protect the environment resides in the effective management of resources that can be replenished or reused, and in the efficient use of those that cannot.

Resources can be divided into three general categories. The first, *renewable resources,* such as water, air, fibers, and timber, are replenished through relatively rapid natural cycles. In theory, a renewable resource can last forever. However, all renewable resources are limited by the capacity of natural systems to renew them. For instance, natural processes that purify water do not occur at an adequate pace to replenish clean water that is consumed and reintroduced into the environment as waste. Learning to manage and use renewable resources is the proper study and practice of conservation. The management or conservation of renewable resources involves practices that preclude over-exploitation (Figure 1.6).

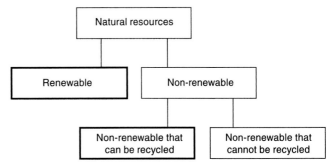

Figure 1.6: To lessen the burden on natural resources, a design process needs to seek use of renewable resources and non-renewable resources that can be recycled.

The second category, *non-renewable resources that can be recycled,* includes all non-energy, mineral resources that are extracted from the earth's crust. Ores of copper, aluminum, mercury, and other metals and minerals are some examples. As these minerals are mined, they are not replaced—at least not at a sufficient pace to be relevant within the human timeframe. However, people can collect these materials after they are used and recycle them.

The third category is *non-renewable resources that cannot be recycled,* such as mineral energy resources—fossil fuels, including coal, oil, and natural gas; and uranium, which is used for nuclear energy. Buchholz (1993) suggests that in 1 year, humans consume the quantity of fossil fuels that it took nature approximately 1 million years to create. There is no way of recycling the energy in fossil fuels, since once the energy has been released, it cannot be regained.

The construction and occupancy of homes uses up resources and generates waste. According to a study by REIC (1991), construction is responsible for 16 percent of the total solid waste production, and approximately 20 percent of this is from new homes. About 80 percent of this waste ends up in landfills, much of which can be avoided. The same study suggests that the construction of an average home produces 2.5 tons of waste, and 20 tons when demolition is required. Approximately 25 percent of the waste is dimensional lumber, and another 15 percent is attributed to manufactured wood products. This situation is not only wasteful in terms of embodied energy, but it also contributes to the problem of waste disposal.

Renewable Energy

Today's homes, larger in size, require more energy for heating and cooling and powering appliances compared to dwellings built decades ago. Much like natural resources, energy sources can be divided into renewable and non-renewable categories. Coal, oil, and natural gas are among the non-renewable sources, whereas solar, tidal, and thermal are among the renewable energies. Designers or sustainable communities should consider and evaluate common sources of energy used, and they should be aware of the renewable sources and their relevance to the domestic sector (Figure 1.7).

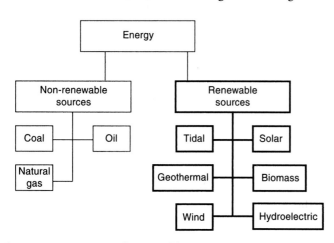

Figure 1.7: Designers of sustainable communities need to incorporate renewable energy sources.

The type of energy used in residences differs from region to region, yet oil, natural gas, and coal are likely to be the main sources in the Western world. Some counties have access to hydroelectric sources, and others draw their energy from nuclear power stations. Studies in the late twentieth century have made it scientifically evident that some part of Earth's energy supply will be exhausted during the twenty-first century. In other words, society is consuming energy at an unsustainable rate. If current consumption patterns continue, lack of energy resources can lead to significant global, social, and economic challenges.

Environmental problems caused by consumption of energy are another challenge. One of the troubling facts is global warming, a result of greenhouse gas emission. Carbon dioxide, which is released by burning fossil fuels, is causing a gradual increase of the average air temperature at the earth's surface. The phenomenon, according to scientists, is said to be responsible for severe droughts in some countries, the rapid melting of glaciers in the arctic and antarctic, and as a result, the rising level of oceanic water that threatens low-lying areas of Earth.

Another cause for concern is acid rain. Some of the gases emitted when fuels are burned, such as sulphur dioxide (SO_2), combine with atmospheric water and create sulphuric acid when they fall to the earth, causing damage to plant material and forests, which are of course necessary to maintain a balanced ecosystem and used as building products and other important goods. The need to halt and, where possible, reverse the damaging process is beyond urgent.

Among the energy consuming sectors in most countries, residential is listed right after transportation and industry in quantity used. According to Alexander (1996), around 85 percent of the energy consumed by dwellings is for low heat, such as space heating, water heating, and cooking. Consumption usually varies with increased activity in areas of colder winters and warmer summers. In Canada, for example, energy consumption in the residential sector increased by 13 percent between 1990 and 2003 (Office of Energy Efficiency, 2006).

Concerns about the unsustainable mode of harvesting non-renewable energy resources and the damage that their use is causing to the environment makes the use of renewable resources relevant as well as economical, considering the mounting costs of energy. The British Renewable Energy Advisory Group (REAG) defined *renewable energy sources* as "Energy flows that occur naturally and repeatedly in the environment and can be harnessed for human benefit" (Alexander, 1996). These sources are limitless and will not be depleted.

Perhaps the most recognized among the renewable energy sources is *solar energy*, which can be divided into *passive* means, those sources that do not require mechanical modes for harvesting, and *active* means. Since the characteristics of these sources will be elaborated later in the book, only general descriptions will be offered here. Tapping the Sun can be accomplished by proper orientation of the structure, placing large windows on south-facing elevations and smaller ones on the north (in the Northern Hemisphere). Suitable materials in the home can retain heat and release it later. *Active solar systems* include roof-mounted panels for water heating and photovoltaic panels.

Wind energy is another source used in the domestic environment with history dating back 5000 years to the ancient Egyptians. Since that time, windmills have been in use throughout the world, especially in the Dutch countryside. The 1970s energy crisis rekindled interest in harvesting wind and by some estimates, thousands of active turbines are now producing energy around the world. Many wind turbines are used to power homes and, in some cases, entire communities.

Geothermal systems, which are also referred to as ground-source heat pumps, are connected to the ground to make use of the very high temperatures within the earth's core. This renewable heat source has been harvested in a number of countries for residential use. The common technique is to drill deep holes through which pipes are inserted to take advantage of the high temperatures underground. Steam, or hot water, is then extracted, brought to the surface, and used as a power or heat source.

Hydroelectric power is another known source of renewable energy in countries that have rivers, both in developed and less-developed countries. The thrust of these systems is the creation of energy in turbines powered by water flow between different elevations. Despite the fact that hydroelectric dams produce renewable energy, opposition to their construction has grown because of the amount of area needed for their construction and the damage they cause to the environment.

Another source of renewable energy is biological, also known as *biomass*. It originates as solar energy absorbed by plants and through photosynthesis is converted into chemical energy. The best-known of this type of energy takes place when wood is burned, and wood provides much of the energy sources consumed by the developing world. Biomass energy can be harvested by burning wooden crops, municipal and industrial organic waste, and animal dung. Bio-gas produced by domestic waste buried in landfills is also included in this category. Other types of biological energy sources are bio-fuels, such as methanol or ethanol, which are produced when corn and other crops are processed.

Taking advantage of Earth's gravitational forces, which generate coastal tides, leads to the production of *tidal energy*. When the tide rises, water flows through gates in a dam to fill a pond behind it. When a sufficient quantity of water accumulates, its energy potential is processed through turbines and power generators.

The use of renewable sources of energy is continuing to expand, though an obvious disparity still exists between the developed and the less-developed world. Nevertheless, the use of energy has become more efficient with improved building practices and more demanding building codes.

Life Cycle Costing and Payback Period

Money often guides decisions by the builder or the occupant to invest in a technique or component that will yield better energy performance. Investors usually want to determine the return on their investment and how long it will take. Two techniques, *life cycle costing (LCC)* and *payback period,* are commonly used to determine these factors.

LCC is explained by Dell'Isola and Kirk (1981) as an economic assessment of competing design alternatives considering all costs of ownership over the economic life of each alternative expressed in dollars. The analysis deals with financial performance over time as a basis for decision-making. Therefore, it includes both "today" and "tomorrow" dollars. Since designing for sustainability involves a long-term view, the building or its parts will require investment, not only in its development and construction, but during its occupancy and renewal. To illustrate the process, consider the following example.

When alternative A, a choice between two heating systems, requires a $1000 initial expenditure, and alternative B requires only $800 now and another $200 in 10 years, which one should you choose? If alternative B is selected, the owner can commit $800 now and place a sum of money in the bank or in another investment opportunity that can grow with interest into $200 in 10 years. If the interest rate is 10 percent compounded annually, then only $77.10 must be deposited now. You could therefore say that the *present worth* of the second alternative is $877.10. This phenomenon is called *discounting*, for it discounts future dollars when comparing them to present spending.

Several terms are commonly used when LCC techniques are investigated. *Baseline date* is the present, today, when costs need not be discounted, as well as the point in time against which investment opportunities are measured (when a house-holder takes possession of a unit, for example). *Sunk costs* are those that occurred before the baseline years (before the householder takes possession). They are called *sunk* because they cannot be recovered. Usually these costs are considered in the analysis only when the technique is being used to assess all the costs associated with a given decision—past, present, and future. *Time horizon* refers to the ending point of the LCC analysis—the cut off, or last year of the analysis. This time horizon may be wholly or at least partially a function of the householder's objectives, which may intentionally stay in the unit for only a limited, predetermined number of years (Figure 1.8).

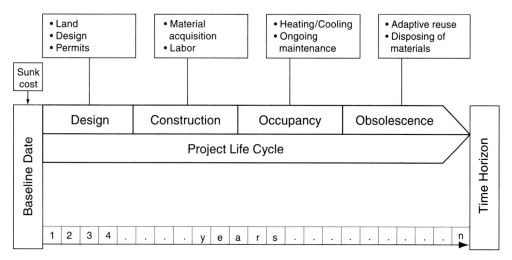

Figure 1.8: Key terms used in LCC analysis.

Some of the investments involved in elevating the building's energy performance, for example, can be referred to as *nonrecurring investments,* as they will be incurred only once. Some of the nonrecurring costs are a result of functional, physical, and economic obsolescence of the building elements. Others are *recurring*, such as the cost of repairing the brick joints periodically.

Before LCC analysis begins, a *measure* must be selected:

• *Total Present Worth (TPW)*   The analyst seeks to relate both today's and tomorrow's expenditures and bring in all costs in the analysis, regardless of when they are incurred, to a single present-day baseline. All future costs are simply reduced to their present worth and the total present worth costs for each alternative are summed.

• *Equivalent Uniform Annual Cost (EUAC)*   The analyst converts today's and tomorrow's expenditures to a uniform annual cost. This translates the total expenditures over a number of years to a constant amount for each year in the lifecycle. This measure indicates how many dollars, if paid uniformly over the lifecycle, would equal the total discounted lifecycle expenditures for each alternative.

The basic procedures of LCC is therefore identification of the alternatives to be analyzed, establishment of a time vocabulary for the analysis (baseline date, time horizon), selection of cost factors relevant to a user, determination of the LCC "measure" to be used, TPW or EUAC, and performance of the analysis and study of its results.

The *payback period* studies the length of time necessary to recover the initial investment of a project. The simplest form of payback makes no allowance for the time value of money. That is, it is an expression of how fast an individual can recover the initial investment. It can be expressed as follows:

$$n = C / S$$

where C is the initial cost (in dollars), S is the annual savings (in dollars per year), and n is the number of years it will take for the initial cost to be recovered, also known as the *simple payback*.

However, the expression does not account for the fact that if the initial amount of money were invested elsewhere, it would earn interest. In addition, to provide an estimate of the true time value of money, it is also necessary to account for inflation. Therefore, true payback is discounted payback expanded to allow for escalation. It can be calculated using the following formula:

$$n = \frac{\log[1 + C/S(1 - 1/k)]}{\log k}$$

where C/S is the simple payback (Brown and Yanuck, 1985). The constant k accounts for the time value of money and is calculated as follows:

$$k = \frac{(1 + e)}{(1 + i)}$$

where e is the escalation rate (inflation rate) and i is the discount rate (interest rate on invested money).

When calculating a payback period, assumptions of interest rates expected in years to come must be considered, as well as the rate of inflation. In addition, the cost value C used in calculations of true payback is not the total initial investment that is made, but rather the difference between the investment made and a traditional investment. For example, in the calculation of the payback of a low-flow toilet that will save on water consumption, the cost used is the cost of a low-flow toilet over and above the cost of a traditional toilet. This strategy has been taken since devices such as toilets, windows, and home heating systems must be bought and installed in a new home, anyway. Therefore, the additional cost of choosing environmentally friendly technologies must be overcome in the design.

The Key Players

Building sustainable communities requires participation and contribution on the part of all players throughout the project's lifecycle. This section distinguishes between types of housing projects to help you recognize each key player's motive, and, at times, barriers to the building of a residential development based on sustainable principles (Figure 1.9).

Governments

All levels of government are, both directly and indirectly, involved in housing their citizens. Another obligation is to manage natural resources efficiently and to contribute to the creation of local sustainable systems. It is, therefore, in the best interest of any government to see that its citizens are not only housed adequately, but also that the resources used in the construction and upkeep of the homes are

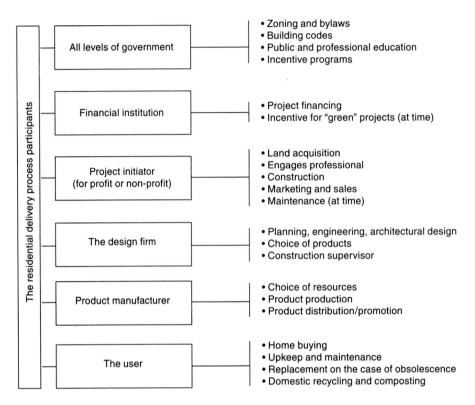

Figure 1.9: The building of sustainable communities requires participation and contribution on the part of all the process's key players.

well-managed. With the growing importance of negotiated environmental protection agreements, such as the Kyoto Protocol, governments also must meet international obligations to keep emission levels within set limits.

In North America, governments traditionally play a modest role in home-building. The act of building is left to the private sector. When governments do build, they produce dwellings known as *public* or *community housing*. Regulation is the primary tool through which authorities control environmental performance of its manufacturing, transport, and building sectors. Different levels of governments set building code standards and zoning laws that exercise control over the end product. It is, therefore, one of the key avenues through which the residential development industry can be affected. Lobbying for change of code standards is the main avenue to achieving sustainability.

Financial Institutions

In a privately managed housing sector, such as that of North America, financial institutions play a critical role. Rarely are residential projects constructed with the builder's own funds. The main objective of a lender is to decrease the risk associated with the loan. Financing experimental projects with untested technology will not commonly be attempted. Bankers want to make sure that funded projects or their parts will last and will not fail while the bank is still owed money. Several financial institutions that hold themselves to a higher "green standard" are now offering loans with reduced interest rates to support environmental projects.

The Initiator

A housing project may be initiated by a *non-profit* or *for-profit* organization. The non-profit sector can either be a government-run agency or a non-governmental organization (NGO). A government-run project uses public funds to create public or community housing. The project will be not only funded initially but will be managed or financially supported through its lifecycle by its initiators or their representatives. NGOs have no legal affiliation with any level of government. The organization can, however, benefit from a subsidy program provided by a government agency. The NGO may organize itself in a variety of legal structures. It can be a cooperative, for example, whose members are affiliated based on their ideological beliefs.

When a non-profit organization undertakes a project, funding sources will likely be governmental. A condition to lending may be that the design holds itself to a higher environmental standard. NGOs, such as cooperatives, are also often motivated by their care and respect of an environmental issue. It is likely, therefore, that the many facets of sustainable design will be included in such a project.

A for-profit initiator can be any private sector firm that sets to develop, build, sell, or rent housing. It can be a land development company that purchased, subdivided, and made land into lots for sale to builders or to be built upon by the development company itself. Despite the fact that construction practices have changed in recent years, the for-profit sector still has a short-term objective to sell homes and invest the profits in another project. Building practices or components that benefit the environment, but are costly, time-consuming to install, and have a long payback period, may not work in the interest of private builders. Attempts to offer "green benefits" may only be made when and if they can assist in the marketing of the home. The number of "green builders," nonetheless, has increased, and many are demonstrating that building communities based on sustainable principles is contributing to their bottom line.

The Design Firm

In design firms, planning, architecture, and engineering provide vital knowledge to developers about strategies and technologies for achieving sustainability in the community or the unit levels. When such firms are engaged, they tend to be the principle source of information about new products to make the home energy or resource efficient, for example. However, design firms are not always asked to participate in a common residential project. Small building firms often tend to use old drawings or engage a technician rather than a licensed design consultant or architect. Builders are also reluctant to get involved in the design process due to the ethical implications. Often, designs are changed on site without advance notice or design fees are held back. Large development companies, however, tend to employ consultants and their input is commonly made in large projects.

Product Manufacturers

Manufacturers and suppliers form a vital part of the building process. For the most part, they are the only participants in the homebuilding industry with sizeable investments in facilities and production equipment. But their greater, more important role has been in the development and promotion of new products that contribute significantly to resource and energy efficiency, for example.

One such product is the prefabricated roof truss, which changed the way roofs on wood-frame buildings were constructed and saved significant amounts of material and labor. Another notable example of significant savings in labor and wood is the plywood board. It altered the way roofs and exterior walls, as well as interior subfloors, were constructed by enabling coverage of large surfaces without using solid sawn lumber.

Products, tools, and new technologies are continuously invented. Some inventions hold promise, but they require time to be accepted by mainstream builders before they will generate the *economy of scale* that contributes to resource savings. Builders and investors must be cautious, however, as past experience shows that a "miracle product" has sometimes resulted in failures that necessitated replacement or additional expenses.

The Buyer/User

The buyer, the ultimate user of the home, has an important role to play throughout the project's lifecycle. When a request to the builder is made, features contributing to resource efficiency can be installed. The occupant can also contribute by upgrading the structure's performance and renovation or by participating in a recycling program. Traditionally, in lower cost housing, it is not affordable to equip the dwelling with many costly resource-saving features or build to higher building standards. For a buyer, it is therefore a balancing act between cost and performance.

Features of a Sustainable Community

Planning sustainable communities based on the principles outlined here represents a challenge for planners and architects. The designs need to aim at repairing some of the damage incurred by mainstream suburbs and must propose new paradigms for an economically, socially, and environmentally integrative approach. Yet, the question still remains: what is a sustainable community? Prior to an in-depth discussion and illustration of different manifestations of sustainability in design, a conceptual framework of such a community is drawn here.

In my view, sustainable communities need to integrate people, land, and buildings. Residents of different backgrounds, who share values and life experiences, should be able to live together successfully. The natural features of the land should be worked with, not around. New buildings should be harmonized with existing structures, reflect the history and spirit of the community, and successfully relate to each other. Development patterns need to consider natural systems and features, which in turn can be set in a context that encourages residents to enjoy the outdoors. Residents should also be able to modify their dwellings to accommodate and reflect their changing needs.

The sustainable community also accommodates diversity within the lives of its inhabitants as well as among them. Families are started and split apart, children move out and come home, and careers are switched and ended. Yet many homes and neighborhoods have not kept pace with the speed of changing lives, having been designed for the needs of past generations. Communities need to house residents throughout their lives by providing different housing types and easily modifiable layouts, as well as a range of services and support required by different age groups, family types, and occupations.

Resource conservation is also encouraged in the sustainable community. Construction and landscaping products should be minimally toxic during their installation and use, and should be disposed of safely or recycled when no longer needed. Biological systems should be used to treat wastewater and compost organic trash within the neighborhood, where space and conditions permit. Landscaping in private and public areas could be bio-regionally appropriate and require little irrigation. Community ties and social bonds need to be called upon to encourage the conservation and maintenance of common resources.

The post–World War II suburb was attractive to many, yet it was isolated and arguably sterile in its appearance. Residents need to be able to take pride in an attractive and orderly neighborhood, and at the same time they require space for children to play, couples to stroll, and seniors to chat. A sustainable community can be more like a well-used living room than a hallway or a formal dining room: comfortable enough to lie back and read the paper, yet nice enough to entertain company. The community should also foster civic-mindedness. Recent public debate in North America has been dominated by themes of alienation and powerlessness contributing to a common climate of fear. While architecture and planning cannot solve political problems, they can certainly design streets and neighborhoods that permit and encourage neighbors to have a friendly civic engagement. Spaces that are shared and enjoyed by the community as a whole require a sense of ownership and pride on the part of the residents if the spaces are to be well-used and well-maintained. Common spaces can help develop a common purpose; when neighbors feel that they can solve problems by working together, it encourages the connection and effectiveness that makes civic action possible.

A community can feel like a place or a series of places. Many residential developments have been laid out in such a way as to disorient drivers, intimidate pedestrians, and cut neighbors off from one another in the name of exclusivity and privacy. Moving through a community by car, on foot, or on a bicycle, a visitor or resident should feel that he or she has come from somewhere and is going somewhere else. While boundaries should not be severe, people need to feel that each community is distinct from adjacent areas, a place unto itself with a particular style and feeling. Similarly, larger communities can be structured by function, visual appearance, or housing type into a series of distinct smaller places to maintain a readily understandable sense of internal coherence.

A sustainable community also needs to be accessible. Its urban form and circulation networks need to permit safe travel by car, foot, public transport, and bicycle. Residents should be able to walk to convenient services and features such as parks or stores. The use of cars should not be discouraged so much as made redundant by accommodating pedestrians and bicyclists with generous sidewalks and separate bike pathways. Transit services should also be appropriate to the size and location of the community, and they should be scheduled and located to enable easy use. Dwellings and facilities need to be accessible to those with limited mobility as well, beyond simple ramps and handrails. As people age and face temporary or permanent difficulty in getting around, intelligent designs can ensure their continued participation in the life of the community.

It is not always clear how to make the leap from general theories to a specific site-oriented plan, but knowing what needs to be taken into account and considered is crucial for designers of new sustainable suburbs. The topics presented in this book are common-sense elements of community building that have too often been overlooked. The premise of twentieth-century design, that newness is progress, led developers to ignore elements that could be adaptively reused. Guiding principles of successful design that already exist within neighborhoods themselves can be integrated with new contemporary ideas. Respecting the inherent integrity of natural and built environments will sustain neighborhood community design for the benefit of not only the suburbs, but also cities.

The Rise of Suburbia

2

The post–World War II evolution of cities and the development of suburbs represented a significant deviation from old urban traditions, with a concurrent decline in community sustainability. To understand how this divergence occurred and what can be done to realign suburban dwellings with sustainable urban patterns, you must first understand the evolution of suburbs and neighborhoods. After you become familiar with the origins of the suburbs and their progress, you may be more able to determine how best to transform contemporary suburban forms into more sustainable communities.

Urban development is an evolutionary process that is affected by a multitude of factors, among them geography, economy, and culture. A key pillar of such a process is the relationship between communities and their surrounding environments and the availability of resources. This chapter reviews milestones in urban history relative to sustainable existence.

The Early Centuries

The neighborhood was an important concept in the early history of cities. In the seventh century B.C., the Greeks developed the first example of a *neighborhood unit*. The *Milesian* form of Greek planning divided cities into relatively autonomous areas. According to Mumford (1961), institutional buildings were not integrated into the neighborhood unit but made part of the town's core. Radiating out from the city center, neighborhood units were organized in an identified form (Figure 2.1). Greek planning also did not differentiate areas near the city cores from those in the periphery. Towns were much smaller than our modern-day cities, with only thousands of inhabitants, and consequently they had little effect on the surrounding natural environment.

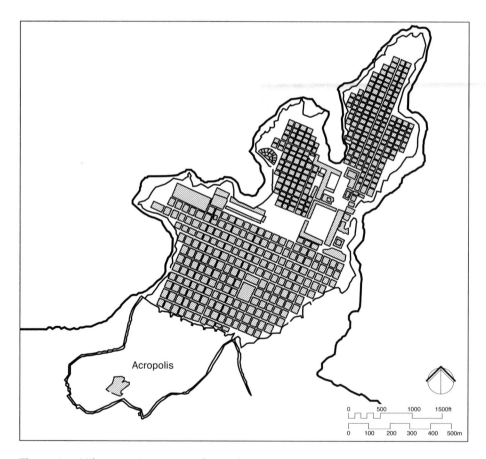

Figure 2.1: Miletus, an Ancient Greek city, demonstrates the early Milesian form of planning that divides the city into a gridiron of neighborhood units.

In the Middle Ages, the first semblance of the "suburb" emerged. Medieval urban forms distinguished settlements inside fortress walls from the outlying communities (Figure 2.2) (Whitehand and Carr, 2001). These peripheral areas, of course, did not resemble modern suburbs in any way other than their locations relative to the city. Immediately outside the walls, they may have included some informal mercantile areas and dwellings, but these quickly dispersed into agricultural plots (Pirenne, 1925). The differences between areas within and outside the walls also included social status, as outsiders were not considered full-fledged citizens, if they were considered citizens at all. They traded goods and services with the city rulers in exchange for protection and fell under the feudal system of law rather than the more flexible merchant or "civil" law (Schoenauer, 1992). Otherwise, medieval conceptions of suburban areas remained geographic in nature, while economic, social, and spatial organization focused on the city within the walls.

Figure 2.2: Walls enclosed the small, confined scale of medieval Florence and separated the outlying settlements from the inner city.

Medieval towns had many features that made them environmentally sustainable in today's terms. The narrow, irregular-patterned street network made commuting by foot or animals necessary, long after other options of transportation became available, and because the towns were smaller than their classical predecessors, the entire city had both a high degree of accessibility and a reduced ecological footprint (Beatley, 2000). Higher densities and the location of the workplace within the home also meant that neighborhoods functioned as well-integrated sustainable entities.

Urban traditions and the heterogeneity changed during the Renaissance (Schoenauer, 1992). This era was a pivotal time in history that would affect both living patterns and sustainability of cities in years to come. During the Renaissance, which began around the year 1450 and is recognized as the beginning of the "Modern Era," humanism placed man at the center of importance and identified him as the shaper of his own destiny (Hollister, 1994). Both humanism and the Renaissance's harkening back to Classical Roman and Greek forms stimulated extensive and grandiose urban designs with large blocks and wide streets, marking a new era, as manifested in the 1776 urban plan of Bath, England (Figure 2.3).

Organic development, a characteristic of the medieval town, diminished with the embellished formal organization and spatial separation of urban activities. The joint location of work and home was first separated during this period, as small industries and businesses were located outside the home. Although the environmental impact of this distinction may have been minimal at the time, it established a norm that would endure for centuries (Elsom, 1996). Urban changes during the Renaissance were largely the result of increased commercial activity and advances in military technology. With greater productivity came greater development, and the growth of trade spurred new investment in communities. A turning point in human history was about to change the structure of neighborhoods once more, however.

The Birth of Suburbia

The *Industrial Revolution* increased production rates to unprecedented levels. The commons, formally part of the feudal land system, were divided and sold, and agricultural machinery replaced manual labor. The result was a massive migration of country folk in search of employment in cities. In the booming economy, cities grew rapidly regardless of availability of amenities, and sanitary conditions were appalling due to overcrowding. Multi-tenant row houses deteriorated as the urban infrastructure could serve only a small portion of the growing population (Figure 2.4).

Overcrowded cities planted the seeds of change and the desire to see neighborhoods as a healthier form of living in the minds of some. These conditions were

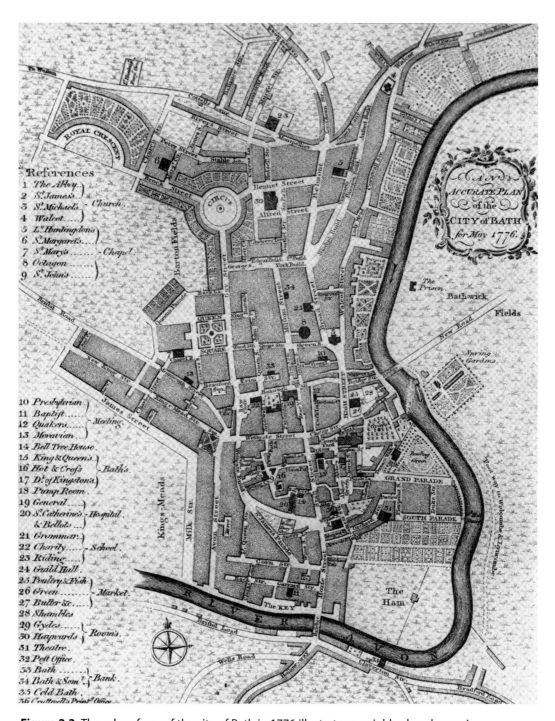

Figure 2.3: The urban form of the city of Bath in 1776 illustrates a neighborhood organization defined by wide streets characteristic of the Renaissance.

Figure 2.4: The industrial revolution led to overcrowding of cities and poor sanitary conditions, as depicted by a nineteenth-century painting of London by Gustave Doré.

an important backdrop to the evolution of the "suburban ideal" from its earliest formulation by theorists such as Robert Owen and Charles Fournier at the turn of the eighteenth century. The establishment of independent, self-sufficient communities was at the heart of these ideas. A relationship between the built component and its natural surroundings was acknowledged. The need to link small towns with large urban centers via public transportation corridors was another feature. Mixed uses and activities were viewed as contributing to the simplification of everyday necessities, as well as creating a balanced social mix and providing an opportunity for people to interact.

Owen's community, perhaps the early version of the contemporary neighborhood unit proposed in 1816, was New Lanark, where, in a repeatable square module, approximately 1200 people could reside (Figure 2.5). Housing enclosed a common space, and communal buildings were located in the public square, while allotment gardens were located behind the houses. Though industry was pushed to the periphery of such a development, Owen was a leading industrialist in England, and he therefore provided for a close living relationship to industry and for the retention of industry by private interests. In fact, Owen's model town could be considered a benevolent dictatorship, as he specified not only the town form but also the hygienic and virtuous manner in which inhabitants should live (Cherry, 1970; Podmore, 1906).

Figure 2.5: Owen's proposed model town is typical of the ideologies of the time. A rigid geometry, consolidated housing, and centralized, enclosed amenities are characteristics that many social models hoped would provide equitable living conditions.

Fourier, a French social reformer, on the other hand created a socialist version of roughly the same type of development. Influenced by the French Revolution and a desire to remove the unemployed from the harsh city environment, he proposed the relocation of society into *phalanxes*. These single buildings could house up to 1600 people in private apartments. Each *phalanstery* had centralized communal amenities and was situated on approximately 5000 acres (2000 hectares) of land that residents were expected to cultivate, thereby ensuring self-sustenance. Though the socialist foundation of such a design was never realized, the palatial treatment of the architecture was realized at Guise, France. This phalanstery was intended to accommodate workers at an iron foundry owned by Jean-Baptiste Godin (Beecher, 1986; Fourier, 1971).

The City Beautiful and Garden City Movements

Two movements that began almost simultaneously at the end of the nineteenth century and that left an indelible mark on the face of North American planning form, both urban and suburban, were the *City Beautiful Movement* and Ebenezer Howard's *Garden City Movement*. In 1898, British planner Howard published a book entitled *Tomorrow: A Peaceful Path to Real Reform*, which was republished in 1902 as *Garden Cities of Tomorrow*. In the book, he proposed the withdrawal from already industrialized cities to communities that combined the social and public conveniences of towns with the healthy and serene aspects of rural life. Howard felt that since private ownership of land led to an exploitation of the city center and inflation of its property values, a community whose land was owned by a limited-dividend company rid of private speculation would allow for free buildings, services, and economy.

With buildings spread out in a small community setting, Howard initially proposed a 30,000-resident limit, and the countryside and its benefits would be accessible to all. The proposal Howard made for a Garden City was diagrammatic, layered circles that did not specify a particular architectural style (Figure 2.6). Industry was located at the town center and surrounded by a ring of parkland. Around the park was a *crystal palace*, a glass arcade that housed a shopping area. The next layers were to be houses with attached gardens. These were enclosed by a Grand Avenue of 420 feet (127 meters) wide, which served to separate the residential from the industrial areas. At the periphery were rail lines and larger farms (Howard, 1902; Macfadyen, 1933). Howard's plan, in fact, laid the foundation for land-use separation that would later influence contemporary town planning.

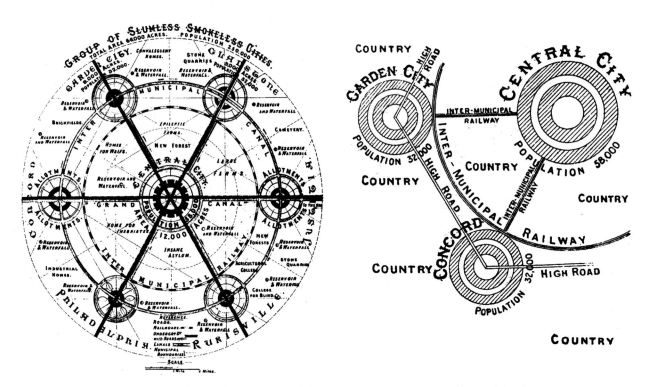

Figure 2.6: With a rigid geometry and diagrammatic nature, Howard layered his design for a Garden City.

The first implementation of Howard's Garden City concepts can be found in the town of Letchworth, England. In 1903, the Garden City Pioneer Company bought 3822 acres (1529 hectares) of land north of London and hired Raymond Unwin and Barry Parker to translate Howard's diagram for the site. Unwin had worked previously in community planning and was involved in the design of New Earswick, a forerunner of sorts to Letchworth, where he developed concepts of low-density housing into a prototype for community design. With Letchworth, the effect was momentous, since he could translate Howard's diagrams into actual plans (Miller, 1992). A centralized civic area in Letchworth is enclosed by a park, and housing radiates from this center. Unfortunately, it initially and ultimately lacked the geometrical clarity of Howard's planning, and certain features of the town were skewed. For instance, the community could not sustain the public buildings planned for the center of town; that left the community somewhat unfocused (Figure 2.7). In addition, the agricultural ventures were unsuccessful (Unwin, 1909; Macfadyen, 1933).

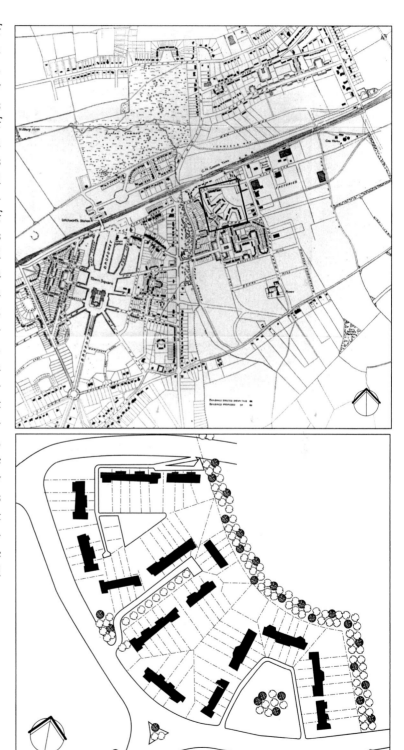

Figure 2.7: The design of Letchworth, which attempted to replicate Howard's Garden City theory, is considered a landmark design in the history of town and neighborhood planning.

Letchworth's citizens have complained of the lack of social amenities and the need to travel to London to find them; in addition, some of the architectural harmony has been sacrificed with the introduction of garages (Jackson, 1985). Nonetheless, the economic principles that Howard proposed remain intact: land has remained in common ownership, in spite of private demand to purchase land in the community (Miller, 1989). The Letchworth Garden City Heritage Foundation owns and manages a 5100 acre (2040 hectare) estate in Letchworth worth millions of dollars; income generated from the property is used to maintain, improve, and develop the estate and to support its charitable activities (Letchworth Garden City Heritage Foundation, 2001).

The cramped and filthy tenements of the typical city of the late nineteenth and early twentieth centuries aroused fear in some citizens. In pursuit of a cleaner and more pleasurable living environment, affluent residents fled industrial cities. Movement to the outskirts of large cities began as resort communities grew. Wealthy city dwellers purchased large tracts of land, located in scenic areas, on which they built summer homes. Lake or river shores and forested areas were among the preferred sites for these residences, which joined existing agricultural settlements whose farmers sold their produce in the city. Eventually, these farms provided basic necessities to vacationers.

The Movements' Effect in North America

The first major North American urban redevelopment movements that affected urban planning were the *Parks Beautiful Movement* in the mid- to late nineteenth century and the *City Beautiful Movement* in the early twentieth century. According to Holcomb and Beauregard (1981) "each emerged as a response to the high densities and environmental degradation brought about by urbanization and industrialization."

The Parks Beautiful Movement created open recreation spaces that also served as buffer zones against the spread of fire and disease. As industrial commerce proliferated in North America, the Parks Beautiful Movement strengthened. Planners and designers realized that adjacent land values increased where parks had been developed. In addition, the clearance of land for park development changed existing urban land uses. Therefore, the Parks Beautiful Movement served to eliminate undesirable districts from certain segments of the city while increasing the land values of others. The first construction within the Parks Beautiful Movement was Central Park in New York City (Figure 2.8), begun in 1857. However, most parks emerged on the urban fringe, where initial land acquisition prices were less expensive and building demolition was not always required.

While speculative development somewhat corrupted the initial ideals of the Parks Beautiful Movement, its philosophy influenced later nineteenth-century urban designers. People began to perceive parks as essential to their physical and psychological well-being. The intrinsic value of nature stimulated a sense of relief as the quiet, undisrupted park space separated visitors from the chaos and confines of the city (Humphrey, 2002). The Parks Beautiful Movement engrained the importance of proximity to nature into the North American perception of ideal living environments (Girling and Hepland, 1994). Nevertheless, the increasing importance of economic development soon overshadowed the nineteenth-century emphasis on park design. The turn of the twentieth century saw the City Beautiful Movement emerge as the dominant philosophy of urban revitalization.

The City Beautiful Movement was born at Chicago's 1893 World's Columbian Exposition. It encouraged the development of civic spaces such as parks, gardens, and shoreline pathways within cities. Holcomb and Beauregard (1981) suggest that the enduring importance of the City Beautiful Movement lies not so much in the plans developed and the few projects implemented, but in its ideas. It recognized that a purposefully designed image could evoke a certain sense of place. In essence, its guiding design principles sought to create holistic places instead of isolated environments.

The concept of creating places, rather than buildings, influenced the development of nineteenth- and twentieth-century "suburbs." For those who could afford to leave the city, ex-urban villages proved to be an inviting residential alternative. In North America, the railroad transported urbanites to the city's periphery and initiated the settlement of early suburbs. The norm of working away from home, which had been established during the Renaissance, was realized on a new scale as the distance between home and work grew from being short and within the same city to longer, working in the city and living in the surrounding countryside.

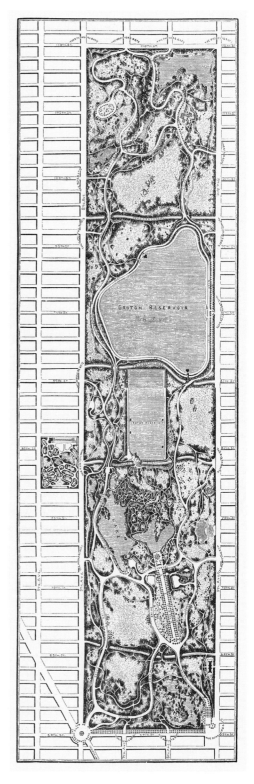

Figure 2.8: Central Park in New York City, designed by Frederick Olmstead, was the first large-scale initiative of the Parks Beautiful Movement.

The origins of these first North American suburbs resulted in large, single-family, detached houses. Forested lands were cleared to make room for recreational estates that first emerged for seasonal use and later became permanent houses for wealthy urbanites. However, as the twentieth century progressed and the automobile became common, the middle class grew and followed its more affluent counterparts to the suburbs. The suburbs became an ideal model of living to which all citizens could one day aspire (Peterman, 2000).

Before World War II, only one more Garden City was built, in Welwyn, England. The Garden Suburb, a variant of Howard's concept, turned out to be a more replicable idea. Forest Hill Gardens in Queens, New York, designed by the Olmsted Brothers and Grosvenor Atterbury in 1911, included sociologist Clarence Perry as a resident. Perry adopted many of its features as elements in his neighborhood unit (Perry, 1929). The notion of the *neighborhood unit* was introduced into twentieth-century planning theory during the Great Depression.

U.S. President Herbert Hoover hosted a conference on home building and home ownership in the 1930s. The conference proposed that urban development should be organized around spatial neighborhood units, much like the early Greek Milesian system. However, early twentieth-century planning concerned itself with the poor social conditions and the dire homelessness among North America's population. Neighborhood units, therefore, were designed to support large residential developments. The proposed generic neighborhood unit was a rectangular grid complete with housing, services, and infrastructure. Perry's neighborhood averaged 160 acres (64 hectares) for 1500 families, or 5000 to 6000 people. The guiding design principles of Perry's plan were elementary schools as a size-defining criteria, safety for pedestrians, provisions for efficient amenities, and building of a socially integrated community. However, a sense of community did not naturally develop from spatially cohesive units as intended, because more than spatial proximity was needed to foster ties among residents (Peterman, 2000).

Radburn

In the years before World War II, great opportunities existed for transforming planning theory into reality, as real towns were carved out of the North American continent. A small group of planners, architects, and historians known as the Regional Planning Association (RPA) became prominent in the planning and execution of new towns. The RPA lasted from 1923 to 1933 and met two to three times a week, acting as a think tank or forum for the exchange of ideas. Led by Clarence Stein and Henry Wright, and including architect and sociologist Lewis Mumford, the diverse group incorporated the sociology of Charles Horton Cooley and Perry, the civic ideas of Patrick Geddes and Howard, and the educational philosophy of John Dewey. Their goal was to design more humane environments, primarily by acknowledging the Garden City's sensitivities. They aimed, according to Stein (1957), to build "balanced communities, in balanced regions." The group produced some of America's most progressively planned communities of the time and they remained influential thinkers and writers in the years that followed.

Radburn, New Jersey, is the most renowned product of the Stein-Wright partnership. It is essentially a realistic translation of several of the principles espoused by Howard and put into practice by Unwin and Parker, although houses were sold in Radburn as opposed to being leased in Garden Cities and New Towns in the United Kingdom. Though elements were sacrificed in this implementation (for example, the greenbelt surrounding the town was never purchased because of financial difficulties, and the proposed industrial areas were abandoned due to the Great Depression), the overall result was a safe, healthy community for young families. A variety of housing types was included in Radburn, and neighborhoods were serviced by small retail centers and defined by cul-de-sacs and scenic, curving streets.

Part of Radburn's success was due to its accommodation of the automobile, whereby the pedestrian and the automobile were completely separated (Parsons, 1992). This new phenomenon stimulated many novel development patterns. Housing was arranged in large blocks with interior greens; the innovative use of the cul-de-sac created these *superblocks*, each one 35 to 50 acres (14 to 20 hectares) in size (Lynch, 1981). Circulation patterns were used to separate pedestrian and vehicular traffic via interior paths and overpasses. Although most dwellings in Radburn were single-family, some rental units existed in garden apartments (Schoenauer, 2000). Individual unit planning was oriented toward the internal open areas rather than to the streets. These design articulations, as can be read from the community plan in Figure 2.9, made Radburn a model of planning in suburbia for the next 30 years. But perhaps the greatest impact on suburban planning emerged when segregated land-use planning took hold.

Euclidean zoning, which separated large swathes of uniquely residential areas from all other land use, emerged in 1926. It was created to simplify the development process and resulted in geographical segregation by income (Logan, 1976). It further contributed to separation of home and work and to increase the distances traveled, which led to long commutes and air pollution (Elsom,

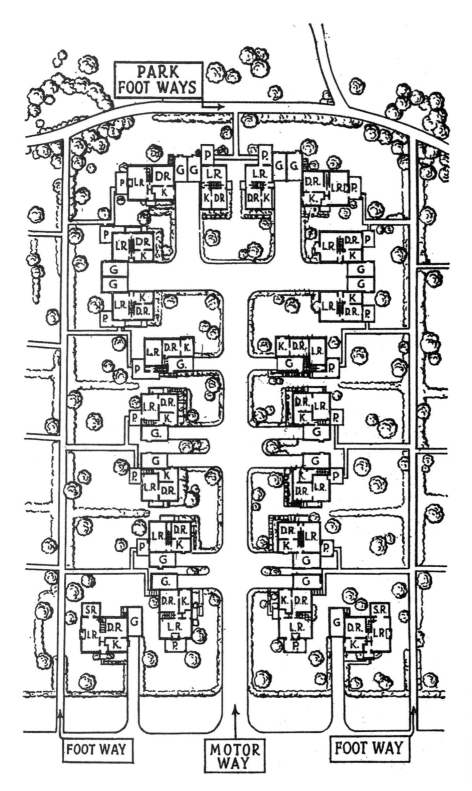

Figure 2.9: Though not a direct translation of Howard's Garden City proposal, Radburn is considered important because of its acknowledgment of the growing importance of the automobile in twentieth-century living.

1996). Early critics of suburbs such as Sharp (1932) commented on this pattern of development and argued that suburbs altered the relationship between North America's countryside and cities. Nonetheless, the continent seemingly offered the best of both worlds by presenting the sophistication of urbanity and the traditions of rural settlements.

The Post–World War II Era

With the wide use of the automobile and the ability to build away from the city center, speculative residential developers began a massive undertaking. The proliferation of suburbia in the post–World War II era had a direct effect on sustainability. Many of the principles that were embedded in novel planning concepts turned into municipal zoning regulations and affected designs in later years.

Levittown, Long Island, was North America's first large-scale planned suburb, developed on former potato fields by the Levitt Corporation, which, in 1947, planned 2000 units. Mass production proved so efficient that by the end of the year, Levittown expanded by 6000 additional units. Upon its 1951 completion, the development contained 17,447 private dwellings (Macionis and Parrillo, 2001). Easy access to government-assisted homeowner mortgages afforded individuals an opportunity to purchase their own homes. The result was a North American common perception in which family-owned, single detached dwellings on private lots must be a desire of most cities (Holcomb and Beauregard, 1981; Whitehand and Carr, 2001) (Figure 2.10).

Figure 2.10: Homes in early mass-produced post–World War II suburban developments were repetitious and monotonous.

Land-use planning is regarded as the overarching reason for current suburban practices. New zoning regulations attempted to maintain the drawing power of suburbia: detached homes with large plots of land away from next door neighbors. Achieving it entailed a density of 7 to 10 units per acre (17 to 25 units per hectare). Such density did not justify the economic viability and frequency of use of most amenities, however. Business owners could not find patrons, transit authorities did not have enough riders, and libraries had too few readers. Residents who bought into the suburban dream were also not content to reside next to businesses, which drew in traffic and created noise. Bylaws strictly objecting to business construction in the heart of communities were initiated. Increasing density went against the grain of the suburban lifestyle. People would have to give up privacy and mix with residences of other income groups and demographic makeup.

The need to access basic amenities, however, did not decline. Suburban residents had to be able to reach stores, medical clinics, and post offices that were located farther away and shared by inhabitants of several developments. Reliance on cars became mandatory. As a necessity, every household needed more than one vehicle that, with low-frequency public transit, was used often. When the number of cars increased, the need to build roads to accommodate them grew as well. Since the 1940s, the amount of road-building in North America expanded significantly. Street width widened and consumed more land in developments that had little traffic most of the day (Figure 2.11). At present, some 30 percent of most community land is allocated to roads, a staggering amount compared to a century ago.

As several cars in each home became the norm, parking garages were constructed adjacent to homes, which meant that a typical residential lot had to be widened as well. When lots widened, street length grew, contributing to decline in density and increasing travel time. Length and expenses associated with infrastructure to serve these homes also grew, prompting the emergence of another social challenge—affordability.

Affordability, or lack of it, had significant ramifications on sustainability. Members of single- or modest-income households had to spend greater shares of their salaries on housing, leaving less disposable income for long-term needs such as healthcare and retirement. Measures that could have offered affordable housing solutions were simply not possible within the new zoning frameworks that mandated costly large lots and wide roads.

Another noticeable factor that affected sustainability and affordability was the transformation of the home from a modest shelter to a swollen token of social status. The increasing sizes of new homes paradoxically paralleled the decline in the number of household members. The postwar-built, 800-square-foot (80-square-meter) bungalow, with an attached, single carport, that dots North American suburbs gradually expanded to an average of 2000 square feet (200 square meters). As the size of homes grew, transporting and consuming more building supplies made them more expensive to construct. Labor costs also rose, as increased housing demands put pressure on a declining number of tradespeople. Unfortunately, the homebuilding industry, which was accustomed to on-site, stick-built construction, did not switch to construction methods that used prefabricated components for cost efficiency.

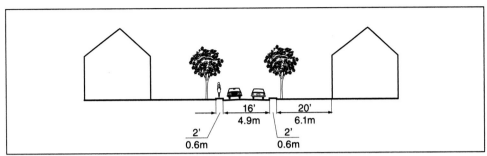

Hampstead Garden Suburb, 1905

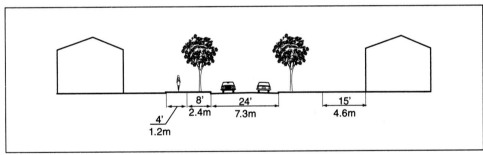

Radburn, New Jersey, 1927

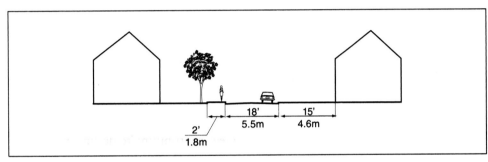

FHA Standards, 1936

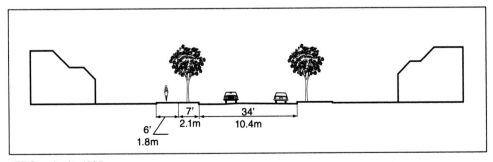

ITE Standards, 1965

Figure 2.11: The planning of suburban neighborhoods saw gradual expansion of street widths.

New spaces and functions continued to be added to home design as lifestyles changed. Today's kitchen has grown in size to become the home's social center and a showcase for costly appliances. Bathrooms with bathtubs, shower stalls, expensive fixtures, and floor-to-ceiling tiles have become the norm. Media centers and bonus rooms are now part of the homebuilder's vocabulary. In addition to the high initial cost of building a home, ongoing maintenance and upkeep expenses have also mushroomed. Large homes also draw an environmental toll. More windows, complex roof shapes, big footprints, and the resulting spreading foundations become sources of energy loss and require large amounts of natural resources—in particular, solid sawn lumber—for their construction.

The linking of a single dwelling to more utilities also means that infrastructure as a whole has required expansion. Water lines, fire hydrants, storm sewers and house drainage systems, electrical grids, telephones, Internet access, and cable TVs are among the services buried below ground and, as a result, development costs have risen.

The social layer, a web of relationships essential to turn a development into a community where interactions among citizens foster a network, has also eroded. When meeting places, shops, and cafés become rare as the car culture prevails, people have begun to disconnect. A single type of dwelling has resulted in a neighborhood with homogenous households. Members of an extended family, young and old, no longer reside close together to create a support system. Long distances, and at times lack of sidewalks, have confined people to their cars or homes, preventing opportunities for meeting and getting to know others.

Unsustainable planning and living patterns have gradually taken hold through the separation of city and suburbs; work and home; single-use zoning; automobile dependency; the desire to live in low-density, single-family homes; and the popular notion of the suburb as the best place to raise a family. Rethinking these planning and living patterns represents one of the greatest challenges for twenty-first–century sustainable community design.

Siting a Community

Decisions made during site selection, an early phase of the residential development process, will largely affect a project's sustainability. These decisions range from where to locate a community, how to design with the site's natural features in mind, and how and where to place roads and dwellings, among other considerations. This chapter focuses on these issues by providing a brief historical background of the relationship between nature and society. It covers planning considerations and principles, and features a project where a neighborhood was built in a densely forested area.

Nature and Society

Since the Ice Age, human settlement has reflected vernacular responses to a site's natural conditions in planning and dwelling design. With the development of agriculture by about 7000 B.C., early civilizations began to modify landscapes. For the first time, trees, for example, were planted for shade, scenic, and spiritual uses. People altered natural conditions to shape environments and foster a sense of place (McBride and Jacobs, 1986; Todd, 1985; Zelov and Cousineau, 1999).

In the medieval and Renaissance periods, Western European civilizations incorporated virgin woodlands into large, domesticated gardens in the countryside. Vast areas of forests, however, were cut down when a demand for timber products arose in the late eighteenth century during the Industrial Revolution. The rapid removal of trees fundamentally altered natural landscapes, and the division and privatization of land consequently changed forever the traditional ways and quality of life. Such unparalleled modification spurred a backlash that was manifested in the Romantic Movement. This movement's ideology centered on self-sufficiency and harmony within the natural order and was an expression of the distress caused by the increasing upheaval of the countryside.

In response to the onslaught of industrialization, the Romantics initiated debates questioning man's inherent right to alter nature. Critics also addressed issues such as pollution and the worsening conditions faced by the poor. Romanticism sought to balance relationships between the organic realm and manmade settlements. Instead of the mass encroachment of chaotic and congested cities into the surrounding countryside, rail linkages were proposed between primary, secondary, and tertiary centers. This proposal led to the establishment of independent communities with a variety of land uses and social compositions (Macionis and Parrillo, 2001). Furthermore, connection between centers of varying sizes, it was believed, would encourage human interaction within a wider context of natural settings.

As late nineteenth-century industrialization helped cities to develop and expand, a gradually growing middle class acquired the means for greater mobility. In North America, increased car ownership and higher standards of living rendered scenic rural landscapes attractive to those with the means to afford a primary or secondary residence away from the crowded city. Farming villages with picturesque landscapes became the new home of city-dwellers. These rural communities not only generated agricultural produce, but also became a commodity in themselves. The rise of the "urban countryside" began with purchases of rural properties for summer homes by the wealthy (Bryant, et al., 2000). Early suburbs were developed as the new, wealthy residents shaped a site's natural conditions to make it more pleasant for strolls, rather than leaving it untamed. Ignoring flora and fauna, roads, paths, commercial strips, and vast estates appeared where forests once reigned. Villages and towns outside the immediate city boundaries were transformed into urban extensions. New land-use regulations directed the type and location of developments. The budding urban planning movement initiated control over environmental features perceived as obstructing the realization of orderly development (Kunstler, 1994; Scarlett, 1999).

The most significant development influencing North American natural sites occurred after World War II. Perceived as underdeveloped land, rural areas were covered with low-density developments that consumed vast areas of farmland. Virgin greenfields were transformed with automobile-centered designs including garages and wide roads. Development first followed the highways and subsequent population movement outward from traditional city limits. Later, large-scale suburban planning not only coincided with highway construction, but at times initiated it. Spurred on by both government-sponsored economic incentives and post-war changes that popularized the desire for more space, modern developments became notorious for razing large tracts of natural land. Forests were unabashedly cleared and designed to be flat, monotonous, and malleable for planners and architects (Duany, et al., 2000). Post–World War II developers approached the environment with the notion that both natural landscapes and traditional rural villages could be altered.

You may ask why Western civilization has minimized the importance of self-sustaining natural environments as essential features of human habitation. Knox and Marston (2001) explain that nature is a social creation as much as it is a physical universe that includes human beings. The concept of nature, they argue, is the product of time and circumstance. Knowing nature, however, is not only inherited from the past, but is also reinterpreted by recent generations to suit contemporary needs.

An attitude of control over nature directs suburban developments as well. Sustainable elements are often ignored or removed from sites because they are viewed as barriers to development. According to Miller (1988), other characteristics, such as reductions in leisure time and transportation costs involved in traveling to natural sites, reduce incentives for preservation and design with the environment. The result is that the intrinsic value of a natural site's conditions has gradually disappeared from the day-to-day experience.

This chapter seeks to demonstrate how a site's environmental characteristics can become generators of design ideas that contribute to a project's sustainability.

Seeking a middle ground between development pressures and sensible site planning is illustrated through the design principles outlined here.

Planning Within a Context

Location is a fundamental concept that affects the sustainability of a project. The site will influence a multitude of aspects, ranging from effects on nature to commuting distance, and, as a result, vehicle fuel consumption and pollution. A careful and systematic process that considers a range of factors must be studied before site planning begins. The U.S. Green Building Council's *LEED for Neighborhood Development* (2007) lists aspects to be considered prior to site selection: location efficiency; environmental preservation; compact, complete, and connected neighborhoods; and resource efficiency. Some of the factors on the LEED list will be studied in other chapters. Other factors dealing with macro issues are considered here.

Infill, Grayfield, and Greenfield

Residential developers are often constrained by availability of lands. Building locations depend on zoning, cost, existence of infrastructure, and environmental assessment, among other factors. Broadly speaking, three types of sites are considered: infill, grayfield, and greenfield. An *infill* site is a plot within an already developed area. The site is likely to be in close proximity to built dwellings and existing amenities. *Grayfield* are sites on which commercial establishments such as shopping malls and buildings are built. Projects on *greenfield* sites are constructed on remote virgin land or on the edge of communities, to which new roads must be constructed and services built.

Suburban developments on greenfield sites contribute to urban sprawl. Highways are extended to reach them and homes are likely to be of low-density configuration. Therefore, when a choice is possible, building on infill or grayfield sites is much preferred. Despite the many advantages of infill housing and its contribution to repairing social and urban fabrics, problems surrounding this type of construction make these projects difficult to build. When an entire area or a single plot of land has remained vacant, there is usually a good reason for it. Prior to acquiring such a lot and beginning design, a developer needs to assess these potential challenges carefully (Figure 3.1).

Soil contamination is common in infill housing developments. When the site is the former location of a plant or storage facility, known as a *brownfield*, poisonous substances may have seeped into the ground, and such materials pose a risk to the people who will inhabit future homes. The soil, therefore, needs to be tested and decisions made as to cleanup methods. When an industrial building is located on the site and cannot be converted, it must be demolished and cleared.

The size, shape, and location of the site may also make infill housing projects more challenging to design and costly to build. At times, a site can be a leftover of a divided, larger plot of land. Designing to these odd shapes efficiently is a challenge; irregular lot shapes may lead to substantial waste, casting doubt on the viability of the entire project. When the site is too small, manipulating machinery and materials will be difficult. When construction begins, noise and pollution can disturb neighboring homes and halt work.

Local opposition to an infill project may arise long before construction begins. This could be due to the introduction of higher density housing or the fear that the new project and its inhabitants will not "fit in" with an existing community. Community involvement and education, preferably in the early stages of the design process, can help mitigate these fears. Innovative design can ensure that infill housing will complement the neighborhood and will not disrupt current residents' quality of life.

Zoning bylaws can further jeopardize the feasibility of infill housing projects. Zoning was originally developed in Europe during the nineteenth century to separate industrial land uses from residential to alleviate pollution leading to severe respiratory illnesses. Whereas past zoning laws served to separate incompatible land uses, today's laws are more specific. Different housing densities and types are separated from each other, residences are set apart from office structures, and one type of commercial activity is distinguished from another. Contemporary zoning is especially prevalent in suburban developments; it no longer simply separates parcels based on use but has evolved to become a tool of economic segregation (Duany, et al., 2000). Working with

Figure 3.1: Sustainable planners seek to develop an existing built area first rather than build on a greenfield.

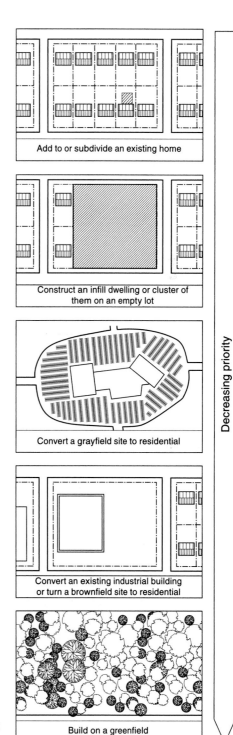

Add to or subdivide an existing home

Construct an infill dwelling or cluster of them on an empty lot

Convert a grayfield site to residential

Convert an existing industrial building or turn a brownfield site to residential

Build on a greenfield

Decreasing priority

49

local governments to ease zoning laws for an infill project can create opportunities for a more diverse, sustainable, and lively community.

Relying on Existing Amenities

Amenity is a catchall term that encompasses the services and community support system a homeowner will need on a regular basis. Amenities include childcare centers, schools, medical clinics, grocery and other shopping centers, and services such as a post office, pharmacy, or bank. Decisions as to which amenities are built are based on the prospective number of users of such facilities, and they are, therefore, a strictly economic venture. New developments built on the urban fringe often do not have enough inhabitants to support such establishments. Several years may pass until the community grows to justify construction of a school or shopping center. Such a scenario is unfortunate when a community based on sustainable principles is to be built. Households made of young, first-time homebuyers with children are most in need of childcare centers, schools, and medical clinics, for example. These families will have to rely on their own transportation in the absence of public transit, thereby incurring additional expenses and not benefiting the environment.

In terms of sustainability, selecting a site with, or adjacent to, existing amenities is preferable. Conceiving a plan that leaves a place for such facilities to be added in the future is also wise. When a regional master plan is prepared, a proper distribution of such facilities can be made to permit easy access of larger numbers of users to them by public transportation and to justify their economic viability (Figure 3.2).

Using Local Resources

Location of development also depends on availability of local building materials and a manual labor force. The amount of energy invested in transporting a product to its final place of use needs to be regarded as part of the "cradle-to-grave" assessment. When the building's design calls for a product whose raw materials travel to an assembly plant from afar, and then a further long distance to the construction site, large amounts of energy are wasted compared to the use of local products. In addition, when local raw materials are used instead of imported materials, their purchase can contribute to the local economy. Jobs in manufacturing and distribution are likely to be created and will support prosperity.

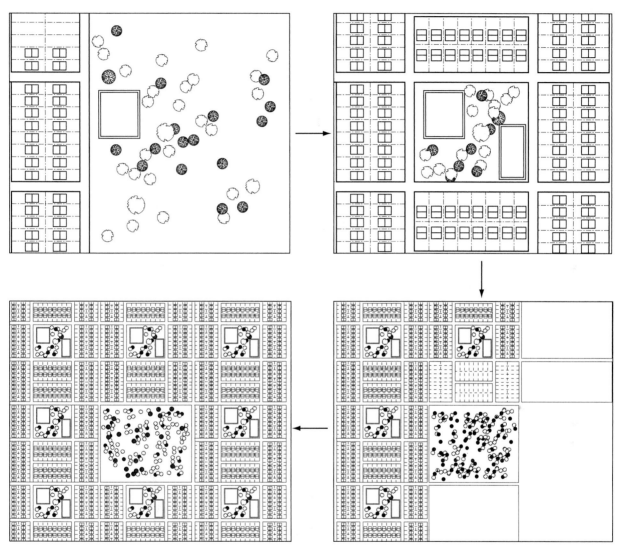

Figure 3.2: Initial siting of a region's and neighborhood's amenities needs to foresee future expansion, making it a shared hub.

Since the rise of globalization in recent decades, outsourcing work to the developing world has become common. In many cases, raw materials harvested on one continent are shipped to foreign manufacturing plants on another, where they are assembled and then shipped back as a product. Packaging and transporting such goods has not only a negative environmental consequence, but it has inflicted devastating damage on local labor forces, and, as a result, local economies.

Zoning Ordinances

Prior to beginning a sustainable residential community design, a developer must understand relevant zoning ordinances. Two alternatives related to a site exist. The first is that regulations are already in place. In an infill site or land adjacent to an existing neighborhood, for example, zoning ordinances specify aspects ranging from road widths, to density permitted and type of dwellings allowed. The second possibility occurs when no zoning or bylaws exist. Known as *direct control* or *plan unit development*, the planner is asked to propose an ordinance along with the design. The proposal is then considered by the municipality's planning officials as to its conformity with safety issues, for example. Some of the zoning proposed, and as a result the design, may be changed or approved.

The principles guiding building of sustainable communities are established at the outset of their design. It is therefore critical that proper zoning be in place early on to ensure conception of such neighborhoods. When zoning laws do exist, it is often difficult or time-consuming to change them. It is better to start from a clean slate and lay down proper principles. Detailed descriptions of the fundamentals of such designs are described in the following chapters; only the main aspects are discussed here.

Mixing land uses is critical to sustainable communities' design. Having public services and amenities in the neighborhood rather than a driving distance away reduces reliance on private cars and fosters healthy transportation habits such as walking or bicycling. The planner needs to ensure that a wide range of uses are permitted. Permitting home businesses, for example, can reduce commuting time as well.

Higher densities will limit sprawl by allowing the building of more dwellings per unit area. It can also result in reduction of road width and an increase in alternative parking solutions. Lanes may be introduced and parking at the rear of structures encouraged, leading to narrower, taller buildings without garages.

Range of housing types will foster an integrated neighborhood with mixed household types and incomes. By proposing *inclusionary zoning*, a greater choice of homes for low- and medium-income families can be offered. Some of the dwellings can accommodate traditional households and others can cater to the needs of singles, single parents, or seniors.

When these factors become the main principles in zoning design, a sustainable community will likely be the outcome.

Regarding Transportation

Reducing sprawl and, as a result, reliance on private cars is a necessary part of achieving community sustainability. Transit options can help reduce significant negative ramifications for the environment. As part of a site-selection process, a sustainable developer must assess the existence or lack of transit systems.

In recent decades, daily commutes in many urban centers have gotten out of hand. Drivers are spending long hours stuck in traffic, time that could be better spent with family members, for example. Some studies also demonstrate that when new roads are constructed, people increase their driving to take advantage of them (Hansen and Huang, 1977). Evidence shows that between 60 to 90 percent of new road capacity is consumed by new driving within five years of the road's opening. Some commuters even switch from using public transit to driving on new roads. With mounting costs of highway construction, loss of productivity, incidents of road rage, and high levels of greenhouse gas emissions and smog, reevaluating transit strategies has become a key priority for all levels of government. Old concepts of transportation need to be reconsidered and new ones proposed.

Several transportation principles are grounded in the idea that movement of people and cars should be regarded as an interconnected system to which various modes of transportation—be they pedestrian, rail, or bus—contribute. In addition, people need to be encouraged in various ways to travel in common to reduce both the number of cars on the road and the cost of constructing new roads. The planning of new transportation arteries needs to be coordinated with other land use allocations to manage commuting across a region. The locations of hospitals, schools, and parks, for example, need to be accessible by public transit.

Public transit also needs to be better designed. Municipalities argue that the systems need to be economically self-sustaining, something that is often hard to achieve. Public transit is arguably a means to achieve sustainability, and its design should be accomplished in conjunction with a community's circulation system for maximum use. The system needs to be hierarchically organized, allowing residents to reach other bus or train lines connecting neighborhoods with major urban centers. Public transit networks should be designed for easy and convenient access by everyone. It should serve both sides of the street and connect with pedestrian paths (Figure 3.3).

In older, denser communities, bus stops should be located approximately every 3300 feet (1000 meters) to foster an average walk of half that distance to a stop. In new, low-density subdivisions, the distance may be twice as long. The common

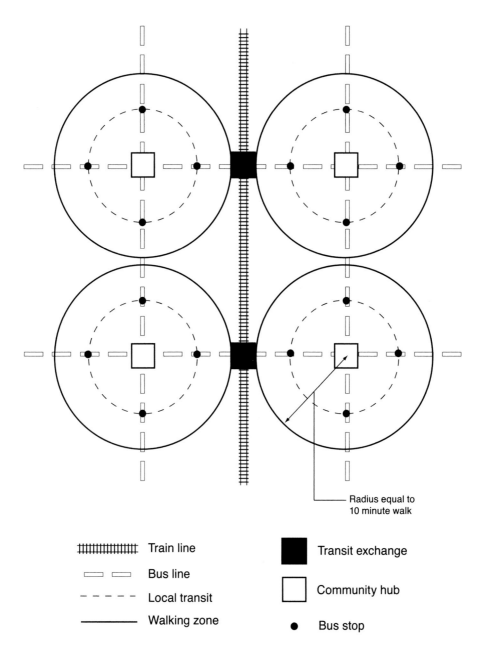

Figure 3.3: Transit networks must be regarded as complementary interconnected systems.

approach to public transit planning in such communities is to have local bus routes that connect with downtown truck routes at main activity points such as shopping centers (CMHC, 1981).

Sheltering people waiting for a bus is also necessary, as it protects them from the elements and acts as a meeting point. Shelters need benches, bus schedules, and maps showing neighborhood streets and the regional transit system. In areas with harshly cold climates, the shelter may be heated. It can also be located near a convenience store, when possible.

Buses or subway line authorities should allow cyclists to bring their bicycles on board during rush hour. Regional trains need to stop at bus depots, and the times of all modes of transit must be coordinated. Locating basic amenities near transit nodes also saves commuting time. People can shop for basic staples on their way home from work to avoid special car trips.

Some other ideas and initiatives have been proposed to encourage more shared commutes. Providing tax incentives to employers in return for covering their employees' public transit expenses or allocating lanes for cars with more than one passenger are some examples. Citizens who mostly use public transit but occasionally need to use a car can get access to a vehicle for a small monthly fee. People can be encouraged to purchase a car with a less polluting engine via monetary incentives. Such measures are meant to reduce the escalating use of private cars, with all their negative consequences.

Sun and Wind

Exposure to the sun should be considered in siting homes to reduce energy consumption and increase entry of natural light. The location and orientation of buildings can maximize and capture solar energy year round, especially during winter months. The daily and yearly changing positions of the sun should be evaluated in the initial planning stages by using sundials and path diagrams. Typically, houses that are angled toward the afternoon sun with the most fenestration (window siting) on the sunny side will catch the sun's most intense rays in the early afternoon (Figure 3.4).

When houses are oriented to catch the sun, their occupants enjoy a maximum amount of sunlight. An alternative siting exemplified in Figure 3.5 takes into consideration the solar arcs created as the sun travels from horizon to horizon. Units oriented along the north-westerly axis (in the Northern Hemisphere), therefore, benefit from a shorter noonday shadow than otherwise might be cast if houses were oriented east-west. Moreover, additional units may be erected upon the cusp of neighboring house shadows if dwelling design follows this layout. Principles considering sunlight and shadow orientation need to avoid obstructions that will prevent the houses from maximizing sunlight.

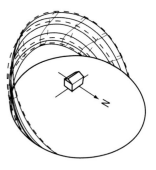

Annual sun path

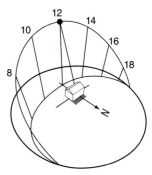

Sun location
at summer solstice

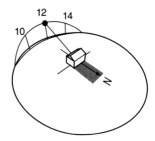

Sun location
at winter solstice

Figure 3.4: Sundials can be used to determine the yearly changing position of the sun and, as a result, road and dwelling orientation.

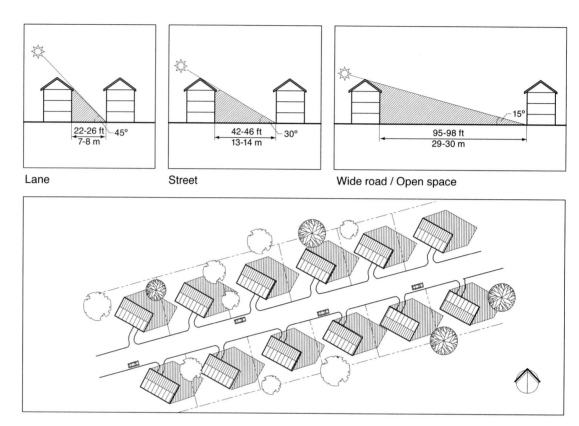

Lane   Street   Wide road / Open space

Figure 3.5: Roads can be oriented and their widths planned so that home siting maximizes sun exposure and dwellings are situated on the cusp of other units' shadows.

Existing natural vegetation and new growth can also be used for shade. To minimize solar heat gain in the summer, deciduous trees can be placed on the sunniest side of the house. The leaves of these trees shade houses from the heat but allow some light to penetrate indoors. In the wintertime, more solar heat and light can filter through their bare branches (Figure 3.6). Other façades that are exposed to sun with lesser intensity should be about 10 to 15 percent fenestrated to allow for natural lighting. Maximizing the solar gain will lower energy consumption, which in turn lowers costs and reduces the amount of emitted pollution necessary to produce this energy (Mendler and Odell, 2000).

Natural ventilation is another important aspect of sustainable design. Trees and other vegetation play an important role in wind flows. Although patterns change from one season to another, the wind is determined by the landscape, time, and weather patterns. Its direction and its speed can be evaluated for each area by looking at a wind square (G. Z. Brown, 1985). For example, near bodies of water, the

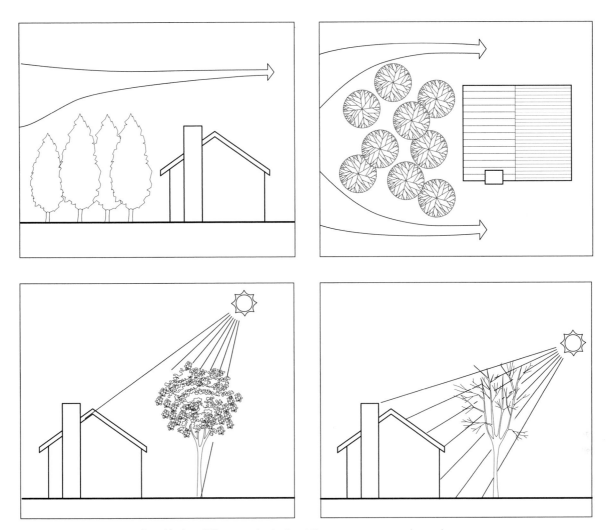

Figure 3.6: Dense woodland helps diffuse cool winds while sun penetrates through deciduous trees on sunny façades in wintertime.

wind will flow from the direction of the water toward the land in the daytime but will reverse in the night. Because of inertia, the wind will flow around objects and keep the same direction of flow. As a result, the vegetation in the surrounding area can greatly reduce wind speed. During the cold months, trees act as a shield from the winter winds that usually originate from the same direction. Consequently, coniferous trees are appropriate winter wind blocks as they maintain their foliage year round. This placement also allows the houses to benefit from summer breezes from the other direction. Favorable positioning will allow for cross-ventilation so that mechanical cooling means will not be necessary.

Trees should be placed at a balanced distance from the developments so as not to create too much shade but to protect against strong winds. The preferred distance of woodland windbreaks from houses should be approximately 10 times the tree-to-house height ratio (Figure 3.7). Trees planted at too great a distance from houses allow wind tunnels to sweep through the area between windbreaks and residences. Houses should also be placed so as not to create a wind tunnel by staggering their setbacks and having gentle curves in the streets. Architectural elements on the façades of houses such as sills and cornices may also act as windbreaks.

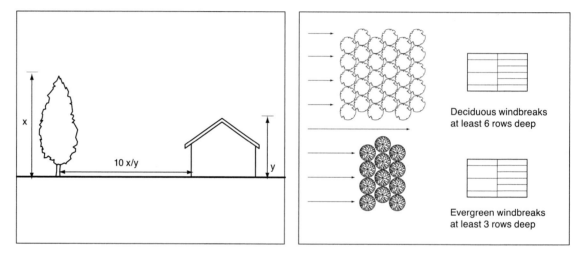

Figure 3.7: The preferred distance of woodland windbreaks from houses should be approximately 10 times the tree-to-house height ratio (left) and several rows deep (right).

The preferred building site is the location at which sun and wind are considered and where different tree species on either side of the homes help control the overall climate. Combining these two aspects can create an energy-efficient and comfortable living environment within a forested area.

Preserving Flora and Fauna

Designers of new developments need to consider vegetation and site conditions, by taking advantage of what is already in place (Figure 3.8). Often, residential developers clear the trees and re-landscape when the buildings are complete. An approach that conserves as many trees as possible and conforms to the site, however, reduces cost and retains the site's natural uniqueness. Minimal disruption of the surrounding environment will also protect the ecosystem's diversity. It is therefore crucial to consider environmental impact on any site's future and begin by evaluating how to build on the site and still retain the natural landscape.

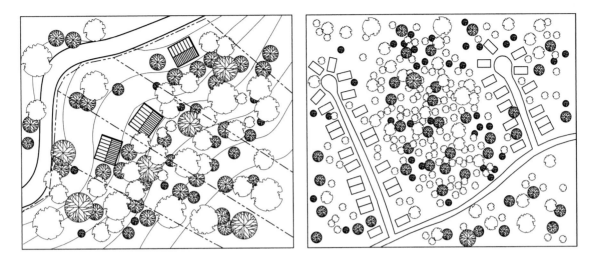

Figure 3.8: The varying amounts of vegetation that cover a site can guide lot division and unit siting (left). Preservation can be enacted upon the most heavily treed sections of the site and the houses can be arranged around it (right).

According to Arendt (1996), woodland areas of 20 to 60 percent tree coverage are appropriate for some developments. The trees should be evaluated as to which are healthy, which need pruning, and which should be removed. Trees that need to be protected, especially mature specimens, can be fenced and/or sectioned off. Some guidelines suggest that a mature tree is any tree with a trunk circumference greater than 18 inches (45 centimeters) as measured from 40 inches (1 meter) above ground level (Figure 3.9). To prevent mechanical damage to the tree trunk, protection should be installed to a height of 60 inches (1.5 meters).

Before construction begins, surrounding trees should be prepared with adequate pruning, watering, and fertilizing (Lamontagne and Brazeau, 1996). Branches and root systems should be protected from breakage and disruption. The grade around the trees should not be changed to avoid damaging the roots or depriving them of oxygen, and barriers should be placed around trees to prevent compaction of the soil around the roots, which can deprive them of oxygen and damage the tree (Fisette, 2002).

Trees and other shrubs catch and absorb stormwater runoff and prevent soil erosion. They also do their part in filtering out noises and offer privacy to homes. Designated regions where trees are preserved share an enhanced character and appearance for all to enjoy. In the end, the trees should reflect the building orientation, height, setback, distribution, and fenestration. According to Arnold (1980), by keeping existing trees healthy on the site, sensitive environmental decisions are responsibly made and natural neighborhoods are created.

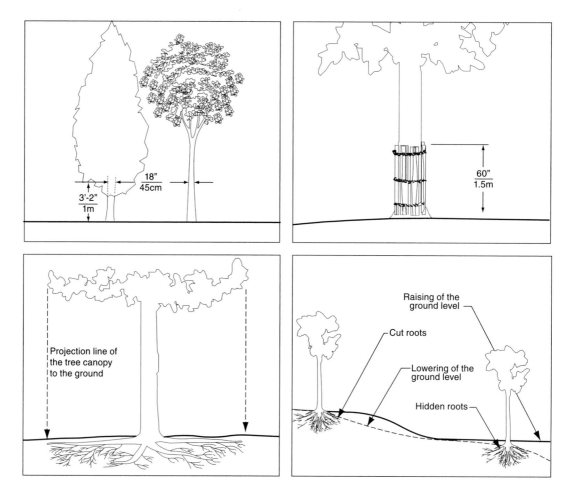

Figure 3.9: Mature trees with a circumference greater than 18 inches (45 cm) need to be protected (top left). To prevent mechanical damage to the tree trunk, install protection to a height of 60 inches (1.5 meters) (top right). Excavation should not occur within the root zone of the tree, which is approximately equal to the spread of its branches to the ground (bottom left). A lowering of the level of the soil can destroy the tree's root system. Raising the level of the soil may cause suffocation of the roots (bottom right).

Preserving the Topography

The site's original topography must be preserved, because, if altered, it may not be restored and can forever change the local ecosystem. Native flora and other natural elements lend the site its distinct character. Roads and buildings should be sited with respect to slopes and changes in elevation and should follow contour patterns, and building on steep slopes should be avoided to reduce construction costs and prevent erosion. When roadways have natural bumps and bends, drivers will travel with more caution, contributing to residents' safety (Figure 3.10).

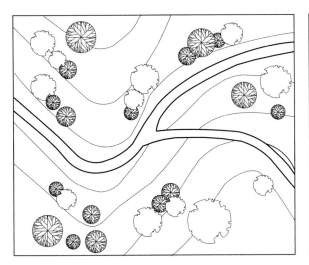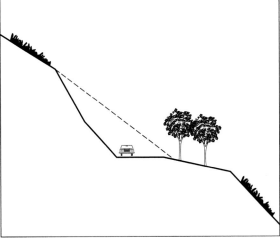

Figure 3.10: The site's contours can guide the road path (left). On a sloped site, roads can be constructed on existing flat areas rather than creating new ones (right).

It is possible to arrange houses on a sloped site using a terracing technique that orients homes to allow for the greatest sun exposure. Placing the homes in rows at different elevations will not obstruct views to subsequent homes and will adhere to the lay of the land (Figure 3.11). Space between succeeding rows creates some private outdoor spaces, decreases obstruction of views, and prevents shadows. A sloped terrain also allows for a simple, natural, and effective drainage system, and reduces construction costs. As well, a community that is located near a body of water can benefit from the tempered effects of evaporation. In the spring and autumn, the land becomes warmer than the surrounding water, thus a thermally induced circulating current is produced, providing a cool breeze.

Grading a site can negatively affect the surrounding ecosystem. Roots of trees and shrubs that reach deep into the ground can easily be affected by soil compaction or water loss. Maintaining the site conditions by constructing retaining walls, terraces, and other structures for stability will reduce chances of soil erosion. Erosion can also disturb the site's natural drainage system and pollute nearby water sources. Less site disruption means a reduced flow of stormwater to nearby sources, so that more water can be absorbed by plants.

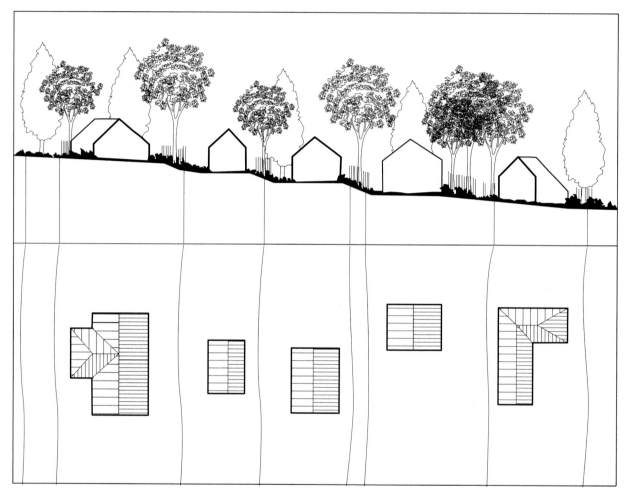

Figure 3.11: When the terrain slopes steeply, homes' grading and footprints should be adjusted to the contours to facilitate views above each other and to maximize sun exposure.

Laying Roads and Paths

Roads, vital to the movement of people and vehicles, should be placed to accommodate mixed use. Streets can be regarded as public spaces for social interaction as well as networks that connect buildings and the community at large. Each road, pedestrian, and cyclist path needs to be woven into the local surroundings and existing flora (Figure 3.12). Accordingly, when building in sites with prominent natural features, roads and sidewalks need not adhere to rigid codes and bylaws. All streets, main and local, can follow the site's contours. Such an approach allows elements such as streams, ponds, and rock formations to be retained, which creates interesting roadside vistas. Keeping natural changes in the terrain, creating gentle curves in the roads, and narrowing streets also slows down traffic. Streets of about 20 feet (6.1 meters), for example, have been observed to benefit pedestrians and drivers, although this width can be varied depending on the flora surrounding the area.

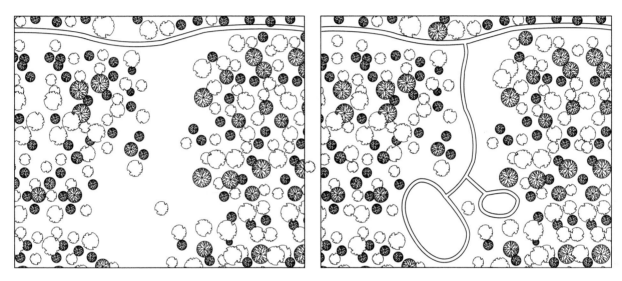

Figure 3.12: The path of a road can run through clearance in the forest and avoid natural features of note.

In limiting traffic speeds, a safer environment is created for pedestrians and walking or cycling can be encouraged over driving, which will increase socialization, physical activity, and interaction with nature (Moughtin, 2003). It is particularly important to balance privacy, car access, and the pedestrian route in residential areas. Sidewalks can be made safer by separating them from the roads with planted vegetation. Trees that are kept or appropriately planted at regular intervals along the street increase the aesthetic pleasure and improve continuity and human scale.

It is also possible to integrate the road and sidewalk systems to make the circulation pedestrian friendly. By eliminating the curb and by having sloped streets, simpler drainage into the ground and existing vegetation is created (Figure 3.13). Roads, streets, and paths in the forest should make use of a permeable material, such as gravel, so that water can be absorbed into the soil (Fisette and Ryan, 2002).

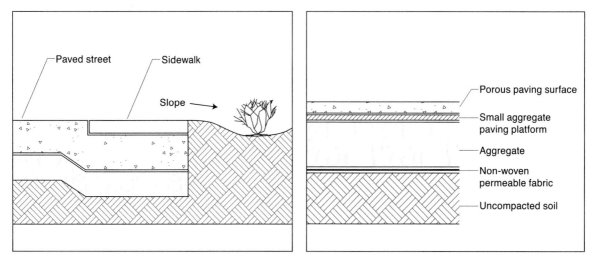

Figure 3.13: Sidewalks can be placed at the same level as roads and sloped to help encourage rainwater flow to natural systems (left). The surface can also be made of porous material to facilitate water absorption (right).

Housing the Car

Preserving a site with ample natural features requires consideration of easily accessible private or public parking. Sufficient yet reduced parking spaces for each home can be provided to minimize tree removal and land waste. In general, outdoor public parking areas reduce the overall allotted space and offer opportunities for social interaction. Shared parking can occur in a defined lot or in a cluster at a reasonable distance from, around, and between existing trees that are close to the road. These unpaved parking spots make efficient use of land and also reduce building and operating cost; hard-surface paving does not let water through and absorbs heat. Natural or planted trees in such spaces can make it more pleasant, provide shade for vehicles, encourage pedestrian walkways, and join shared parking spaces with each home (Figure 3.14).

Private parking can also be provided in garages or driveways adjacent to or behind houses to maintain a consistent visual streetscape. The driveways leading up to the garage can provide room for other vehicles. Parking places should be oriented according to natural features, perhaps at an angle, leaving ample room for vehicular access. The free space in front of the houses can then be left for landscaping. Instead of garages, open parking can be accommodated between shrubs and trees. These spaces need to be planned according to the status of mature trees and other flora. Also, at times it may be more suitable to have on-street parking and avoid additional tree clearing (Figure 3.15). Such practice is the simplest and most economic parking alternative as parked cars also slow down oncoming traffic and increase pedestrian safety (Mayerovitch, 1973).

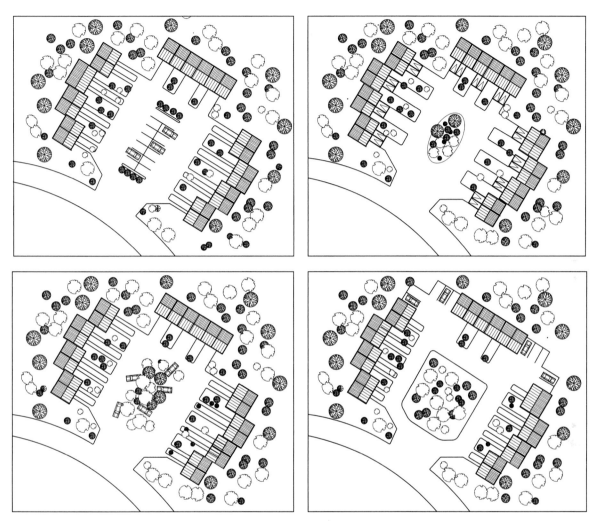

Figure 3.14: In conservation projects, parking should be integrated into the units, arranged between trees and clustered in the center or at a corner.

Natural Open Spaces

Public outdoor spaces are used for recreation, social interaction, and physical activity. Retreats such as parks should be designed in multipurpose fashion to appeal to young and old alike. They should be well-distributed, visible, and accessible to all. Accordingly, open public spaces could be located to face clusters of row houses, in the center of built-up areas, or in between streets and lanes. A site plan that allows views of a green space is more desirable than one facing neighboring homes and can be integrated into the natural surroundings. In a site with bold natural elements, location and arrangement of green area is, therefore, very important.

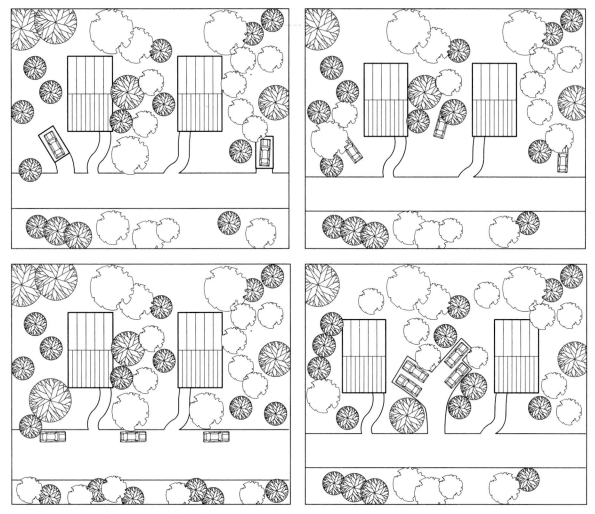

Figure 3.15: Alternative parking solutions near homes need to be explored in a conservation site.

Areas of dense preserved trees can also be designated as public areas. Parks and other types of open spaces should inhabit landscaped areas that have been carved out of the original natural system. Planners can incorporate mature trees and vegetation with their design so that there is less need to remove old growth and plant anew (Arnold, 1980). The parkland, for example, can continue and spread into private lots to maintain continuity, which also makes these areas more accessible to residents. Cleared or felled playing fields can foster proper human scale and be set away from main roads (Figure 3.16).

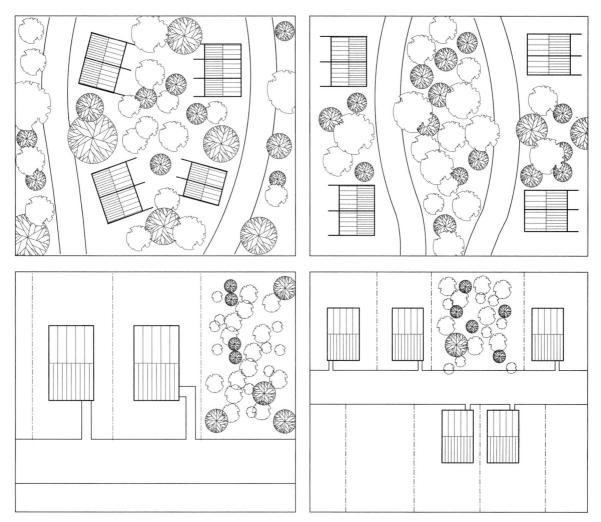

Figure 3.16: Concentration of natural dense forested areas can become the community's open space (top). Houses can be sited to have a direct access to, and view of, dense forested areas at the side or front (bottom).

Smaller pockets of open space are more appropriate as they are safer and less intimidating than less private, vast open spaces. Also, more trees may be conserved in such a design. Large, open cleared areas can be separated from the more serene areas by other flora. Adequate roads or pedestrian paths encourage use of open space bounded by buildings. Access points can be readily visible and accommodating, creating a sense of public place. Benches and other stopping places, such as steps and ledges, are also essential to draw and keep people in green spaces. Benches that are grouped or angled toward one another increase opportunities for contact between individuals.

Planning Lots and Siting Homes

When planning lots and siting homes, natural features should be considered for personal, environmental, and economic reasons. Landscaped areas can provide attractive screening for privacy and be integrated with dwelling layout so that the areas can be shared by all residents. Cluster developments are an appropriate design because the units occupy less land and minimize areas needed for roads. When planning lot, road, open space, and path patterns, unit arrangements should ensure shared access to preserved natural environments (Figures 3.17 and 3.18).

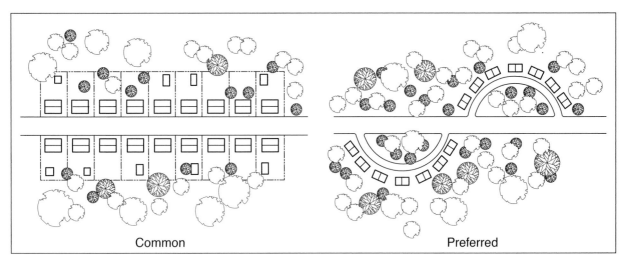

Common   Preferred

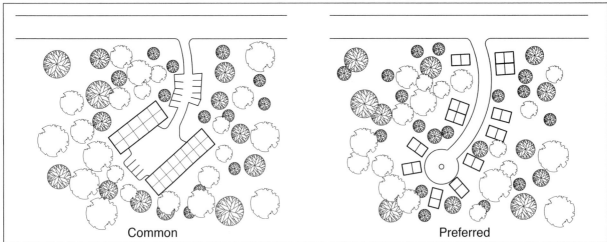

Common   Preferred

Figure 3.17: In sites with prominent natural features, cluster developments are more suitable than conventional grid layouts (top). Smaller dwellings rather than larger buildings are better suited to these areas as well (bottom).

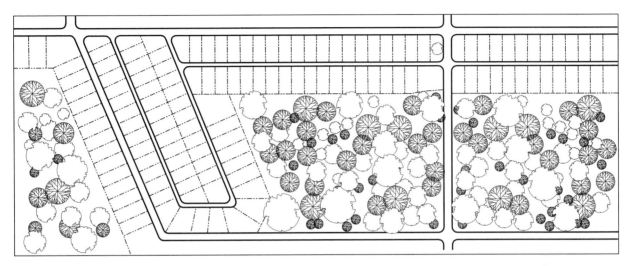

Figure 3.18: Master plans are more prone to preservation principles when they make natural areas an integral part of the design.

Shared amenities also help with greater preservation of natural elements and reduction of forest clearance. To avoid construction of private swimming pools on each lot, for example, the community can offer a large public pool. Also, to prevent excessive tree removal, the houses can be placed as close to streets as possible. An important exception to this considers mature tree cover on property fronts. In such cases, houses should be placed further back on the lots to preserve vegetation, and this will affect the distances between houses. Arrangements providing greater than 10 feet (3 meters) between units can ensure that windowless walls face lot lines. Otherwise, dense lot designs should confirm that windows of neighboring units do not face each other.

Planning for Change

One of the attributes of sustainable planning is the ability to accommodate changes. Rather than construct communities according to the last century's design principles, planners can use emerging social and architectural trends when creating designs. Rather than demolish and rebuild, the process of adaptation can be used. The need to facilitate changes can occur in the short run as well. In a large-scale development with hundreds or thousands of units, which take several years to complete, rethinking the master plan or the types of chosen dwellings could occur as circumstances change.

The scope of change in society can be seen in its shifting demographic makeup. Following World War II, builders viewed buyers as a homogenous group consisting of a breadwinner father, stay-at-home mother, and three or four children. The single-family home dominated the marketplace, demand exceeded supply, and there was no reason to change the dwellings' design. Since the 1960s, however, traditional families account for a smaller segment of all households, with a quarter of all clients looking to buy a home being single or single-parent families, for example. Looking to the future, between the years 2011 and 2027, the post-war baby boom generation born between 1946 and 1962 will retire and search for diverse housing types.

Such unpredictable housing trends make it difficult, if not impossible, to predetermine the type of buildings that are most appropriate for a large, multi-phased development. The choice of housing type has become more complex as the makeup of the family unit changes. To accommodate the fluctuations in the housing requirements in an increasingly diverse market, an adaptive and flexible process that is sensitive to the accelerated change of sustainable urban systems is needed.

The Conventional Process

In a conventional design process, planners are asked to predict the types of dwellings that will be in demand in the future. Municipalities require the submission of a master plan with any application for residential developments that claim new, previously uninhabited land. The master plan must be approved through a political process and includes primary and secondary roads, with accompanying utilities and infrastructure, and land subdivisions. Everything from the location of lamp posts to the dimensions of sidewalks, building setbacks, and parking arrangements is determined early on. In other words, the entire development is designed in detail years before these dwellings will be inhabited.

Once approved, the master plan becomes an absolute point of reference for the duration of the development's construction, however long it lasts. If a project is not built in its entirety, the construction of one of its phases may occur several years after the actual design but will still be limited to that design long after it has outlasted its usefulness. Issues and concerns that were considered to be important at the time of design might well be obsolete and contradictory to the issues and concerns at the time of construction.

The Alternative Design Process

To allow change to occur, a simple breakdown of a project's design in accordance with the anticipated construction schedule will allow each stage of the development to be created immediately prior to its construction. It will limit the possibility of drastic market shifts between the design and construction phases. This would preclude the need for planners to predict the future of the housing market and create a sustainable design that would have continued relevance well into the future. Rather than designing an entire community in advance and building a section at a time—as is often the case today—only those sections for which financing has been secured and that are ready for construction would be designed in the greatest detail. The design of subsequent sections would take place before implementation. This process would give developers more freedom in responding to changes in market demands. A mechanism that ensured a certain degree of continuity and harmony between the different sections of a development could be included at the beginning of the process. If, however, the degree of municipal control is divided along hierarchical levels, then flexibility can be achieved without compromising harmony and overburdening authorities.

In this alternative process, developers guided by planners would begin their design by creating a *vision* of the kind of community that they expect to build. This vision would include the general concept layout of the development as opposed to the detailed characteristics. In the form of a written description, it would be general enough to allow for various alternatives yet descriptive enough to define the community's character.

Having created this vision, the developer would engage the services of a planner who would establish a general concept for the entire development. This concept would further define the vision and begin to influence the design concept physically. Along with this concept and as a manifestation of it, the planner would design the major roads traversing the site. Because at this stage the roads and services will be planned according to specific dimensions and capacities, designers will also have to outline the envisioned overall density of the development to avoid overloading or overbuilding the infrastructure. The developer would implement the general design concept by determining the shapes, sizes, and quantities of subsections into which the development will be divided, and as a result, define the community's proposed scale.

La Forêt de Marie-Victorin

The La Forêt de Marie-Victorin project began when retired architects Jean-Marie Lavoie and Paul Brassard purchased a 102 acre (41 hectare) plot of densely forested land near a small town called Saint-Nicolas in Quebec, Canada (Figure 3.19). Proximity to the St. Lawrence River with a view of the city made the site a prime location for a residential development.

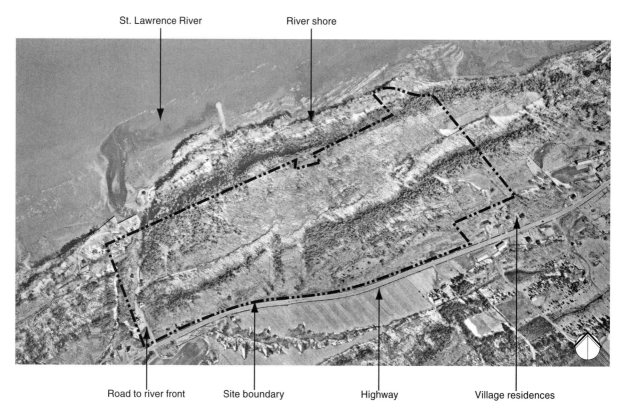

Figure 3.19: The Forêt de Marie-Victorin site is a 102 acre (41 hectare) plot of densely forested land near the town of Saint-Nicolas, Quebec, Canada.

When Lavoie and Brassard contemplated their approach to site planning and the type of homes they wished to build, they realized that they must apply unconventional thinking. They recognized that common approaches to contemporary development—those that involve clearing the forest and building wide boulevards, for example—would alter the beauty of the site. They also assumed that conserving the site's assets could become a marketing draw and attract homebuyers seeking proximity to nature. These clients, Lavoie and Brassard argued, would want to trade private swimming pools or large parking garages for trees. The homes, they decided, should not be sprawling suburban dwellings whose construction would mean extensive landscape alteration. They instead agreed that adaptability to the topography would play a pivotal role in both urban planning and unit design. In their search for a housing prototype that would satisfy these requirements, they became familiar with my work, and they invited me to collaborate in both the planning of the community and the design of the homes. The ultimate goal was to promote sustainable living and create a community that contributed to such an endeavor.

We started the first stage in the development of the master plan by studying regional and urban issues and their potential effect on the site. We correlated the contribution of these aspects to sustainability. We documented the presence and location of amenities such as daycares, schools, medical clinics, and shops to determine whether such facilities would be needed on the site. Further study attempted to identify the anticipated buyers. Their socioeconomic characteristics were gathered from census data, marketing surveys, and visits to other projects. The possibility of buyers of different age groups and incomes was the goal from the beginning. Once we made key background decisions, we directed our attention to the site.

We began a careful study of the site's natural assets. A soil test revealed an elevated level of rock, and the study of aboveground and underground water showed that several streams and a deep ravine crossed the site. We analyzed existing microclimates and the site orientation in relation to the sun's path.

The extreme climatic conditions found in Quebec that produce cold winters and hot, humid summers are typical of the site. Temperatures fluctuate between winter lows of 5° to −22° F (−15° to −30° C) in January, to summer highs of 79° to 95° F (26° to 35° C). Similar to other low-latitude areas, the sun at the site peaks at a relatively low 68 degrees on the summer solstice and only 21 degrees on the winter solstice. Climatic conditions characterizing the site are not only influenced by solar reception: winds also affect the environment. Wind patterns tend to differ seasonally, as northwesterly winter winds strongly bluster while southeasterly breezes cool summertime heat. Importantly, within the context of the site, the woodlands act as windbreaks by diluting severe airstreams. Creating energy-efficient housing considers not only temperatures but also wind receptiveness, and we decided that a sustainable design must, therefore, consider the interdependent relationships governing microclimates.

Identifying the site's flora and fauna was the next stage. The concentration of trees was documented throughout the site using aerial maps. In addition, an expert was engaged to map and indicate the location of each tree in each area that was slated for construction. Judgment as to whether a tree was worth preserving was also made based on the tree's age and diameter. Two areas with dense concentrations of trees in an east-west direction were immediately recognized and set aside for conservation: the first on the northern edge of the site, and the second in a ravine in the middle (Figure 3.20). In general, woodlands cover 90 percent of the area and the flora is composed of mixed growth. Most of the trees are deciduous, with maple dominating over other species such as birch, elm, beech, and alder. These trees represent several stages of growth and range from early successive to mature woodlands. Tree undergrowth also varies in maturation stage (Figure 3.21). Animal migration paths and large rock formations are also visible.

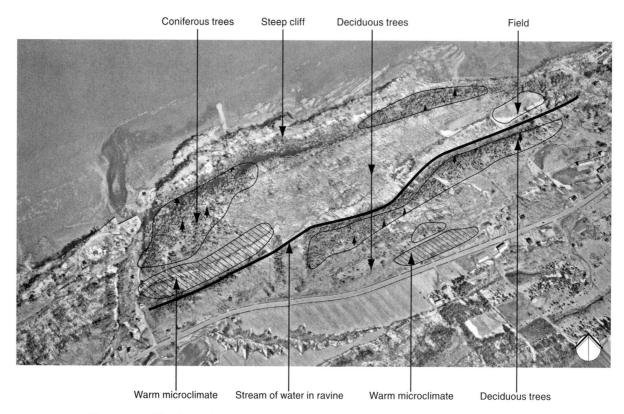

Figure 3.20: The Forêt de Marie-Victorin site has several areas with dense concentration of deciduous trees.

Site Planning

When study of the site characteristics was completed, construction of roads and pedestrian paths began. To keep the natural conditions intact, we decided that circulation routes should be as short as possible. Also, unlike typical suburban streets measuring 40 feet (12 meters) wide, a 20 foot (6 meter) road was designed. The sidewalks were only 24 inches (61 centimeters) wide and were at the same level as the street's asphalt surface, so that rain water could return to the ground and existing flora. An earlier tree survey revealed several patches with fewer, much younger trees. These areas were more suitable for roads rather than clearing areas with older trees, and vehicular circulation, as a result, connect these patches. The street path was also routed according to the site elevations, bypassing boulders and refraining from clearing additional trees. During construction, all the services were buried under the roads to maintain the natural beauty (Figure 3.22).

Land subdivision to lots was another aspect that required deviation from common practices. Rather than create lots with 60 by 100 foot (18 by 31 meter) proportions, we decided that long, narrow parcels of land would be more suitable. Smaller homes in denser configurations could be encouraged rather than dwellings with large footprints. While considering the design, we recognized that the practice of clearing trees from the entire lot should be discouraged and enacted a requirement in the deed of sale that only those trees that grew under the footprint of the home would be cut. The rest would be protected during construction and remain untouched. Special precautions were taken during construction to protect tree trunks, which were wrapped and guarded against damage. The dense areas in the middle and at the top of the site would be turned into a communal path and a narrow linear park to be used by all residents (Figure 3.23).

To preserve the site's natural state, homes were placed as close as possible to roads. Carport parking structures were offered as an option in front of or next to the home (Figure 3.24). To avoid utility poles for telephone, electricity, and TV cables, a service column was constructed in front of each house. The column would be the exit point for underground cables and would also house a domestic recycling box.

Figure 3.21: Most of the trees on the site are deciduous, with maple dominating over other species.

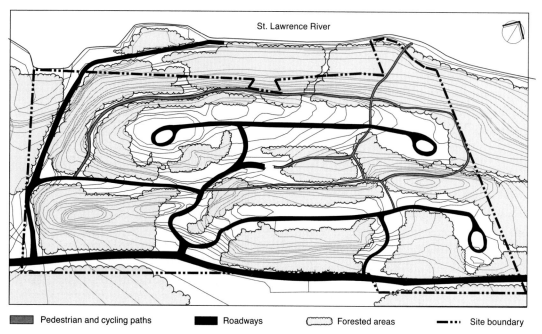

| | Pedestrian and cycling paths | | Roadways | | Forested areas | | Site boundary |

Figure 3.22: The routes of the roads and the pedestrian paths were determined by the concentration of mature trees, the site's elevations, and locations of other natural features.

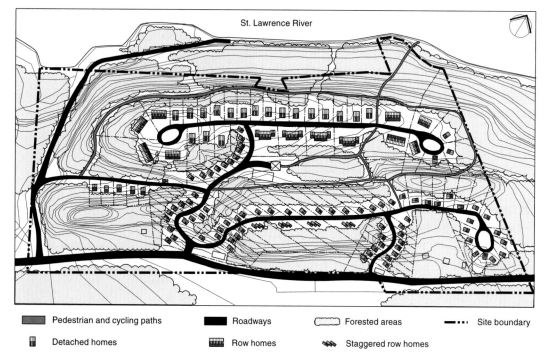

| | Pedestrian and cycling paths | | Roadways | | Forested areas | | Site boundary |
| | Detached homes | | Row homes | | Staggered row homes | | |

Figure 3.23: Rather than having large lots, narrow and long lots were introduced. The homes were clustered near the road to prevent excessive tree clearing.

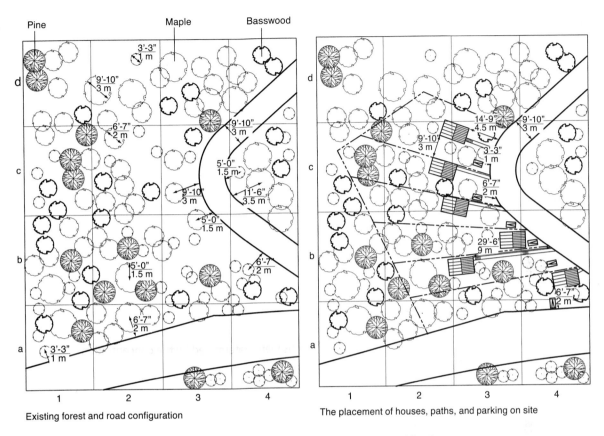

Figure 3.24: The siting of each home and parking structure was determined by the position of mature trees on the lot.

Unit Design

The quest for a home with a long and narrow footprint led to the design of a unit measuring 20 by 32 feet (6 by 10 meters). It created floors with a footprint of 640 square feet (64 square meters), each of which could become a small self-contained, one-bedroom apartment. The open-ended approach to the design led to the creation of a variety of interior configurations and alternative layouts for each floor. The options created a possible scenario whereby the ground floor could be used as an independent dwelling unit to house an elderly member of the family. Alternatively, the floor could become a home office for a resident of the upper two floors. Developers expected that buyers would regard these options as a menu from which they would select their needed number of floors, desired interior layout, and suitable finishes (Figure 3.25).

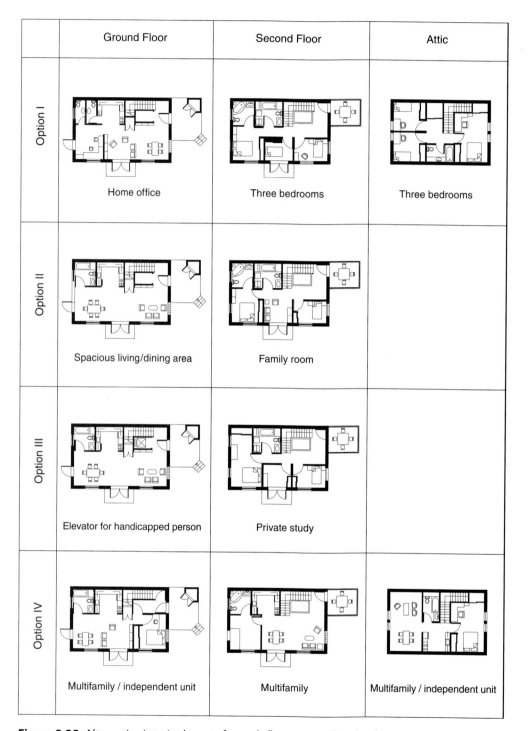

	Ground Floor	Second Floor	Attic
Option I	Home office	Three bedrooms	Three bedrooms
Option II	Spacious living/dining area	Family room	
Option III	Elevator for handicapped person	Private study	
Option IV	Multifamily / independent unit	Multifamily	Multifamily / independent unit

Figure 3.25: Alternative interior layouts for each floor were offered to buyers.

To maximize the flexibility of the overall space arrangement, two front doors were designed. This enabled the structure to function as a single- or multifamily home. Also, the configuration of the stairs permitted the installation of an internal elevator to allow a disabled occupant to reach upper levels.

Recognizing the effect that extensive excavation and dynamiting would have, developers avoided excavating basement levels and constructed shallow foundations instead. A special prefabricated truss was selected to allow the use of the roof space. Turning the attic into a habitable area also aided in resource conservation since warm air rises, creating a reduced need to heat upper floors during winter months (Figure 3.26).

To maximize the dwelling's interior space and adaptability, an appropriate floor plan was created. Locating the unit's mechanical and service functions along one of the walls proved to be a suitable strategy, as it freed the rest of the space for interior partitioning that fit the occupant's needs and budgets. As a result, the stairs, kitchen, bathrooms, and utilities were all placed against the north wall. Avoiding fenestration of that wall also contributed to reduced energy losses and increased privacy from the neighboring home. Openings were, therefore, placed instead on the other façades and mostly on the southern elevation to maximize passive solar gain (Figure 3.27).

A Balancing Act

The site planning and dwelling design of La Forêt de Marie-Victorin project was the outcome of an integrated approach that paid direct and indirect attention to key sustainable principles. This section reviews the effects of these principles on the project's decision-making process and the outcome.

The employment of the *path of least impact* in this project is clear. Most planning decisions avoided alteration and

Figure 3.26: The dwellings in the site have small footprints, shallow foundations, and utilize roof space.

Figure 3.27: To enhance the dwelling's energy performance and increase privacy, the north façade was left unfenestrated. Other elevations, particularly the southern, had more openings.

destruction of the site's environmental conditions. These decisions, however, had other consequences. Economically, developers saved substantial amounts of money by constructing narrower roads and sidewalks. Also, by avoiding dynamiting rocks and constructing attics rather than basements, the developers were able to lower the dwelling costs and offer more competitive housing prices. By opting to construct tall and narrow—rather than sprawling—homes and thus saving trees, an overall higher density was achieved, which led to a potential larger number of units arranged in a denser configuration and a higher profit. The design was more suitable to a site with a dense tree population. Having a flexible lot size contributed to a least-impact approach. Another innovative approach was a result of the fact that the site was a *planned unit development* permitted to have its own zoning.

Design decisions made in the project can also be seen as contributing to a *self-sustaining* process. Saving trees was promoted as a marketing advantage and used to attract buyers who wanted to reside in a "green" environment. The opportunity offered to clients a home office that not only saved commuting time and avoided air pollution from car exhaust, but enabled income-tax deduction of expenses associated with maintaining an office. Also, by not building a basement and offering an attic instead, each home's energy performance was improved. Basements are known to be a source of energy loss, whereas because heat rises, attics remain warm. When a fan is installed at the top of the stairs, the heat can be pushed downstairs and circulated during colder months.

By avoiding clearing the forest, spending on creating green public and private open spaces was avoided. The forested area can be regarded as part of the 10 percent commonly allocated to public open space. In addition, smaller expenses can be made annually on maintaining those spaces. It is likely that the trees will have to be pruned, but water consumed in watering large grassed areas, as is the case in most suburban developments, will be saved.

A number of examples demonstrate a strong *supporting relation* in La Forêt de Marie-Victorin project. Construction and maintenance of narrow roads result in slower car speeds and greater communal safety. To save trees, private swimming pools cannot be constructed at the rear of each home; instead, residents are allowed access to a public pool, which contributes to fostering a stronger bond between residents. By choosing a housing prototype that can be converted to accommodate extended family, a support system between two generations is also in place. Also, the mixing of unit types and an offer made by the developers to sell floors in the building rather than an entire building not only increased their profit, but contributed to forming a community made of residents of mixed ages and incomes.

By avoiding windows on the north walls, not only was the amount of energy lost from the building diminished, but greater privacy was maintained. Views of and from the neighboring properties were reduced. Moreover, the placement of large openings on the south sides contributed to passive solar gain.

In this project, the developers decided to leave a gap between the northern lots and the project's edge and create a linear pedestrian path. It is shared by all community members who are able to stroll, fostering a stronger bond among them.

The notion of "cradle to grave" was a key feature of this project. Perhaps the most noticeable aspect is the flexibility offered in the dwellings' design. The units are configured to be modified from single-family dwellings to two-family dwellings, so that each building's lifecycle can be extended and demolition later in life prevented. The placement of the mechanical and service functions along the north wall while avoiding windows also facilitates ongoing maintenance and prevents heat lost throughout the buildings' life.

In the design of La Forêt de Marie-Victorin, environmental, social, and economic aspects were considered. The project's initiators chose to employ principles that, when implemented, contributed to the creation of a sustainable residential community.

High-Density Neighborhoods 4

In recent years, policymakers and planners have been faced with urban sprawl that needs to be controlled by building higher density neighborhoods. In addition to environmental degradation, demographic transformation is an argument for introducing higher densities. Childless couples, single-parent families, and singles make up a significant segment of today's population, who, although interested in suburban living, are not necessarily the type of residents who wish to reside in large homes. In addition, people are living longer, and the large, difficult-to-maintain single-family home may not be seniors' preferred retirement residence.

To accommodate the changing urban environment, we must propose and implement models of denser suburban communities based on sustainable principles. This chapter recalls the historical evolution of high-density living, describes contemporary precedence models, outlines guidelines a designer should consider in planning livable compact neighborhoods, and demonstrates their implementation in real-world projects.

High-Density Living Through History

Throughout history, people have congregated for food-gathering, security, and social disposition. Settlements, agriculture, and trade contributed to the development of civilization. Exchange of ideas and information helped fuel technological and cultural development and took place in communities. Several landmarks contributed to the urban evolution of high-density living, and we can learn much from the experiences gained.

The departure from the predominance of cities as commercial and population centers, common in ancient civilizations, occurred with the onset of the early medieval period, around the sixth century A.D. After the fall of Rome, marauders raided towns and scoured the countryside, causing people to retreat to remote areas. Others chose to remain in the cities and settled within the fortified ruins of amphitheaters, such as the one in Arles, France, which reinforced the notion that walls were the best way to safeguard people. Given the impermeable perimeters, urban development within the walls was compacted into dense forms. Schoenauer (1992) explains that the city's form was the result of organic or natural growth. Initially, topography shaped the urban form, but thereafter cities grew in an uncontrolled fashion. Often, the city nucleus was ecclesial or military in origin, with narrow arterial streets to accommodate movement of goods. Narrower roads and lanes connected residential districts to main streets densely lined with houses and enclosed rear alleys.

Centuries later, medieval society viewed domesticity and work as complementary and industrial or commercial activities began occurring within homes (Bemis and Burchard, 1933). Buildings with street frontages were of higher value due to the increasing importance of commerce. As a result, narrow, deep plots developed with an average width-to-depth ratio of 1:6. Even in larger medieval cities, the density rendered the distance from the walled peripheries to the city centers to be less than a third of a mile (half a kilometer) (Schoenauer). A compacted city size resulted from not only the impervious fortressed walls, but also from the need for foot travel and self-sufficiency. Agricultural products and goods were transported from the outlying countryside, and all other goods and services were produced and exchanged within city walls.

Dubrovnik, a city in present-day Croatia, is an example of a medieval urban settlement. It illustrates that neither density nor disaster forced urban development to take place outside the fortressed walls. Instead, the city internally accommodated physical changes that resulted from economic and social pressures (Figure 4.1). Trade agreements with Italian maritime city-states helped make the town a significant port city. As Dubrovnik prospered, it expanded to more than 40 acres

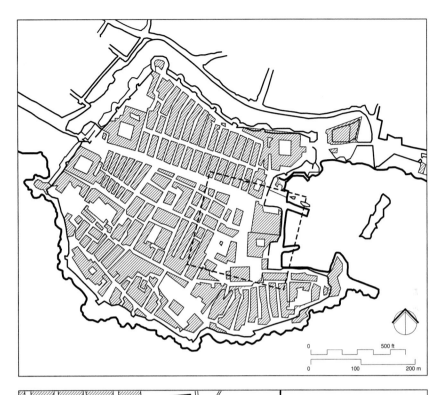

Figure 4.1: Dubrovnik, situated at a harbor, is a typical example of a medieval city with dense urban form, walls, and nonlinear pattern of narrow streets (top) and civic and religious centers (bottom).

Palaca

Sponza Palace

St. Biaggio

Harbor

Market Place

Rector's Palace

Cathedral

(16 hectares) by the end of the thirteenth century. Then, successive disasters such as earthquakes, fires, barbarian invasions, and political conquests ravaged the settlement. Despite being weakened, its inhabitants survived and continued to adapt. As a measure against the spread of fire, for example, north-south streets that averaged 7.5 feet (2.3 meters) in width and east-west streets that averaged 11.8 feet (3.6 meters) in width were built. The arterial route running through the city's commercial area was 984 feet (300 meters) long and wide enough to accommodate transport of goods to and from the harbor. Many narrow secondary and tertiary lanes dispersed from the arterial route to join residential and workshop units. Three-story dwellings averaged 23 to 30 feet (7 to 9 meters) in width and 33 to 43 feet (10 to 13 meters) in height.

Typically, a workshop adorned the ground floor, a reception room occupied the second, and a family living space was on the third floor of a building in Dubrovnik. According to Schoenauer, most residential lanes accommodated pedestrians only. Concentrated at the harbor front, the civic center linked a series of grouped squares—that is, public squares fed into one another as they wove through narrow streets and dense buildings. Key governments or clergy buildings dominated some squares, while monuments were featured in the center in others (Zucker, 1959). All grouped civic squares centralized trade and social congregation. Throughout history, both the city's population and economy adapted to the constraints of dense urban form. Dubrovnik, which exists and flourishes to this day, exemplifies a typical medieval city's capacity to adjust to high-density living in modern times.

Another example of innovative, mixed-use, dense urban form from the medieval period is the city of Chester, England. Chester's land use and housing form, like Dubrovnik's, are characteristic of their time of construction. What makes Chester unique is The Rows, which were narrow, wooden, multi-use dwellings elevated above street level (Figure 4.2). Perched atop vaulted cellars, shops with residential quarters above were connected by raised sidewalks. Beneath these shops were streets that freely accommodated vehicles. Schoenauer suggests that these covered, elevated sidewalks illustrate the viability of some modern planning concepts that separate vehicular and pedestrian traffic. Unfortunately, much of Chester's innovative urban concepts were lost during the Renaissance era.

The Renaissance involved a great deal of urban reconstruction. Both new development and building rehabilitation sought to restore existing cities to the glory of classical civilizations (Bemis and Burchard; Gardiner, 1974). Schoenauer suggests that the human scale of the medieval city was gradually replaced by a monumental and impressive scale. Guiding design principles endorsed straight, wide boulevards; prominent sweeping vistas; gregarious civic squares; and rectilin-

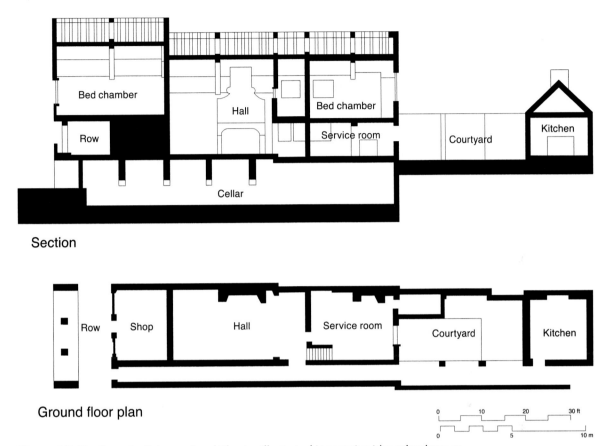

Section

Ground floor plan

Figure 4.2: The Rows built in medieval Chester illustrated innovative ideas that have re-emerged in current planning concepts. The dense, mixed-use units effectively separated pedestrians from vehicles.

ear block layouts. In the city, small industries and businesses were moved out of the home into separate buildings. The separation of home and work altered community relations. According to Mumford (1961), the city became "nobody's business." As a result, cities prospered with economic and artistic wealth but faltered with community impoverishment.

Renaissance development had both an upside and a downside on the faith of neighborhoods. While community cohesion subsided, economic empowerment spawned the rise of a new social class. With the Renaissance, commerce swept from the continent into Britain. In imitation of the powerful aristocracy, the middle class created a demand for new housing. As a result, sectors of row houses called *town houses* were built with elevations that emulated the façades of royal palaces.

By the close of the eighteenth century, residential rowhouse squares established London's unique character. Rear units contained personalized open spaces but were largely used for kitchen and domestic activities. Communal squares across from residential units were the focus of family recreation. Immaculately landscaped, semi-private parks provided benches, gardens, and green space for residents' enjoyment as well as places for family and personal interactions.

In the aftermath of the Industrial Revolution, efficient construction techniques sparked the building of many homes. Early in the era, designers were still sensitive to public perception. To ensure the sale or rent of units, attractive details, such as bay windows and elevated entrances, were added to houses. However, over time, a dramatic increase in demand allowed builders to sell lower quality, shorter, and narrower home units. Overcrowded conditions at the time occurred neither rapidly nor extensively within all cities. The monotonous, dreary, nineteenth-century worker rowhouse was generally confined to a certain segment of a city. Moreover, as Rudlin and Falk (1999) suggest, the back-to-back terrace homes were relatively desirable since they were self-contained and afforded a degree of privacy to a family. Rowhouses were attached on three sides to neighboring units, and windows adorned only the entrance side, resulting in lack of cross-ventilation and stifling air (Figure 4.3).

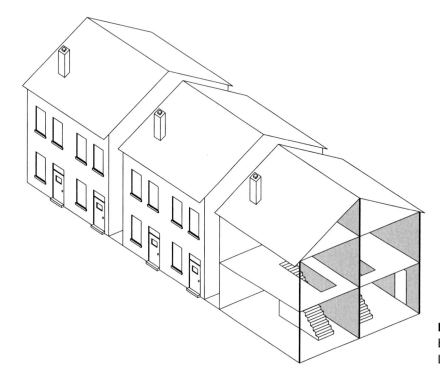

Figure 4.3: Typical back-to-back nineteenth-century London townhouses

North American urban development patterns were similar to those implemented during the British Industrial Revolution, which also resulted in poor living conditions for lower income families. Philadelphia was the first American city to adopt the English residential concept, although higher land values and gridiron street plans created blocks of up to 10 to 12 attached units. As the Industrial Era progressed in North America, rowhouses became smaller. For example, it was common that two, 25 foot (7.6 meter) lots were divided into houses with three rooms and one "dark room," which was a third of the size of a typical room and had no windows. With increasing rural-urban migration, the working poor and immigrant groups began to face housing shortages, leading to the conversion of old middle-class rowhouses into tenement buildings. Five families were housed in a unit with a 10 by 12 foot (3 by 3.6 meter) living room and a 6 by 7 foot (2 by 2 meter) bedroom (Schoenauer). The drastic urban overcrowding spawned a dire concern. Wealthier families in both Britain and North America left cities for fear of diseases and moral depravity, which were believed to breed within their congested grounds (Rudlin and Falk).

Throughout European urban history, the understanding of dense city neighborhoods changed from safe havens that protected citizens to places of pollution, disease, and poverty. Consequently, perceptions of the countryside also changed. Whereas it was previously seen as a backward place to live, it became a desirable place to reside. People began to crave open space, nature, and healthy living environments, all within a commutable proximity to urban employment. Moreover, people not only wanted to flee the pollution and poverty of cities, but they sought to avoid the overcrowding. The undeveloped countryside provided opportunities for the pursuit of spacious living environments, which led to the birth of the suburbs.

Strategies for High-Density Communities

Public notions that associate low-density suburban housing with personal wealth can prompt potential homeowners to regard high-density developments unfavorably, even if they are otherwise attractive communities. Therefore, reintroduction of high-density dwellings needs to be undertaken with caution. The advantageous aspects of suburbia, such as privacy and open space, must be incorporated in new designs. Simultaneous elimination of environmentally unsustainable elements such as excessive road coverage must also be considered. Several key aspects that affect the design of such developments have been assembled here, selected in accordance with their contribution to the environmental, economic, and social viability of a place.

Urban Form

Determining the development's main concept is a first stage in planning a high-density community. The planner must adhere to the site's natural conditions and zoning, among other considerations. However, the features that will most affect the design are the roads and parking patterns, the system of open spaces, and the type, density, and layout of dwellings (Figure 4.4).

Community location and urban form are often related to the presence of major transit systems. A community may have a main arterial road nearby, may be located a short distance from a major highway, or have a railway line and a station at its heart. Such features can dictate other key features of the entire road network that needs to regard a range of uses and users including motorists, cyclists, and pedestrians. Since the beginning of the twentieth century and with the proliferation of cars, road configuration has changed as a result of parallel evolution in planning concepts. The rise of suburbia and landmark developments such as Riverside, Illinois, and Radburn, New Jersey, cast a model that influences residential design to this day. In general, concepts that reduce area allocated to roads and increase dwelling density are more appropriate to high-density communities. Circulation networks that connect places rather than facilitate movement are likely to be more successful.

Determining areas of open space is another conceptual stage in a high-density neighborhood. Open spaces are easily accessible networks of green areas that range from the regional to individual unit levels. Large-scale parks, located outside the development, form the most public green spaces. Enclosed outdoor areas, on the other end, are the private. Within these two extremes are neighborhood parks and communal areas for clusters of homes. As density increases, the importance of open spaces rises, since the amount of area allocated to each home declines. In addition to traditional roles, open spaces serve to let sunlight into the heart of the neighborhood and accommodate the needs of people of all ages and mobility.

Deciding about the type of homes and how they should relate to each other is another phase in conceiving a community. To reach high density, the traditional single-family dwelling on a large lot needs to be replaced with multi-family configurations. Apartment houses or stacked dwellings need to be considered. Clustering structures of various densities will lead to a variety of dwelling types and mixed households. In addition, the combination of land uses will also foster a different neighborhood dynamic and will affect mobility. These issues are elaborated in the following sections.

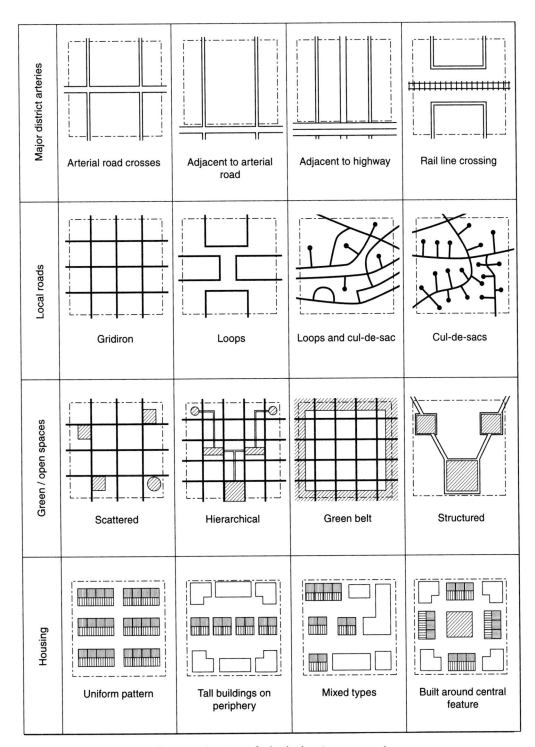

Figure 4.4: Key features affecting planning of a high-density community

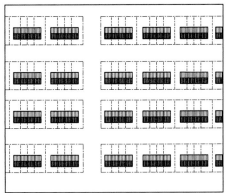

High-density developments from the twentieth century with 31 units per acre (77.5 units per hectare) are likely to be unwelcome by many suburban towns and deemed unfavorable by buyers.

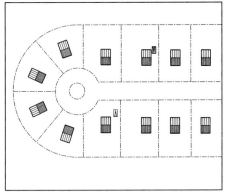

Dwellings with a density of 7 units per acre (17 units per hectare) are common in contemporary suburbs.

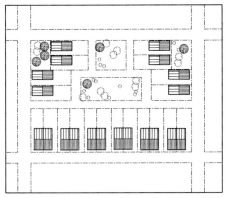

A community with a medium density of 20 to 25 units per acre (50 to 63 units per hectare) can leave open space for residents to enjoy when properly planned.

Density Yardsticks

Urban density is a subjective term that relates to a particular location and culture. An Asian neighborhood is likely to be much denser than its North American counterpart, for example. The question is, therefore, how should density be regarded and what are the common yardsticks of such neighborhoods?

Typical twentieth century suburban and city forms have two distinct densities. The first is of considerably lower density and averages 7 units per acre (17 units per hectare) (Figure 4.5). The large lot size, land, and infrastructure costs per unit are high and result in higher dwelling costs and foster suburban sprawl. In contrast, a high-density city has 31 units per acre (77.5 units per hectare), which is likely to be unpopular with the typical buying public. Would-be buyers will be reluctant to accept crowded communities that lack public and private open spaces, for example.

By combining planning features from low-density and high-density designs, you can introduce urban forms that mix both. Such a design averages 22 units per acre (55 units per hectare), with rear private parking and yards for each unit. Minimal, though acceptable, widths separate the houses. Moreover, green open space located at the center of the cluster can be made accessible from each unit, which is associated with the notion that public parks are crucial to community interaction. The new design for high-density communities mixes ideas taken from traditional, late nineteenth century high-density communities with contemporary designs.

Lot Dimensions and Siting

The choice of lot dimensions and home siting is a rudimentary phase in higher density planning. A typical lot

Figure 4.5: Mixing aspects of high-density neighborhoods with privacy and green open spaces can create livable denser communities.

size in post–World War II traditional suburban design was 50 by 100 feet (15 by 30 meters). Over time, similar lot sizes have been written into the bylaws of many municipalities. Increasing density, however, is mandating choice of a narrower lot. To do this, the planner must transform the house's traditional siting and move the garage, often located at the front, to the rear, which also requires the introduction of a lanes system. The front setback can be reduced and the home can be pushed forward. The length of the lot can then be shortened from the common 100 feet (30 meters) to 92 feet (28 meters), with a 16-foot (5-meter) rear lane. Narrow streets with slightly taller buildings will also foster a more pleasant human scale (Figure 4.6).

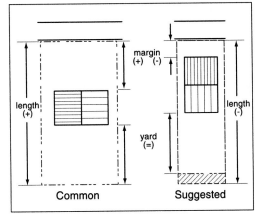

Changing the house orientation will contribute to an increase in density.

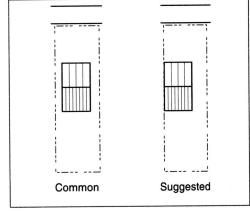

Maximizing the lot's useable area can be achieved by placing the home on the lot line.

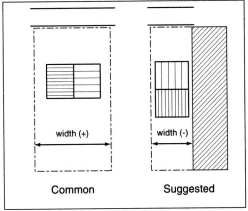

Reduction of the lot's length and front setback will increase density.

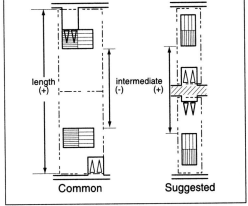

Introduction of rear lane parking helps reduce the lot's width.

Figure 4.6: To increase density without compromising livability, homes can be placed closer to the street, and a rear lane with parking can help avoid the front garage.

93

When subdividing land, the tendency in suburban development is to have more homes face a green open space, be it a park or a golf course. This practice needs to be used with care in higher density developments. A desirable situation will be to have double-loaded streets (streets with homes on either side) that make efficient use of costly infrastructure. The intermittent introduction of small squares and parks can help alleviate feelings of crowdedness.

Reduction of lot sizes means that arrangements for privacy and landscaping must be reconfigured to accommodate higher density. Houses, for example, can be clustered, which preserves any natural areas around the build site. Clustered dwellings work well for groups of eight to twelve units where open, shared spaces can be placed between buildings and smaller private open spaces can be included with each home. The different orientation of the dwellings also allows for views onto green areas as opposed to views into other units (Figure 4.7). In past high-density developments, individual private open spaces, even though small, were appreciated and used for such activities as clothes drying, children's play, sitting, and gardening (Lozier, 2005).

Roads

Although roadways provide efficient access for vehicles, many suburban municipalities over-design vehicular trafficways to the detriment of other amenities such as green space. The total area allocated to roads and public parking can account for between 30 to 50 percent of the total area. This can be somewhat explained by the peripheral locations of new communities. As the distances from residential areas to employment and commercial nodes increase, car dependency also increases. The common approach is to plan wider streets. The average neighborhood regulates 49- to 59-foot (15 to 18 meter) rights of way that break down to 26-foot (9-meter) road widths and 10-foot (3-meter) sidewalks, for example. Yet excessive road widths create neither efficiency nor safety. As illustrated in Figure 4.8, the minimum passing space required between two vehicles is 1 foot (30 centimeters) if cars are driving 20 miles (32 kilometers) per hour (Southworth and Ben-Joseph, 1997). Moreover, vehicle speeds increase on wider roads. In contrast, narrow, hierarchical road networks efficiently accommodate automobiles while enhancing safety by reducing traffic speed (Figure 4.9).

Southworth and Ben-Joseph also encourage a social perspective when considering street designs. They argue that roads should be integrated into living environments, not form them, because both vehicular and social activities can occur on the pavement. An interesting example is the practice of traffic-calming features implemented in the Netherlands, where roads for cars and pedestrians known as

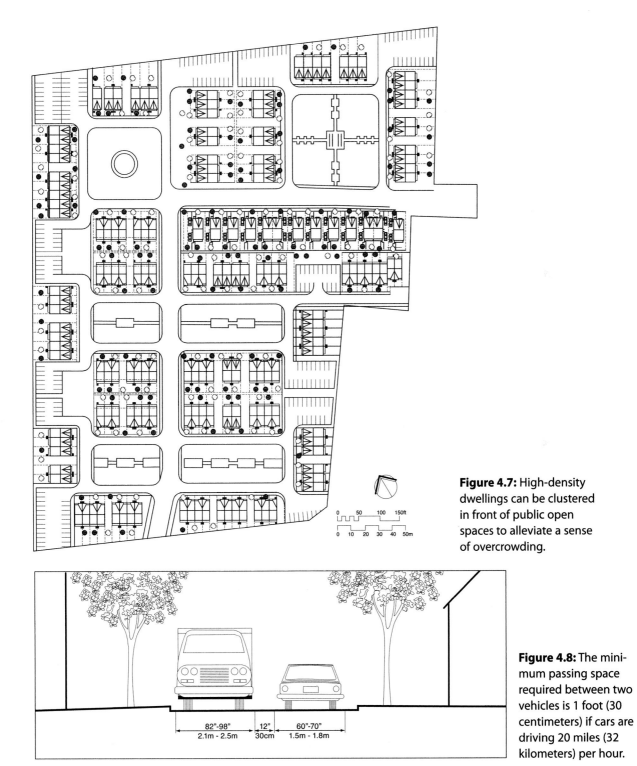

Figure 4.7: High-density dwellings can be clustered in front of public open spaces to alleviate a sense of overcrowding.

0   50   100   150ft

0   10   20   30   40   50m

Figure 4.8: The minimum passing space required between two vehicles is 1 foot (30 centimeters) if cars are driving 20 miles (32 kilometers) per hour.

82"-98"   12"   60"-70"
2.1m - 2.5m 30cm   1.5m - 1.8m

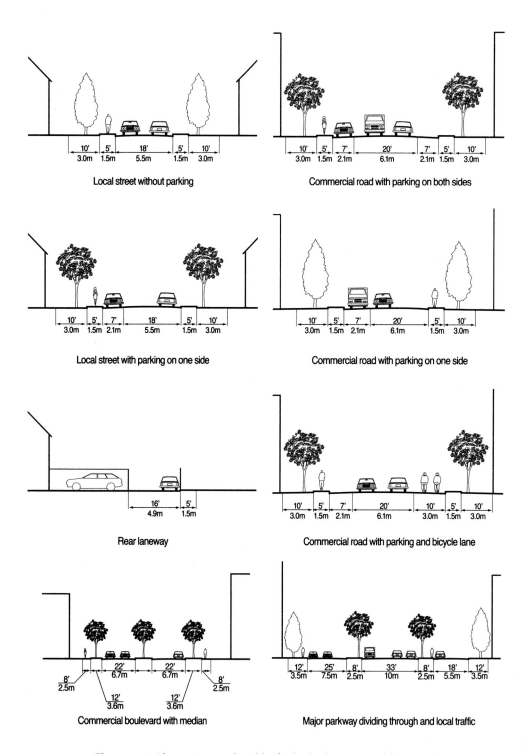

Figure 4.9: Alternative road widths for high-density neighborhoods

Woonorf include street furniture and plants. The result is a narrower road for moving vehicles, fostering both slower speeds and greater pedestrian activity. This concept can also be applied to existing streets without the need of major expenditures on reconstruction (Figure 4.10).

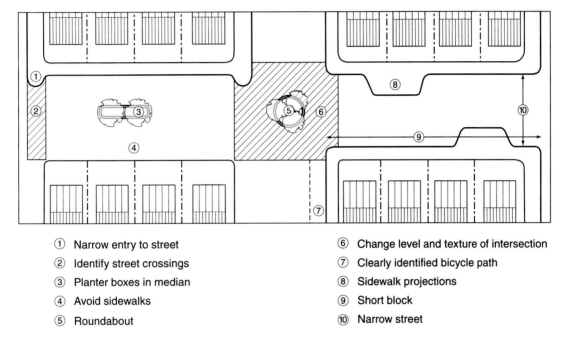

①	Narrow entry to street	⑥	Change level and texture of intersection
②	Identify street crossings	⑦	Clearly identified bicycle path
③	Planter boxes in median	⑧	Sidewalk projections
④	Avoid sidewalks	⑨	Short block
⑤	Roundabout	⑩	Narrow street

Figure 4.10: A road shared by motorists and pedestrians is designed to slow traffic.

Walkable Communities

Small numbers of suburban homes per unit area lower the use and economic viability of neighborhood amenities. Several residential developments share the same commercial establishments, as a result. The distance between homes and these establishments in most suburban neighborhoods has grown beyond walking distance, producing a negative effect on sustainable living in two main areas: excessive use of the car and vast amounts of land needed for its accommodation, and people's poor state of fitness. Planning walkable communities can address these issues by considering the needs of pedestrians alongside those of car users. Here we review some of the facts for the need to consider walking and cycling paths.

The amount of time that people spend at the wheel of a car has grown significantly. In Canada, some 75 percent of the population uses a private car on a typical weekday. People spend on average an hour a day commuting to work. Overall,

72 percent of those who live within 5 miles (8 kilometers) distance never choose cycling as a mode of transportation, for example. According to Dan Burden, Director of the Orlando-based Walkable Communities, Inc., the average Atlanta, Georgia, resident spends more than 12 hours a week stuck in traffic (2001). The environmental ramifications are staggering, with the need to expand arterial roads, build more local streets, and endure the resulting pollution.

The effect on personal health is also significant. A survey by the Canadian Heart and Stroke Foundation (2005) found that people who live in suburbs, smaller towns, and rural areas are often at a higher risk of heart disease and stroke than their city dwelling counterparts. An outcome of physical inactivity is the rapid increase of obesity among North Americans. A 1999 article in the *New England Journal of Medicine* suggested that overweight and obese people are at four-fold risk of cardiovascular illnesses, and a five-fold risk of diabetes as well as hypertension, gallbladder disease, and some cancer (Willet, Dietz, and Colditz, 1999). The authors go on to suggest that the overall mortality risk is more than two-fold for the group. Studies have also shown, on the other hand, that each additional 0.6 mile (1 kilometer) walked per day reduces a person's likelihood of becoming obese by nearly 5 percent, while each hour per day spent in a car increases the likelihood of becoming obese by 6 percent.

The design of walkable communities must regard the needs of pedestrians, cyclists, and drivers equally. Burden suggests several principles for guiding the planning of such neighborhoods. Citing Portland, Oregon, as an example, he suggests that affordable and reliable public transportation that reaches across neighborhoods and links them to city centers can "unchain" people from their cars. Using the term *walkable scale*, Burden argues that towns and neighborhoods can be planned from the outset with walkers in mind. Location of commercial and institutional buildings need not exceed a comfortable 10-minute walk from home. Once the place of community public functions has been determined, a network of pathways can link them to one another and to the homes (Figure 4.11). To make walking efficient and safe, short blocks are preferred as cars slow down when they approach intersections. Burden also suggests that roads need to have multiple uses. They can elicit appropriate behavior and increase neighborliness, association, belonging, acceptance, pride, and play. When a street intersects a pathway, pedestrian crossings should be easy. To keep speed and volume of cars low, the number and lanes can be reduced, street width narrowed, and the road surface changed from asphalt to brick, for example.

Sidewalks cannot be too narrow and need to have buffers and be well-maintained year-round. Icy pavement will keep walkers, primarily the elderly, indoors

Figure 4.11: A network of lanes and pedestrian paths needs to connect community amenities located within a 10-minute walking distance from residences.

in wintertime. When sidewalks are landscaped to include a buffer between them and the road, they are more comfortable and safer for pedestrians. Trees can shade benches and create a pleasant sound as the wind blows. Design of sidewalks and pathways needs to foresee all users: parents pushing strollers, elderly assisted by walkers, and wheelchair users should all be comfortable. The number of interruptions to the continuity of a sidewalk, and in particular cut-offs by driveways, should be minimized.

Public open spaces and functions that, in recent years, have been stripped from neighborhoods need to be redesigned into them. The culture of *big*, which saw the amalgamation of small play areas into large fields all on the edge of communities, can be downsized. Destinations a walking distance away need to be reintroduced as well as bylaws prohibiting them from being altered. These spots can also be viewed as social generators and magnets, a place to meet an acquaintance or make a new friend.

Bicycle paths can be used for leisure or can have a utilitarian purpose. They enable residents to travel longer distances while transporting small objects. They can also be used by people of almost all ages. The path can be part of a special network distinguished from a road or can be made part of it. When part of the street, the bike path should be separated by special markings and should allow cyclists to ride in both directions. Unlike pedestrian paths, bicycle paths can span longer distances. They may link homes with regional amenities such as libraries, sports centers, and schools. Bike racks for safekeeping can be placed near such amenities (Figure 4.12).

Parking

Substantial areas of a typical suburban development are devoted to parking, be it on private lots or street-side. The average automobile spends half its life parked outside or near an owner's house; allowing excessive amounts of space for this single function is wasteful, especially since the length of suburban driveways averages 23 feet (7 meters) in 4844 square feet (450 square meter) lots (Southworth and Ben-Joseph, 1997). Dense design alternatives encourage street parking, which simultaneously slows traffic speeds and acts as a buffer between automobiles and pedestrians. Cooper Marcus and Sarkissian (1986) suggest that a housing development pleasing to its inhabitants can be stigmatized by inadequate parking. They contend that design principles should guide vehicles reasonably close to dwellings without disturbing the quiet, pedestrian orientation of a site. Parking provisions should complement building sizes, as shown in Figure 4.13.

Developments may also offer "cluster" residential parking (Figure 4.14). Such lots, averaging 4306 square feet (400 square meters) for 20 vehicles, create opportunities not only for denser lot design, but also for more open spaces. Typical

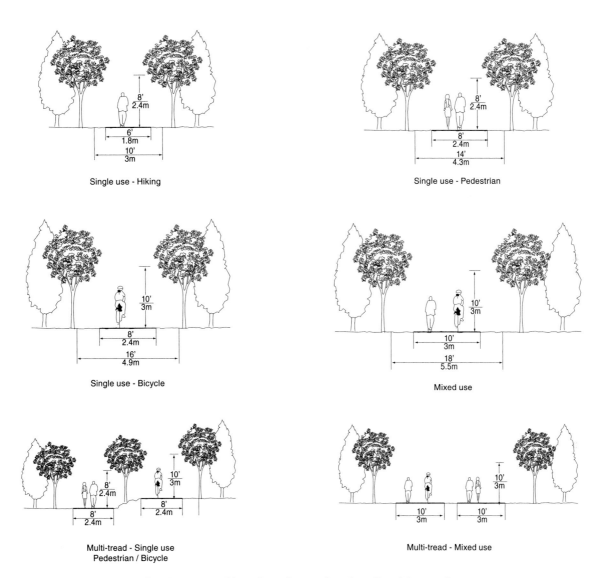

Single use - Hiking

Single use - Pedestrian

Single use - Bicycle

Mixed use

Multi-tread - Single use
Pedestrian / Bicycle

Multi-tread - Mixed use

Figure 4.12: A variety of pedestrian and bicycle paths needs to be offered for a wide range of users and uses.

suburban land use allocates 4844 square feet lots (450 square meter) to dwellings, with an extra 23 feet (7 meters) for driveways and 172 square feet (16 square meters) for rights of way. In total, paving can consume up to 50 percent of an entire development (Southworth and Ben-Joseph). Minimizing expansive circulation and parking for densely designed communities facilitates both automobile and pedestrian flows and increases green open spaces.

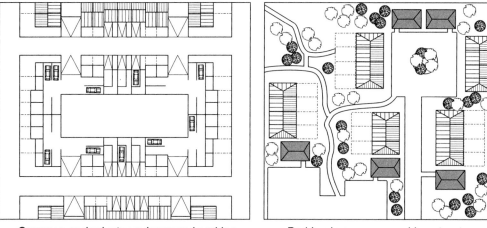

Common and private underground parking   Parking in common parking structures

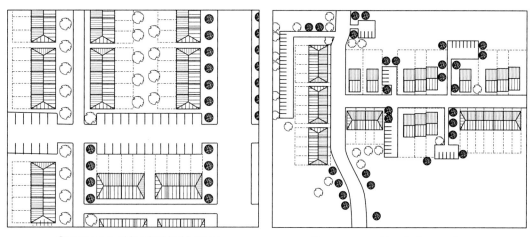

Common parking behind homes   Common parking between homes

Figure 4.13: Alternative parking options can be offered in high-density communities.

Open Spaces

If an extensive road network is an example of a misconceived notion about high-density neighborhoods, another misconception is that rowhouses are overcrowded and leave no room for outdoor private space. Some developers and buyers shy away from rowhouse development because of this perception. However, while high density lessens the amount of personal space available, appropriate design can provide the desirable attributes also found in single-family detached dwellings, such as open spaces and privacy. Communal space becomes an important attribute in dense developments, since multi-use open spaces with clear demarcations and

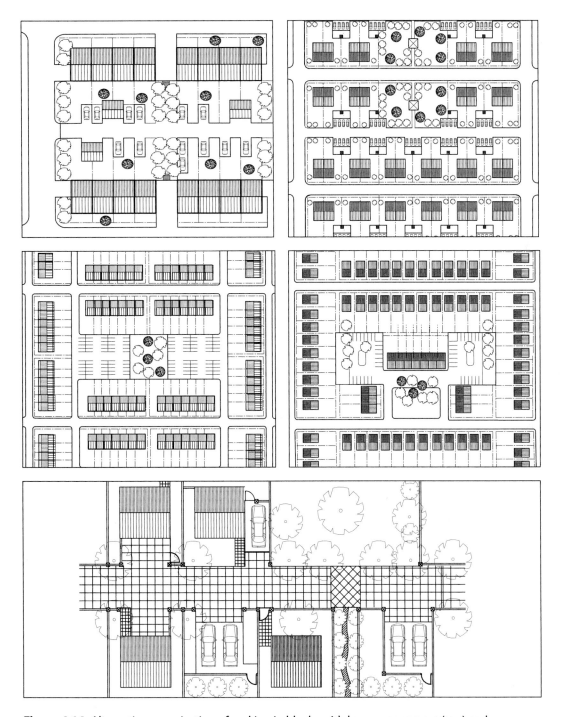

Figure 4.14: Alternative organization of parking in blocks with lane arrangement (top) and example of possible lane design for various uses (bottom)

fine landscaping establish edges, and in turn, edges establish privacy. According to Jacobs (1961), the demarcation between public and private space in high-density areas is essential. Front yards act as key transitional spaces between the private and the public realms. Moreover, landscaping increases curb appeal and contributes to a unit's identity and value in a row of dense townhouses. Landscaping in small yards enhances sustainability not only because of lower land consumption, but also because of a reduction in energy and pesticide use. In some designs, dense dwellings may have backyards with trellises and hedges to create enclosures.

Public open space, lost in many suburban developments, contributes to overall community cohesion. Residential parks, similar to those introduced in historic London, provide opportunities for collective interaction. Density may alleviate a sense of isolation as people become more community oriented. Street amenities encourage foot travel, lessening the need for vehicular traffic. Commerce enjoys increased sales in active local areas that are easily accessed by pedestrians. Essentially, shopping becomes a local activity, not a chore accessible only by vehicle (Barton, 2000). Open spaces are, therefore, essential to creating a sense of place in dense dwelling design.

As density increases, the amount of space allocated to each dwelling decreases. Lack of ample private open space can be mitigated by creating more appealing public areas. They can be placed in proximity to clusters of homes, instead of being located as a large regional park that serves several neighborhoods. Tall homes can frame a local park and enhance a better human scale (Figure 4.15).

Community gardens can also be regarded as open spaces. Set as allotment lots next to homes, gardens not only provide sources of fresh vegetables, but they engage residents in physical activities and foster better relationships. People can use composted materials to fertilize their gardens. By regarding public open spaces as a system, connecting them, creating a variety of landscape typologies, and introducing play areas for toddlers near homes, opportunities for engaging the residents in physical activities are created.

Mixing Land Uses

When considering land use allocation in a contemporary suburban community, the common tendency is to segregate between residential and non-residential activities. Such practice forces reliance on private cars and the building of an extensive road network. The rationale for the segregation by developers is that low-density developments do not provide the economy of scale necessary to justify introduction of commerce into the heart of neighborhoods. This argument has less bearing in the

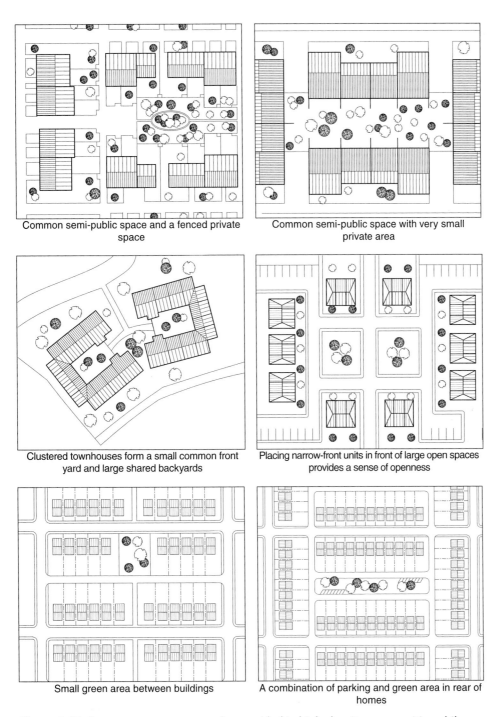

Common semi-public space and a fenced private space

Common semi-public space with very small private area

Clustered townhouses form a small common front yard and large shared backyards

Placing narrow-front units in front of large open spaces provides a sense of openness

Small green area between buildings

A combination of parking and green area in rear of homes

Figure 4.15: Common green areas can be provided in high-density communities while ensuring private spaces.

planning of communities with a higher density. Commerce or other communal functions, such as libraries or medical clinics, can be placed in a central location to which pedestrian paths will lead. When these functions are located on the edge of a community, they can be accessed by residents of neighboring communities, further supporting these uses economically (Figure 4.16).

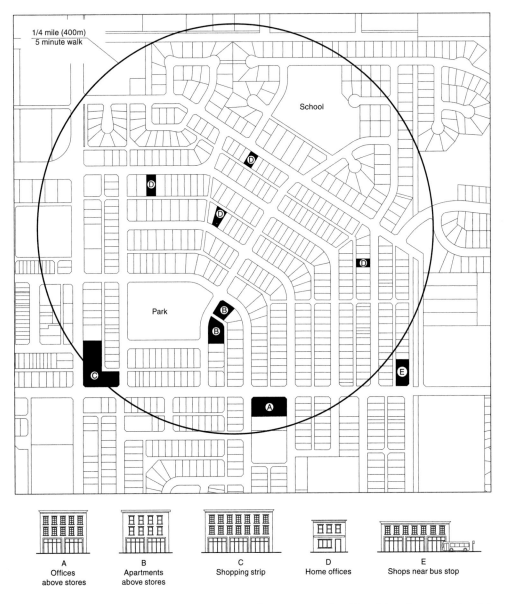

Figure 4.16: In sustainable communities, the weaving of residential and non-residential land uses carries a broader importance as it helps reduce reliance on private cars.

According to Van der Ryn and Calthorpe (1986), many of the trips taken daily by drivers are to non-residential destinations. Some car trips can be avoided if these functions could be closer to homes. In addition, walking or riding a bike to local stores, schools, or a library can contribute to improving fitness of residents of all ages.

The wide use of the Internet has also led to the proliferation of home offices. At present, many municipalities do not permit home businesses, a decree that needs to be reconsidered. Home offices can also contribute to reduction of travel time as businesses and services will be used by local residents. The placement of schools in the community's heart can also foster a culture of walking or bike riding by children. The same school can also house a library or a sports facility that is open after hours and shared by all.

Waste Management

The conventional methods of dealing with waste entail shipping garbage to a seemingly limitless, out-of-sight landfill. However, present landfills are becoming an increasing concern as waste levels rise, leachates pollute groundwater, and odors permeate inhabited areas. According to studies by the city of Halifax and Environment Canada (1992; 1992a and b), about a third of the total non-hazardous waste from residential sources is personal waste. The burden of waste collection and removal on the environment and community's finances can be greatly reduced if sustainable recycling programs are made available and attractive. The potential of such actions becomes evident as up to approximately 75 percent of this waste could be recycled, reused, or composted, diverting it away from the taxed and toxic landfill systems around the country.

By virtue of its layout, a high-density community already contributes to reduction of waste in construction material and energy needed to construct and provide basic services such as roads, electrical wiring, and wastewater treatment. The additional impact of the dense housing offers opportunity for communal composting and recycling centers that require less land and storage space for waste and recyclables than personal composters or recycling boxes (Figure 4.17). Composters, purchased or made from recycled wood pallets, are size-adjustable to accommodate more than one household. Leaves, lawn clippings, fruit and vegetable wastes and scraps, and wood ash from fireplaces or wood stoves can all be added to a compost pile. The bin can be located away from uncontrolled water sources, placed far away from the edge of a roof, and aerated to speed composting.

The combined savings from composting waste from landfills reduces landfill costs to the community and slows extraction of natural resources for new materials.

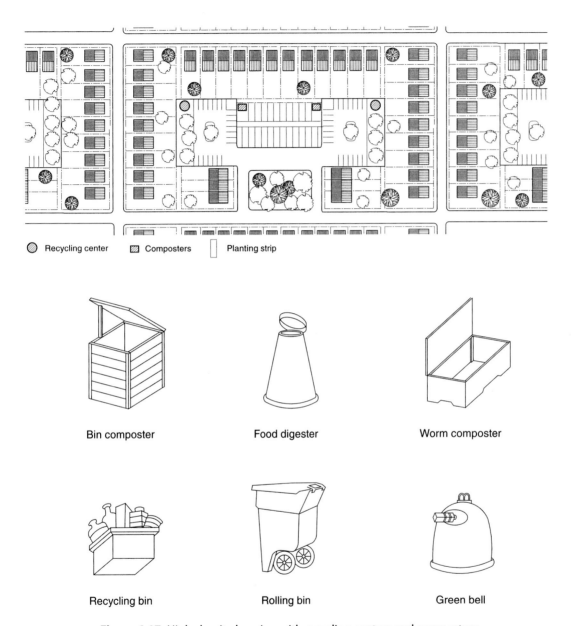

Recycling center ⬤ Composters ▨ Planting strip ▯

Bin composter

Food digester

Worm composter

Recycling bin

Rolling bin

Green bell

Figure 4.17: High-density housing with recycling centers and composters

Implementing composting and recycling strategies in a new or existing neighborhood could be accomplished with little disruption to original plans. Communal and personal composters can be installed in backyards and common areas. By designing areas for compostable waste, inhabitants will be encouraged to reduce their impacts on the environment.

Xeriscapes

Derived from the Greek word *xeros*, meaning dry, *xeriscapes* promote water conservation through careful plant selection and integrated approaches to design and maintenance of land surrounding a home or group of homes. According to Ferguson (1987), without diminishing aesthetic value or human accessibility, xeriscapes can save 60 to 70 percent of, or even eliminate, water requirements for irrigation.

Water demand can increase by 50 percent or more during summer months due to plant watering. Excessive residential use of water for landscape irrigation can account for up to 40 percent of total household water consumption (Regional Municipality of Waterloo, 1990). Irrigation not only drains local aquifers but also pollutes groundwater with fertilizers, pesticides, or herbicides used in lawn maintenance. As such, many communities are adopting water conservation ordinances for landscape irrigation, limiting turf installation, or offering rebates to homeowners who install xeriscapes (McPherson, 1989).

Xeriscaping is based on eight basic principles. Water is conserved by first limiting turf use to specific social and recreational areas due to its high water requirements. In addition, watering requirements can be mitigated by selecting water-efficient plants suited to local soil, drainage, and climate; clustering of plants with similar water requirements; and grouping of trees and shrubs in beds. Improving the water capacity of soil, the use of mulches, and the installation of an efficient irrigation system can all reduce evaporation. Collecting rainwater from rooftops and pathways provides an extra source of water for irrigation and returns rainfall of an area back into the ground.

Yards for single-family residences commonly vary in use and required water intensity. Identifying these zones will direct water and energy to areas with high human impact and eliminate unnecessary and high-energy turf grass that is used for ornamental groundcover where native species could be better suited (Figure 4.18). Identifying these zones is essential to the development of a xeriscape. Implementing these principles will not only conserve water and reduce land pollutants, but it will also reduce labor and fuel needed to maintain a traditional turf-based landscape.

Although "payback periods" of xeriscaping alternatives is not immediate, the benefits of such landscaping are well worth the investment. Choosing local plants and promoting resource conservation and natural habitats are benefits to xeriscaping that escape typical cost-saving calculations.

Figure 4.18: An alternative to a turf-covered front lawn

Farming in Suburbia

Crop cultivation can be a domestic activity of residents who can harvest produce from *community gardens* that are smaller and located within a residential project. Produce from private horticulture can both feed and flower households. Desirable design would site the gardens in the core of each residential cluster. Buildings enclosing communal gardens can create pleasing living environments with each unit having a view. In addition, individual units can have their own horticultural opportunities. Vertical planting, for example, makes efficient use of limited spaces and is a solution relevant to a small yard, greenhouse, and rooftop garden. It is an efficient garden design that incorporates a variety of plants on cable trellises and shades surfaces in summer while insulating them in winter.

Private *greenhouses* absorb and trap heat from thermal radiation. As a result, vegetation flourishes as growing seasons are extended beyond natural cycles (Puma, 1985). Greenhouses can be constructed as separate structures or be part of a main dwelling. As additions, greenhouses can heat and provide fresh air for houses if proper ventilation systems are installed. Greenhouses are best located beside or atop units facing the direction of most sun to maximize exposure (Figure 4.19).

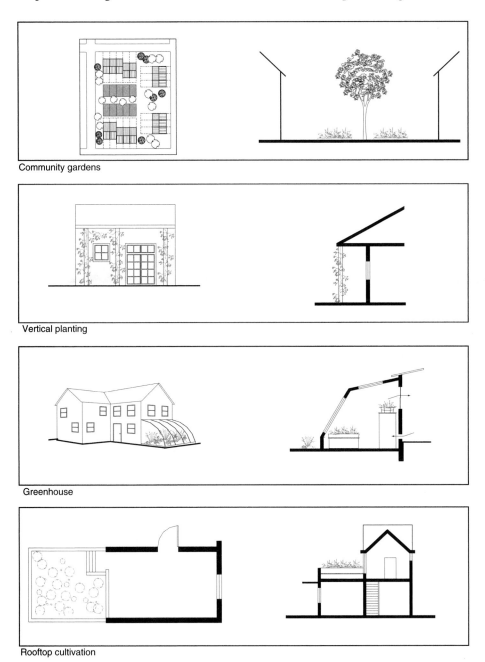

Community gardens

Vertical planting

Greenhouse

Rooftop cultivation

Figure 4.19: Several methods can be used by residents to grow their produce, and gardens can be fertilized using compost.

May (1993) suggests that the shrinking space left over for building and the great demand for green spaces and gardens in our cities make the creation of roof gardens highly desirable. Similarly, rooftops are flat and often under-used and offer a relatively inexpensive large space for production. Roofs can provide surface for vegetation growth, when structurally reinforced and appropriate water protection is installed. Since standard roof design does not take into account the additional weight of soil, plant material, and gardening implements, technical adjustments must be made and accessibility considered.

District Heating

When a central, common source of heating is powering a neighborhood, it is referred to as *district heating*. The source can be of any kind, including solar, geothermal, or even fuel-based. The advantage of such a system is the savings that it offers to each household. No heating system has to be purchased by individual homeowners. The system is installed by the developing firm, which charges each dweller based on consumption. It offers savings through economies of scale that reduces the cost for each individual homeowner. To be economically viable, large numbers of users must be connected to the system.

District heating is common in some countries. In Iceland, for example, geothermal water sources are used to heat residences. Solar heating systems were implemented in Herlev near Copenhagen in Denmark (Boyle, 1996), providing space heating to 92 dwelling units. There, a central solar collector field of 11,000 square feet (1025 square meters) heats a large insulated water tank to 176°F (80°C). The system also satisfies the community's hot water requirement (Figure 4.20).

The Southampton Geothermal District Heating Scheme in Southampton, U.K., is another example of a district heating system. In this project, a borehole was drilled near the city to a depth of 6000 feet (1800 meters) to encounter water at 158°F (70°C). Through a system of coils and pipes, the water is brought to the surface and then distributed within a 1.2 mile (2 kilometer) radius to several buildings. Studies demonstrate that the system saved the town substantial amounts of money in energy costs (Boyle).

Dwelling Forms

Socioeconomic realities with direct effects on sustainable living need to be considered in the design of contemporary dwellings. Chief among these realities is the transformation of the family, since statistics show that single parents, singles, same-sex partnerships, and seniors make up large percentages of today's society. These households, at times, cannot find suitable accommodation within the dwellings

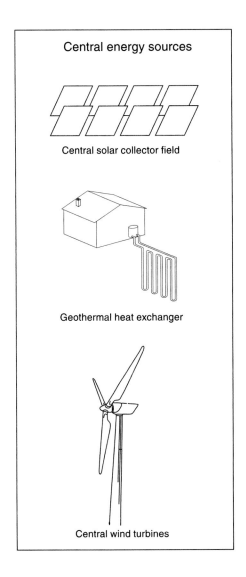

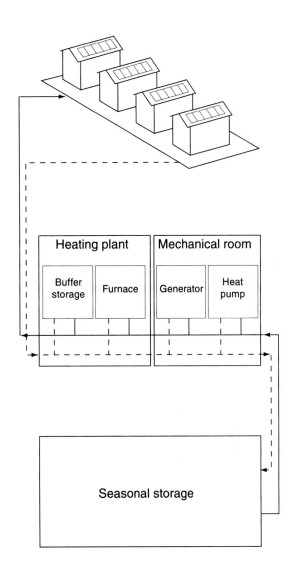

Figure 4.20: District heating

offered by private-sector builders. Rethinking space needs of all users is, therefore, paramount if the building of sustainable communities is to be pursued.

Key features of such an approach are diversity and choice. At present, most residential developments are segregated by price and types of homes. It is common to find the same dwellings with a relatively similar price tag and design in the same neighborhood. Better integration and a variety of housing types need to be offered instead. Integration of homes for seniors, for example, along with dwellings for young households will attract extended family and help facilitate a mutual support system.

Another hindrance for personal economic sustainability has to do with the fact that, often, from lack of suitable housing, small households are obliged to purchase or rent homes with excessive space they do not need or cannot afford. Having an option to reside in a smaller dwelling will not only foster economic sustainability by reducing initial costs, but it will diminish the amount of ongoing expenses.

The need to develop denser housing prototypes that offer greater flexibility to buyers leads to some key design principles:

- *Smaller footprint*   To consume less land, the home's footprint needs to be small. Narrow and long proportions are recommended as it will save on infrastructure costs.

- *Taller buildings*   To increase density, more floors need to be placed on the same foundation.

- *Attached dwellings*   Planners need to be given a choice as to the degree and type of attachment they wish to achieve. Joining more units will reduce land needed and contribute to energy management, as lost heat from one unit can be transferred to the next.

- *Design for internal subdivision*   Designing an adaptable structure to accommodate a variety of households requires consideration of flexibility principles from the outset.

Similar principles guided my design of the Next Home (Friedman, 2002). The three-story structure was designed to demonstrate how flexibility could be employed to achieve affordability and sustainability. One of the fundamental distinguishing features of the Next Home was the option extended to buyers of purchasing the type and "quantity" of house that they needed and could afford. This option was made possible by designing a three-story structure that could be built, sold, and inhabited as a single-family house, a duplex, or a triplex. If three separate households each bought one floor in the Next Home, the structure could become a triplex as easily as it could become a single-family home when a couple with children, for example, decided to purchase all three floors. Alternatively, if a household bought two floors while a single person bought the third, the Next Home could become a duplex. In a row of such structures, therefore, triplex residents could be neighbors to single-family homeowners, who in turn could live next door to duplexes.

The Next Home was designed as volumes to be subdivided and rearranged both pre- and post-occupancy and to accommodate transformation from one house type to another with minimal inconvenience and cost. A hallmark of the design is its non-static allocation of units by floor. A structure originally built as a duplex could at a later date be changed either to a triplex or a single-family home, according to the dictates of future owners. This built-in capacity for transformation is an inherent element of the design, which considered such aspects as the location of entrance and stairs and the placement of building systems (Figure 4.21).

In another example, rapid migration coupled with lack of land and environmental pressures caused cities on the American West Coast to consider high-density mixed-housing–type developments. San Jose, California, is characterized by a low-rise, low-density urban form. In an attempt to break away from its suburban image, the local government initiated development of urban nodes complemented with transit systems radiating out from the core. The Jackson-Taylor Revitalization Strategy proposed the integration of two ethnically diverse Japanese and Hispanic areas amidst new housing, employment, and commercial units within a 75 acre (31 hectare) area. Peter Calthorpe, a leading proponent of higher density development and the scheme's planner, explains (1993) that the design established a network of neighborhood parks, plazas, daycares, and community centers connected by comfortable, landscaped, pedestrian-oriented streets. In the design of the proposed residential buildings, Calthorpe attempted to maintain the rhythm and character of the surrounding single-family neighborhood and provide integration with the surrounding residences.

The Jackson-Taylor proposal includes 2100 residential units and more than 800,000 square feet (74,320 square meters) of building space. Of that, three building types define the development. Sorted according to height, bulk, and density requirements, each design has specific guidelines to ensure that neighborhood quality is maintained. Building types include triplexes with a density of 15 units per acre (37 units per hectare), walk-up apartments with 50 units per acre (125 units per hectare), and mixed-use buildings. Open space is provided through a clustered development and is located adjacent to dense building sites. The Revitalization Strategy is a good example of a medium- to high-density development that was inserted into a low-rise, low-density suburban neighborhood to offer diversity of housing types.

Adaptable Interiors

Choices presented to buyers in the speculative housing market are commonly limited to finishing products, such as fixtures and textures. An option to acquire

Layouts

Elements

Combinations

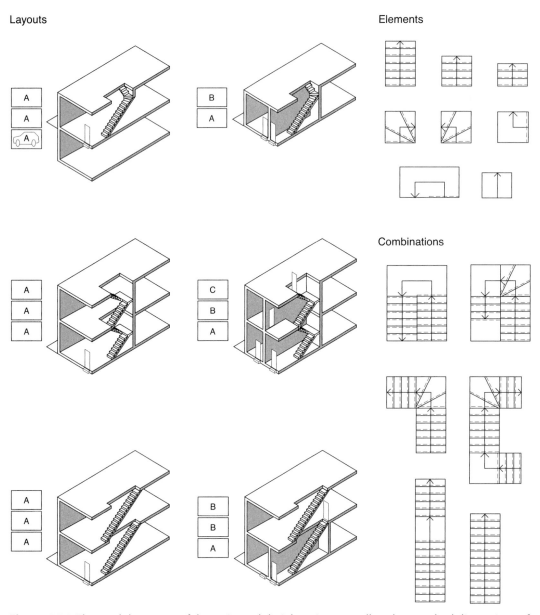

Figure 4.21: The modular nature of the stairs and their location, as well as the standard dimensions of the floor plans in the Next Home, led to flexibility in arranging the volumes as well as interior layout prior to or after occupancy by the builder and the occupants.

only the items that suit the buyer's needs and leave out others is not common. The home, on its interior features, in other words, is never regarded as a catalog of offerings. By limiting consumption in residential design, however, a form of sustainability can result, with flexibility in the dwelling's interior occurring prior to or after occupancy.

To increase adaptability, the space needs to be free of support walls and permit location of selected functions, such as kitchen, bathrooms, and storage compartments, in whichever place the occupant wants. Once located, these items should be easy to remove and relocate. Flexibility includes not only reduced consumption by the first occupant, but allows adjustment to the needs of subsequent occupants. The dwelling can also be modified according to the ongoing needs and lifecycle changes of every user.

Similar thinking guided the design of the Next Home's interior. To facilitate future transformation of dwelling units within the structure and to maximize the sense of open space, the mechanical systems were designed for simple adjustment at the pre-occupancy stage by incorporating a vertical shaft throughout the entire building height. The vertical shaft encloses the water supply, drainage, venting, electrical, telephone, and cable TV lines. In conjunction with a horizontal channel, which can be installed optimally by the builder to run the length of each floor and which would facilitate future relationship of rooms, issues of post-occupancy flexibility have also been addressed (Figure 4.22). Such an arrangement of channels permits access to utilities through the floor—not the ceilings or walls—therefore facilitating all changes for each occupant, making changes as unobtrusive as possible to neighboring units.

Several technical components can be introduced to a design to permit such flexibility. They include, in wood-frame construction, space joists with a wider span, flexible tubing for hot and cold water, demountable partitions, and hollow floor moldings through which insertion of wiring is possible.

In the growing home-improvement industry, consumers may choose from catalogs of hundreds of bathroom types and an even greater number of faucet and towel rack models, for example. Despite this, the homebuilding industry has failed to facilitate post-occupancy adaptation. Components and appliances are installed into new homes with the expectation that they will be permanent. The designs most commonly offered do not permit change and make several assumptions about lifestyle and values.

The truly responsive home needs to be considered as a system into which items of all kinds may be easily plugged in at various locations and removed or relocated with equal ease. Accommodation of pre-occupancy choice in the design stage allows occupants to tailor their home to their specific lifestyles and budgets. By offering a catalog of interior components, they can select which items they

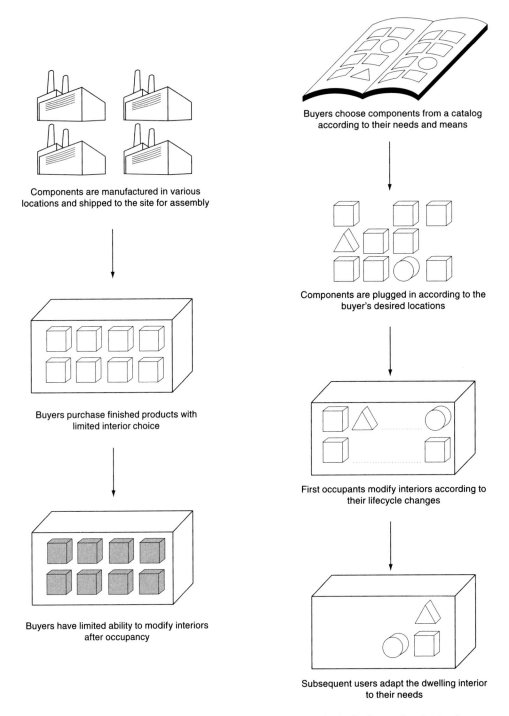

Figure 4.22: Unlike traditional homebuying processes in which the buyer has limited choices (left), regarding the dwelling as an open system with infill components offers a user greater flexibility in the pre- and post-occupancy stages (right).

would like installed into their home and where they would like them installed. Other items can be purchased separately later on, when interests change or means permit. In this way, buyers are not forced to consume more than they think is necessary. For example, a couple who is buying a first home may desire a range, sink, fridge, and pantry installed in the kitchen. After some time, they may then wish to add a dishwasher or additional storage units. When the couple later buys a dishwasher, they want to place it beside the sink for convenience, which would require the range to be moved aside.

Lifecycle Homes

Enabling the elderly to age in place or disabled individuals to function in their own residence is regarded as contributing to the occupants' health and self-esteem and to societal sustainability. Such consideration is a result of recognition by public authorities that the number of elderly is expected to rise and institutional care will not be available to, or affordable by, all. Rather, encouraging people to use their homes and installing appropriate accommodations is the preferred approach. This notion is also largely supported by legislation in many countries that mandates accommodation of disabled people in their homes and in public places. In the United States, for example, under the access requirement for housing programs receiving federal financial assistance covered by Section 504 of the Rehabilitation Act of 1973, 5 percent of new apartments constructed within a funded project must be wheelchair accessible.

Fitting a home for use by the occupants at a later stage of their lives or by persons with special needs might have a limited advantage as opposed to making it usable throughout the residency. *Universal design* promotes the need to design housing—or any building, for that matter—to be usable by everybody at all times. An example of this approach is raising the height of electrical receptacles from their current low position so that plugging in appliances becomes simple for all. Despite the fact that special assistance is offered in the projects described here, the general approach of universal design—that of incorporating consumer projects and design features that are easily usable and commonly available—was adopted.

When a catalog of items is developed for elderly users, it must address their needs and concerns. In addition, buyers with limited mobility may require a unique assortment of accessible components, such as handrails, raised toilets, and stair lifts. The necessity for modules to be easily exchangeable is of paramount importance. If a middle-aged person purchases a home and lives there for a long time, at some point their mobility may decrease. The home must never be a source of physical stress on those with limited mobility, who are unable or unwilling to purchase an entirely new home at that time. If needed, the regular sink module, for example, may be easily swapped for one from the accessibility catalog that permits a wheelchair to roll beneath it for easier use. The stairs can be fitted to provide better traction, or a retractable seat can be installed in the shower (Figure 4.23).

Another approach to enabling the elderly to remain part of the community is to permit the building of *accessory structures* at the rear of an existing dwelling that can have different uses. Such a structure, sometimes known as a *granny flat*, can be constructed along with the main dwelling or added later. Placement of the unit, which is common and encouraged in several Australian towns, for example, is often prohibited in North America. Cities fear that such structures may cause parking problems and load utilities. Where these structures have been constructed, however, these fears have proven unfounded. Granny flats can be constructed via conventional methods or prefabricated in a plant and brought to a site. Avoidance of a basement makes the dwelling accessible to a person with reduced mobility. It can be independent from or connected to the main structure. Years later, where permitted, the main dwelling can be expanded to the granny flat. Alternatively, the flat can be rented out to another person when a rear entryway is introduced.

Communal and Residential Identity

In high-density, moderate-cost housing, the tendency on the part of developers is to replicate dwelling exteriors for cost-saving purposes. This often leads to repetitive and sterile environments. Communal and residential identity and personalization is important. A place's identity evolves over a long time with many small interventions (Figure 4.24). However, even in the initial phase, conditions can be provided to create a sense of place. It is important to note, however, that a neighborhood image is defined not only by its physical layout, but by a social identity created over time. According to Barton (2000), this can be a network of people with similar interests, mutual recognition, support, and friendship.

Strategies for fostering a sense of identity may include attention to public open spaces. A bandstand, statue, or unique landscape arrangement can be placed at the center of a cluster, giving each cluster of homes a unique appearance, for example. A similar approach can be taken when the homes are designed. To avoid creation of a theme-park motif, with each home having a different exterior, overriding guidelines can be created. Within these guidelines, choices can be presented to homebuyers to select such items as doors, windows, or even brick shades.

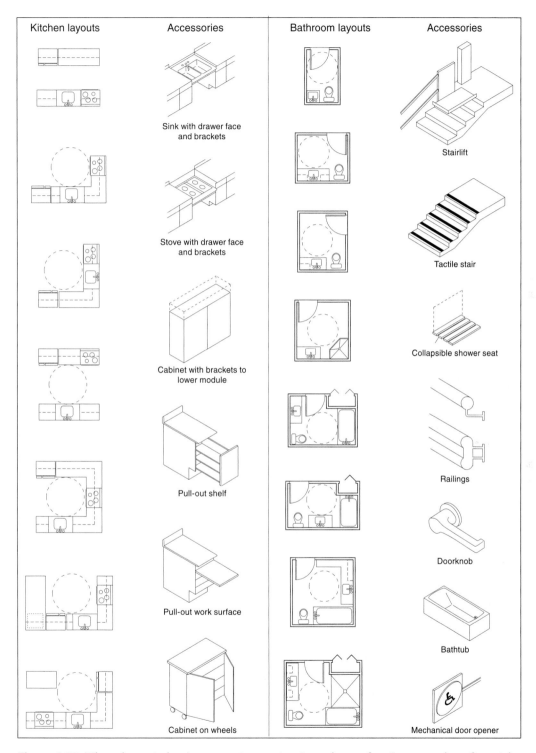

Kitchen layouts

Accessories

Sink with drawer face
and brackets

Stove with drawer face
and brackets

Cabinet with brackets to
lower module

Pull-out shelf

Pull-out work surface

Cabinet on wheels

Bathroom layouts

Accessories

Stairlift

Tactile stair

Collapsible shower seat

Railings

Doorknob

Bathtub

Mechanical door opener

Figure 4.23: When the main buying group in a project is made up of seniors, a catalog of special items and layouts can be prepared to permit the easy and continuous use of the dwellings.

Dwelling unit	Alternate façade features and colors	Different roof elevations in row housing	Preparation for windowsill planters
Community	Similar architectural features on all buildings	Bandstand or statues in public spaces	Unique pavement

Figure 4.24: Features fostering greater personal and communal identity have been included in these communities.

A Livable Denser Neighborhood: Quartier Jardin

The development *Quartier Jardin* is a private initiative that demonstrates a successful systematic approach to planning a high-density sustainable neighborhood. The project began when a development firm that owned 102 acres (41 hectares) wanted to build a community and approached me for assistance. Located 6 miles (10 kilometers) northeast of Montreal, Canada, on the edge of a small town called L'Assomption with a population of 16,000, the project offered an opportunity to consider a neighborhood based on sustainable principles.

Several programmatic attributes were combined to pose both a planning challenge and an opportunity. The developer foresaw that the majority of the clients would be young, first-time homebuyers from L'Assomption and other neighboring towns. Another significant segment of buyers were forecasted to be seniors who might trade large, high-maintenance homes for smaller units in this sustainable community. Both buyer groups, it was assumed, were likely to opt for a smaller, energy-efficient dwelling that in turn would lead to the design of a denser community.

The project's size ran the risk of launching the town onto a sprawl path. It became clear that appropriate strategy and better practice must be followed early on to avoid such an outcome. Another imposing issue was the site's location and natural conditions. Surrounded by the L'Assomption River, the town served as a hub and provided services to the neighboring farming communities. In fact, the property was a former farm. The flat terrain had hardly any remaining flora, and soil tests demonstrated that it was suitable for building low-rise residential structures. The southeast edge of the site was bordered by the L'Assomption River, which was regarded by the developer as an important feature. The town's land use planning prohibited building near the river so a strip of land along the bank had to remain a park (Figure 4.25).

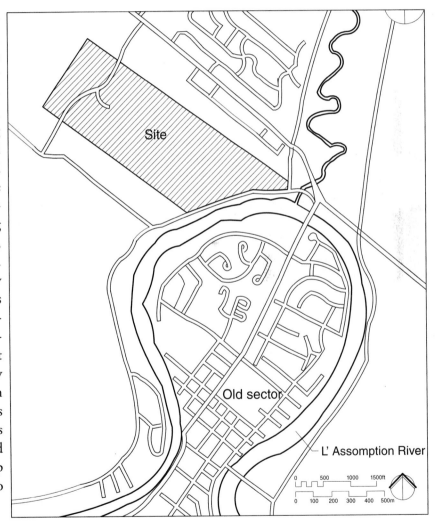

Figure 4.25: The town of L'Assomption, northeast of Montreal, is surrounded by a river that also borders the site's southeast edge.

123

Other considerations had to do with the economic, social, and cultural makeup of the town. Established as a village in 1717, the center of L'Assomption used old Quebec graystone-clad buildings dating back to its beginning (Figure 4.26). It was, therefore, recognized that the proposed new design needed to consider and build upon the old. Be it in its planning or architectural style, the new neighborhood would not be regarded as a stand-alone entity and would need to be integrated with the old. Also, housing young, first-time homebuyers was seen by the developer and the city's administration as a contribution to a well-balanced demographic continuum, and so it was decided that early on in the life of the neighborhood, an elementary school would be built in its heart to serve the community.

Figure 4.26: The center of L'Assomption includes old vernacular graystone buildings that date back to the town's establishment in 1717.

As for the approval process, the project's planning was proceeded as a *planned unit development*. A wider range of flexibility as to the makeup, type, location of residences, roads, and public open spaces was granted to the designers.

Site Planning

The choice to build a high-density community was made in Quartier Jardin to address the housing needs of homebuyers with modest means and those looking for smaller homes. A planning process followed, and several decisions were made early on to address economic, social, and environmental concerns. Weaving the proposed neighborhood into the old fabric of L'Assomption was meant to include Quartier Jardin as part of the town, rather than as a new and isolated enclave. Documentation of existing streets and building typologies, as well as the community's sociodemographics, provided a background for the design and a detailed understanding of local needs. Also, a strong sense of community emerged through interviews of residents and civic leaders, a sense that the new design attempted to consider.

The need to increase density was clear when the target unit costs were set. Yet, the site's location in proximity to rural areas, where wide open spaces and fields are common, was a challenge. Buyers, it was feared, might not be willing to trade rental dwellings for a home in a community with a dense urban feel; thus, higher density was balanced with a number of open spaces tucked in between clusters of homes, and streets were oriented toward the river to provide the neighborhood with a sense of openness (Figure 4.27).

Planning a walkable community was a central design feature of Quartier Jardin. It began by including features that would encourage walking and reduce reliance on automobiles. The location of the school in the neighborhood's center, walking distance away from each home, was meant to instill in young people the habit of biking or walking. The school would also be used after hours and would house a library and a community center. Introduction of commercial spaces on both the edge and the heart of the community offered residents access to basic amenities. When the community matured, these would likely become locations for a convenience store or a café, for example.

To make walking safe, narrower streets were proposed as a car-slowing measure. The homes were clustered around looped roads that encourage slow speeds. Whenever possible, pedestrian paths were introduced. The main avenues, those that cross the community in the east-west direction, would have clearly marked bicycle paths. Because harsh Canadian winters often restrict walking and biking

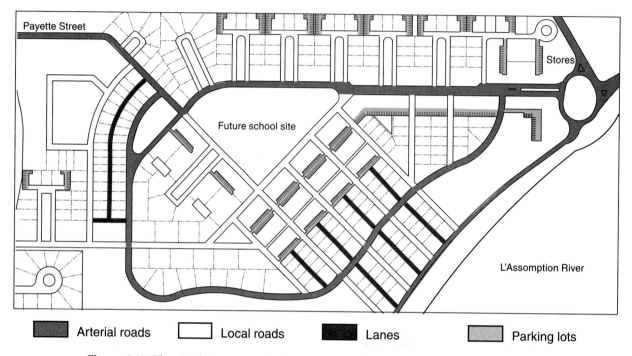

Payette Street

Future school site

Stores

L'Assomption River

| Arterial roads | Local roads | Lanes | Parking lots |

Figure 4.27: The circulation system in Quartier Jardin

activities during this part of the year, orienting the streets away from the wind and creating windbreakers was of the utmost necessity.

Once the general objectives had been established, their integration into the planning began. Roads of different widths reflected anticipated traffic loads. Linking the new neighborhood to the existing community was accomplished through an entry boulevard and a square on the eastern end and an access from the west. Another artery, Payette Street, would permit access from the northwest and would lead, like other parallel streets, to the river. To make efficient use of costly infrastructure, most of the streets would have homes on both sides. Yet, so as not to create a tunnel effect, green open spaces were placed at many of the streets' ends or intersections. Also, to enhance a better sense of human scale, taller buildings "framed" wider roads.

Due to the high density, parking design in Quartier Jardin was challenging. Several alternatives were considered—for example, lower-cost homes had common parking lots placed behind them. To alleviate the negative impact of massive parking lots, smaller areas were placed on the northern edge in between groups of homes. In other dwellings, parking was offered indoors.

When outdoor space design began, it became clear, given the site's natural conditions and lack of vegetation or other topographic features, that green areas would have to be created. This process began with an examination and decision as to what kind of open spaces would be offered and what their scale should be. It is common to see regional parks serve several new developments. However, such an approach discourages physical activity among residents, as they need to drive or be driven to faraway places. The open space strategy in Quartier Jardin was to integrate the linear park along the L'Assomption riverbank into the community. This approach also served to draw residents of the older part of town into the new. The proposed school's open space would also be available for use by all citizens. Another aspect of the public open space design was to place homes at the site's north end, in front of a narrow landscaped area that provided a play space for toddlers and young children under the watch of parents (Figure 4.28).

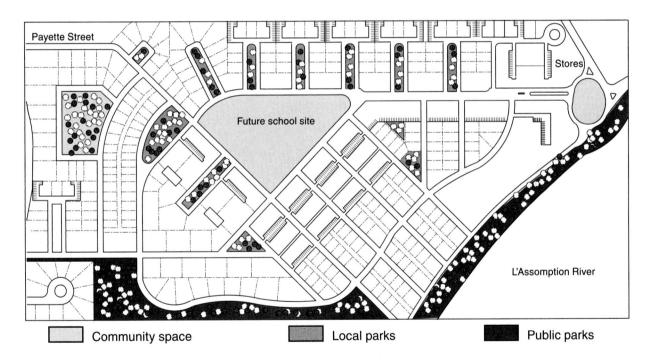

Figure 4.28: Small public open spaces were arranged near clusters of homes to encourage play by children.

Dwellings' Design

Regarding societal, economic, and environmental issues was the thrust of the homes' design. Their choice and integration was seen as part of the overall approach to the community's planning. The need to mix unit types led to the consideration of both apartments and single-family homes totaling 889 units, with the majority being single-family attached homes. It was anticipated that seniors would be more inclined to reside in the lower floors of these units. To achieve a range of prices, single-family detached, semi-detached, and row homes were proposed. Flexibility was a prime objective in designing the units' interiors. A wide range of options was offered, with a variety of kitchens and bathrooms. A built model made of four different homes was constructed so that buyers could see and purchase only the items that they needed and could afford (Figure 4.29).

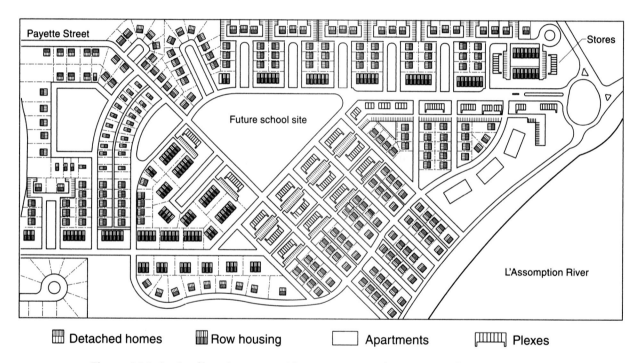

Figure 4.29: A mix of housing types with varying interior layouts was offered to buyers.

The evolving needs of the household were also considered. The basements were unfinished for residents who lacked the means at time of occupancy to complete later. The space above the garage was also left for the homebuyers to arrange as per their space needs and lifestyle. Some residents, it was envisioned, would turn the space into a home office, while others might house an older member of the family in that space. An extended family member could, for example, reside in an independent dwelling on the ground floor or in a room of their own in the combined space. By regarding a single structure and, in fact, the entire community in a flexible, open-ended manner, a mix of ages, incomes, and uses was established (Figure 4.30).

Designers of high-density residential environments run the risk of diminishing the level of personal identity. Creating diversity within overall harmony, therefore, was the strategy adopted in Quartier Jardin. Each cluster of homes was provided its own identity with unique landscaping, architectural style, and brick color, although all the clusters conformed to the same overall guiding principles. Also, in the design of each home, areas were left for personal intervention through choice of roof tile colors, shade of door frame, door style, and landscaping (Figure 4.31).

The design of Quartier Jardin was a balancing act between a program set by a developer, and the needs of the town and the community's future residents.

Considering Sustainability Aspects

Unlike the design of La Forêt de Marie-Victorin project that was described earlier in the book, where keeping the site's natural conditions intact was emphasized, the Quartier Jardin site did not pose an environmental challenge. Built on former farmland, the

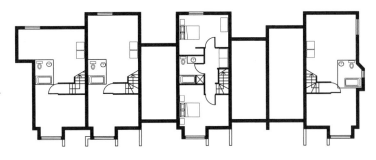

Basement

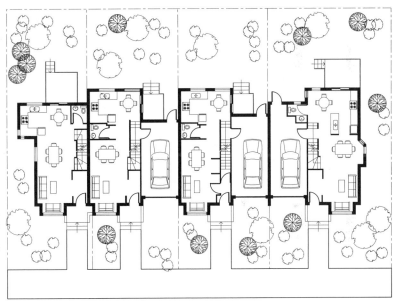

Lower level

Upper level

Figure 4.30: Floor plans of a typical unit in a rowhousing structure

Figure 4.31: An effort was made to distinguish façades of one rowhouse cluster from the next to allow personalization.

developer's intention was to initiate a community with a higher density, and this led to the integration of principles that contributed to the project's sustainability.

The decision to build a "compact" community also had a significant positive environmental effect. It was bound to leave the least impact by avoiding construction of permanent service roads and reducing commuting time, and as a result, pollution. Avoiding the building of vast common parking lots and tucking parking spaces between and behind homes left fewer marks that would have visually stigmatized the neighborhood and instead fostered more pride among its members regarding the curb appeal of their homes. A decree by the town's administration to prohibit construction along the riverbank also ensured that much-needed forested area contributed to the social and environmental integrity of the community. The common tendency is to offer this prime location to builders of luxury estates or tall apartment buildings that may block the view, and this tendency was avoided here to benefit the entire neighborhood.

Construction of smaller rowhousing helped save valuable natural resources as well. The amount of materials consumed in the construction of these homes was far less than that required for larger houses. The strategy of letting buyers select and pay for the components that they needed and could afford not only benefited the occupants monetarily, but reduced consumption of unnecessary goods. Placing the school in the heart of the community contributed to a *least negative impact* effect as students would not have to be driven to and from their school. Similarly, including stores in the community had the same effect by reducing commuting.

Other design decisions contributed to the view of the project as a *self-sustaining* entity. The construction of taller homes and their attachment led to energy savings. Since hot air rises, lower floors would keep upper ones warm. Also, heat loss in one dwelling would be likely to find its way to next-door units in the row. Orienting as many homes as possible to a southern exposure would contribute to passive solar gain that benefited the homes' energy management. Offering the option to buyers to have a home business helped with the homes' acquisition as office expenses could be deducted from income tax (and the arrangement lowers commuting time). Having one parent work at home also helps families with toddlers and reduces the need for commuting to and from daycares. The building of smaller, affordable homes for young, first-time buyers and the elderly also contributes to the self-sustaining nature of the community. Rather than lose a segment of its young population and care for its elderly, the new project helped the city of L'Assomption house both. It is likely that older residents and their married children will reside in the project, thereby fostering supporting relations.

Locating public open spaces near homes also helped bond the community. As 10 percent of the development area was required to be allocated to green space, a decision not to concentrate the area but place small patches near clusters of homes permits encounters among residents and allows more physical activities by children and adults. Also, by allocating special pedestrian and cyclist paths, reliance on cars is reduced and contribution to a healthy society is achieved. The decision to have higher density housing drew buyers to the project but also provided economic justification to the construction of commercial nodes. In initial discussions about the school design, it was recognized that the building would also house the local library and community center. Investment in a public building, therefore, would have additional benefits.

Many of the planning decisions were affected by a long-term view of the project and the needs of its occupants. The designs of the homes were perhaps the best manifestation of such an approach. Regarding the dwellings and, in fact, the entire community as a continuously changing entity contributed to its sustainability. Occupants can complete and modify their homes as needs arise rather than move to other communities.

The design of narrow roads also benefited the community. Not only were funds saved initially, but savings on repair and maintenance throughout the project's life will also be possible. Less area allocated to streets also reduces sprawl and saves on pollution caused by extensive commuting.

The tendency is often to assume that the mark of a sustainable development is strong environmental components. Quartier Jardin demonstrates that by seeing issues related to society, economy, and the environment as a system, contributions can be made to each and benefits from the relationship among them can be achieved.

Green Homes 5

Rising energy costs, dwindling natural resources, and concerns about occupant health have all prompted architects to reimagine the design and construction of dwellings. Houses that address residents' environmental, economic, and social needs are rapidly becoming common in the marketplace. This chapter focuses on the home. It draws conclusions from the way earlier civilizations housed themselves, outlines principles and examples of sustainable dwellings, and describes a community whose residents chose such homes.

Indigenous Environments

Since early history, people have sustained themselves by making use of the resources provided by their environments, including natural resources, at a renewable rate. No waste collection or water treatment was necessary because communities were small and largely self-sufficient. Rivers were potable, soil was cultivable, and local fuel sources were available and renewable. Built of earth, stone, or plant material and designed to fit within their surroundings, most structures of indigenous peoples were sustainable out of necessity. Architect Frank Lloyd Wright (Stitt, 1999) once suggested that the basis for serious study of architecture could be found in these humble buildings.

The earliest settlements were formed when hunter-gatherers in southwest Asia began farming approximately 10,000 years ago. Circular houses of up to 30 feet (9 meters) in diameter were built on a rough foundation of one course of stones. Walls were made of a perishable material, most likely reed matting and mud, and internal post holes indicate that roofs were in place. Fireplaces were also common, and raised rectangular areas acted as food preparation sites. By the seventh millennium B.C., village-based farming communities, such as Jarmo in present-day northeastern Iraq, were constructing rectangular houses of several rooms made of molded and pressed mud on a stone foundation. Beds of reeds served as a base for clay floors. Storage bins and domed clay ovens, possibly for drying grains, were found at the site, which comprised no more than 25 houses and approximately 150 people at one time (Palmqvist, 1993).

Earth has been a sustainable building material since prehistoric times. In hot, arid regions, the insulating value of mud was suitably efficient. The tools and supplies necessary for the simplest of buildings were minimal—hands, intelligence, sunshine, and an abundance of mud produced a strong structure. The Dogon people of Mali still live in villages of mud housing in a desert climate (Figure 5.1). Baked by sun, the structures are sturdy, easily repaired, and able to be constructed from and returned to the earth. Although many buildings are small, more complex constructions such as the Grand Mosque in Djenné have adapted earthen buildings to a larger and more aesthetically intricate scale.

In the American Southwest, the Anasazi people built high-mass, adobe dwellings in south-facing cliff caves that took advantage of passive solar heat gain in the winter but that blocked heat and sun in the summer (Figure 5.2). *Kivas*, or family units built into existing pueblo structures or partially underground, were fairly comfortable year-round, were well-ventilated, and relied on the thermal mass of the enclosing earth. The inhabitants often aggregated and then dispersed, moving

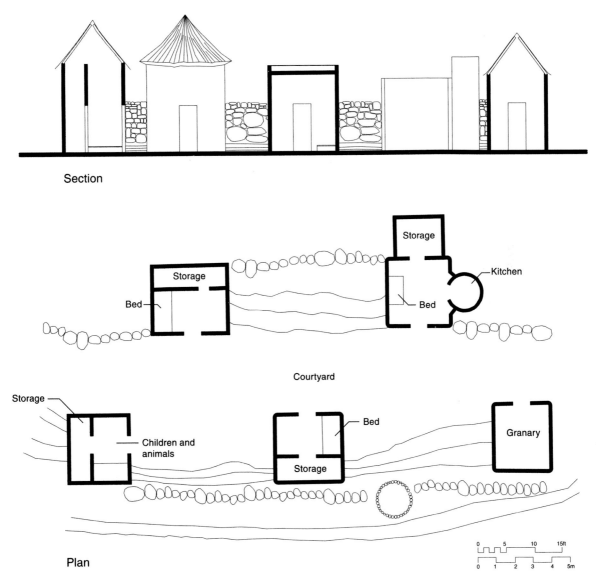

Section

Storage

Storage

Kitchen

Bed

Bed

Courtyard

Storage

Bed

Children and
animals

Granary

Storage

Plan

0   5   10   15ft
0 1 2 3 4 5m

Figure 5.1: Dogon villages in Mali use mud to finish all buildings.

into other homes or building new communities. The largest Anasazi assemblages
are believed to have peaked at 2000 or 2500 people, the most the social structure
could support (Ferguson, 1996). According to Wines (2000), these communities
intuitively recognized that Earth's resources were finite and that humans should
not greatly alter nature.

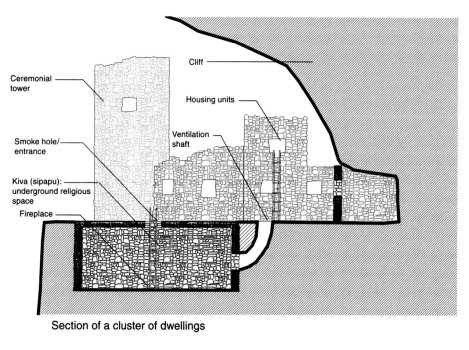

Section of a cluster of dwellings

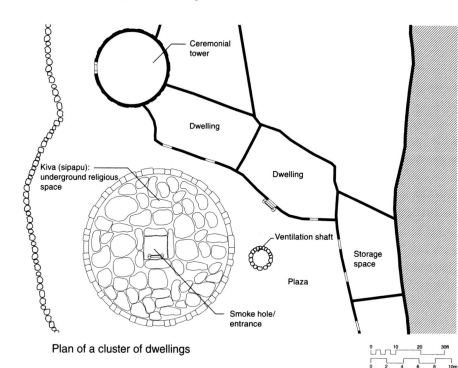

Plan of a cluster of dwellings

Figure 5.2: Anasazi cliff dwellings in Colorado's Mesa Verde National Park were built with high mass to take advantage of sun exposure.

Across the ocean, changes in climate after the last Ice Age caused many tribes to move from southwest France and the Italian and Iberian peninsulas into what is now northern Europe. Many relics of civilizations in this area are made of stone, a durable and easily preserved building material. Although the most famous sites are thought to have been built for ceremonial occasions or burials, such as Poulnabrone in western Ireland and Stonehenge in southern England, many stone buildings and entire villages indicate the prevalence of masonry construction in Atlantic Europe (Burenhult, 1993).

Skara Brae, a remarkably well-preserved village in the Orkney Islands of Scotland, consists of stone houses with walls of at least 10 feet (3 meters) in height. The roofs were made of timber and whale rib framework with an outer covering of living turf. Each home consisted of a single spacious room of about 388 square feet (36 square meters), with a stone hearth and furniture, including beds, shelves, and boxes (Figure 5.3). Excavation of the site showed that *midden*, or piles of domestic garbage, were used as building materials once the heap became stable. Houses were constructed of stone in pits in the midden, embedding them in a warm, insulative material. During good weather, people lived atop the midden but retreated partially underground when the weather became rough. The village dates back to between 3100 B.C. and 2500 B.C., and its remains today indicate that the sturdy and natural construction was intelligently designed, meant to be preserved over time (Ritchie, 1995).

Subterranean homes were used in traditional towns and villages in the Chinese loess belt in the provinces of Honnan, Shansi, and Kansu. Loess is silt that has been transported and deposited by wind. Soft and porous, it is suitable for carving. The pits of these structures were about one-eighth of an acre (one-twentieth of a hectare), carved 25 to 30 feet (7.6 to 9 meters) deep (Figure 5.4). Apartments of about 30 feet (9 meters) in depth and 15 feet (4.5 meters) in width were accessed through an L-shaped staircase from a central courtyard. Homes, schools, hotels, government offices, and factories were all built underneath fields, providing warmth in the winter and staying cool in the summer (Rudofsky, 1965).

According to Duly (1979), respecting human scale has always been the practice of indigenous cultures, whose people have constructed buildings based on personal need. Such a principle is illustrated in the *igloo*, an archetypal building that arose as a migrating people faced harsh climates and a single building material: snow. Its simplistic dome structure encloses the largest volume for the smallest surface area, creating an energy-efficient dwelling. Snow is cut into rectangular blocks that are stacked in a spiral fashion and finished with a key block on top, creating a self-supporting structure. The exit is a tunnel of snow blocks, made small to reduce heat

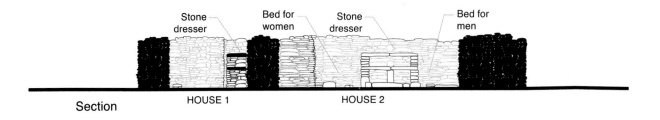

Section   HOUSE 1   HOUSE 2

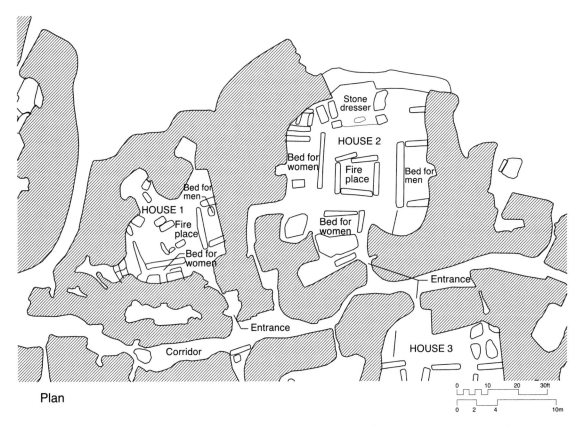

Plan

Figure 5.3: A house at Skara Brae has remained intact after 4000 to 5000 years, a durability certainly lacking in modern construction.

loss and below the main igloo floor level to encourage the exit of colder air. The structure may serve as an overnight shelter or may be enlarged in a radial pattern from the main room if more space and permanence is required (Figure 5.5).

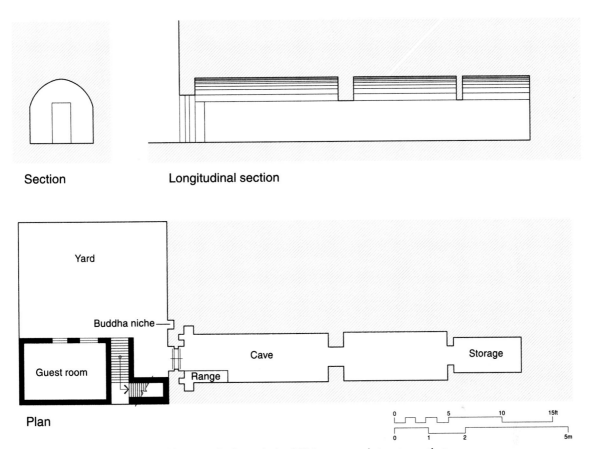

Section   Longitudinal section

Yard

Buddha niche

Cave   Storage

Guest room

Range

Plan

0   5   10   15ft
0   1   2   5m

Figure 5.4: Subterranean buildings in the loess belt of China conceal structures that, due to the insulative properties of the ground, remained warm in the winter and cool in the summer.

Although used by some Inuit cultures, the igloo is not the only method of creating shelter in northern extremes. Igloo builders in the winter, such as the Caribou Inuit, created conical tents of animal hide during the summer, and other northern indigenous cultures, such as the Tareumuit, lived in semi-subterranean houses of sod or stone. All structures were transportable or easily re-created and constructed from local and often abundant materials that could return to the earth once the inhabitants discontinued maintenance (Duly).

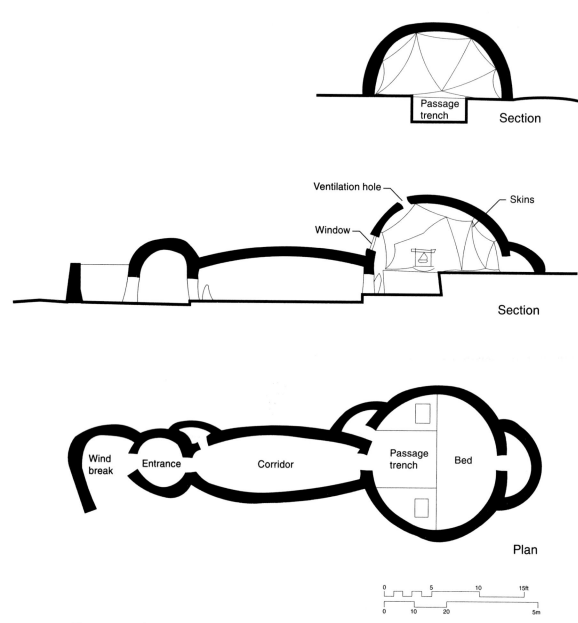

Figure 5.5: Igloos are constructed as temporary solitary structures or enlarged in a radial pattern.

While these dwellings are rare to nonexistent today, many modern architects are reviving the logic of indigenous people's building practices. Earth and stone are still sustainable, are locally available materials in developed countries, and retain the same efficient building properties that existed millennia ago. Modern-day requirements of housing have become more complex, diverging from the interdependence that buildings once had with the surrounding landscape. However, the sense of place present in the structures of indigenous people is indispensable in creating a community that is in harmony with the surrounding environment. Modern innovations and reclamation of construction techniques, such as rammed-earth walls, turf or green roofs, and structures made of untreated wood, are re-creating sustainable human habitat.

Strategies for Sustainable Homes

The design of a sustainable dwelling is affected by aspects that extend from site planning to construction. A sustainable dwelling must not only have little environmental impact but must also increase the inhabitants' quality of life, as such homes are healthy, comfortable, and adaptable. Four major components are incorporated to achieve green building: First, the design must minimize environmental impacts by using building materials with low embodied energy and high durability that do not compromise the occupants' health or standard of living. Second, the building envelope (the building shell, through which thermal energy can be transferred to or from the exterior, unconditioned spaces, or the ground) must be efficient, requiring minimal energy for heating, cooling, and lighting. Third, the use of natural resources, such as water and fuel, must be minimal within the home; this is a priority that can be accomplished by incorporating technologies and designs such as low-flow toilets and high-efficiency heaters that rely on alternative sources of power. Last, generated waste during construction should be reduced by building with materials that are recyclable or recycled during production, reducing the environmental impacts and costs associated with waste management.

As environmental concerns and building costs rise, buying small, suitably designed homes is becoming increasingly attractive. In turn, the educational benefits of such dwellings can be far-reaching, sensitizing the public about the environmental, economic, and social benefits of sustainability. The elements listed here present what is currently practical in conserving energy, land, water, and other natural resources, given available technologies and the cost of using them. This discussion is by no means exhaustive, but it illustrates what is possible at the unit level.

Solar Energy

Incorporating passive design strategies and active solar features for solar gain in residential design yields a reduction in utility expenses and an increase in the occupants' level of comfort. Buildings oriented for maximum sun exposure will benefit from greater amounts of daylight, passive gain in walls and floors, and additional benefits from active solar systems such as photovoltaics and collectors. Planning considerations made for passive solar gain, such as house orientation and window overhangs, will also provide the surface area for active energy collection that requires unobstructed access to direct sunlight. Fans, pumps, valves, thermostats, and other mechanical systems, all of which require electricity, can be used to collect and distribute heat.

The most well-known component of active solar systems is the *photovoltaic (PV) panel*, which can be installed on any surface with maximum exposure to the sun. Photovoltaic is a renewable form of energy obtained by the conversion of light into voltage between two layers of semiconducting materials, an effect first discovered in the nineteenth century. In one form of production, thin silicon wafers are cut from large crystalline silicon cells, which are then connected and laminated onto structural modules. Alternatively, silicon can be vaporized and deposited onto a glass or stainless steel module. Both types of production will not degrade in performance if contained and maintained, and can be expected to operate for at least 20 years if certified to the *International Electrotechnical Commission Standards* (with occasional cleaning to remove dirt buildup).

Photovoltaic systems, if not connected to the electrical grid, require an inverter and batteries to store and discharge electricity (Figure 5.6). The battery is currently the "weakest link" of the system. However, homes can also connect photovoltaic generators directly to the electricity grid via an inverter, supplying the grid when a surplus of energy builds up in the home and taking electricity from the grid if insufficient supply is available for the current needs (El Bassam and Maegaard, 2004).

Photovoltaic energy is silent, reliable, renewable, and environmentally safe. It can be used to provide lighting to homes and power to water pumps or other appliances that service an entire community. Although the price of photovoltaic panels is relatively high due to the energy required to create the pure silicon crystals, the cost is dropping as demand rises. Currently, solar cell arrays are being integrated into building elements such as roofs and cladding, widely practiced in parts of Europe and Japan. Switzerland, for example, has developed arrays alongside highways that also act as sound barriers. Decentralized and increasingly cost-effective, photovoltaic systems are becoming feasible options for local and sustainable energy production (Ramage, 1997).

Solar collectors are a popular, less expensive, and simpler alternative to capturing the power of the sun. Unlike photovoltaic panels, solar collectors do not

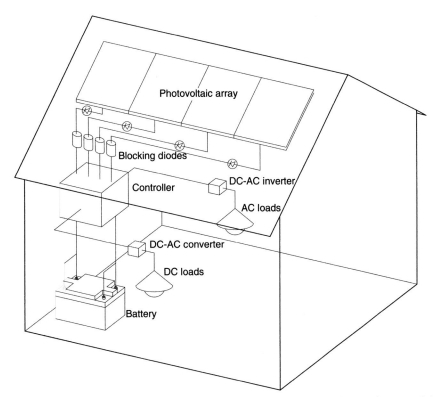

Photovoltaic array

Blocking diodes

Controller

DC-AC inverter

AC loads

DC-AC converter

DC loads

Battery

Figure 5.6: Photovoltaic systems require a crystalline silicon photovoltaic module, an inverter, some protection control, and a battery installed in an independent system.

generate electricity. Instead, they collect the heat of solar radiation in air and water for space heating, hot water, pool heating, desalinization, solar cooking, and crop drying. They require no pumps or motors to distribute hot air or water, relying instead on the building's orientation and the hardware. Very little additional construction costs are required for their installation, and such units can contribute to reduced heating bills.

Active systems pump water or another heat-absorbing fluid through a solar collector. This collector is set on a roof or exposed area and usually consists of copper or rubber tubing passed between a metal plate and glass covering that form an insulated box (Figure 5.7). Such systems can be technologically advanced, supplying hot water and central heating in colder climates, while other systems, particularly in subtropical climates, may simply be a black bucket or rubber tubing on a roof fed directly to the shower or tap. High-temperature solar thermal systems reflect sunlight via parabolic mirrors to a single point that can potentially be producing temperatures greater than 1830°F (1000°C), creating steam to drive electric turbine generators or power chemical processes (El Bassam and Maegaard). For the home, however, the efficiency of a solar collector is often insufficient to provide 120°F to 140°F (50°C to 60°C) hot water to an average household, so the solar collector is instead used to preheat water to around 95°F (35°C) to reduce the load placed on alternative heating systems (Ramage).

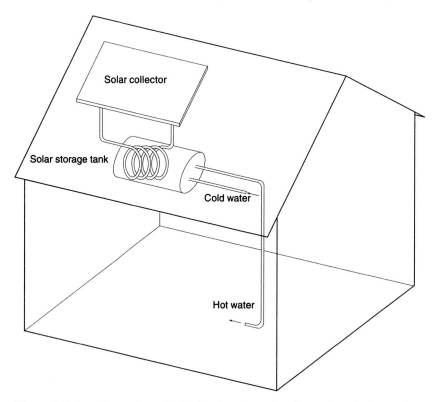

Figure 5.7: An active solar collector heats water using the sun's radiation and pumps it to an insulated storage tank.

Home Perimeter and Form

At present, construction, renovation, and demolition of housing account for a large amount of material consumption and direct or embodied energy required to produce, or dispose of, them. Resources sent to landfills during these processes also create problems. In addition, heating, cooling, and house operating requirements are growing, especially in very hot and very cold climates. By changing unit dimensions, configurations, and size, and by grouping homes, the buyer and builder's material needs, energy requirements, costs, and time can all be decreased. This is accomplished by increasing the ratio of floor area to perimeter, which not only reduces inherent heating costs but leads to a simpler design that requires less corners, skin, and framing (Figure 5.8).

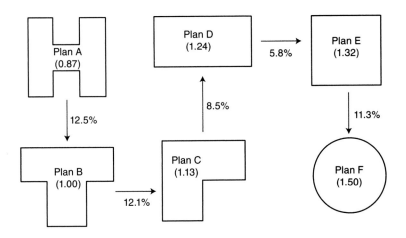

Plan Configuration	Wall Area sq.ft. (sq.m.)	Energy Required (KWh)
Plan A (H)	1720 (160)	2856
Plan B (T)	1505 (140)	2501
Plan C (L)	1320 (123)	2198
Plan D (rectangle)	1205 (112)	2001
Plan E (square)	1140 (106)	1894
Plan F (circle)	1010 (94)	1679

Figure 5.8: Changes in building configuration affect the perimeter and floor area, thereby altering factors such as materials and energy requirements.

Conserving resources and improving the thermal performance of the envelope through simple, efficient, modular design helps reduce energy consumption and waste in any home. By designing for modular configuration of building material, such as studs, joists, plywood, and sheetrock, waste from off-cuts is reduced. For example, designing for a 4-foot (2200-millimeter) module and 24-inch (610-millimeter) stud spacing can reduce lumber requirements by 8 percent. Efficient framing, sheathing, and layout of interior finishes also result in significant material, energy, cost, and waste disposal savings. While sheathing and wall framing material requirements remain fairly consistent, waste generation decreases significantly as module size increases (Figure 5.9), ranging from 6 to 7 percent wasted material for Plan 1 (no module) to no waste at all in Plan 4, the 48-inch (1220-millimeter) module. Vertical stacking, grouping and joining units, and size reduction all increase energy efficiency in the home by limiting the perimeter area, building footprint, and cost per square foot. Vertical stacking also reduces the excavation and foundation requirements as well as basement and attic sizes.

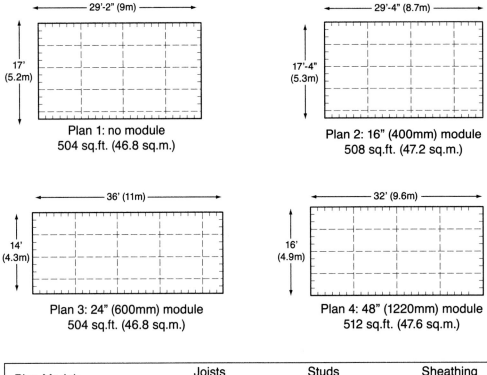

Plan Module	Joists ft (m)	Studs ft (m)	Sheathing sq.ft. (sq.m.)
Plan 1: no module	1240 (378.2)	1840 (561.1)	2502 (232.5)
Plan 2: 16" (400mm)	1261 (384.4)	1706 (520.1)	2511 (233.3)
Plan 3: 24" (600mm)	984 (299.9)	1834 (559.2)	2609 (242.4)
Plan 4: 48" (1220mm)	992 (302.4)	1751 (534.0)	2560 (237.9)

Plan Module	Joists		Sheathing	
	Ordered ft (m)	Wasted ft (m)	Ordered sq.ft. (sq.m.)	Wasted sq.ft. (sq.m.)
Plan 1: no module	1324 (403.6)	83 (25.4)	2688 (249.7)	185 (17.2)
Plan 2: 16" (400mm)	1340 (408.4)	79 (24.0)	2688 (249.7)	174 (16.2)
Plan 3: 24" (600mm)	992 (302.4)	8 (2.5)	2688 (249.7)	78 (7.3)
Plan 4: 48" (1220mm)	992 (302.4)	0 (0.0)	2560 (237.9)	0 (0.0)

Figure 5.9: Four simple plans with the same floor area and configuration were designed with increasing building material module sizes and reduced waste.

"Trimming the fat" from houses achieves a reduction in size and maintains the usable floor space. Considerable amounts of energy can be saved by building taller rather than wider. Since heat rises, warm air from lower floors is likely to contribute to heating the upper floors. Also, by reducing the unit footprint, less energy escapes from the building foundation and roof. In addition, attics may actually be reclaimed by using knee-type trusses or stick-built framing methods in the roof. An 8-foot (2.4-meter) clearance, for example, could be achieved on a 14 by 36 foot (4.3 by 11 meter) area by using a 6:12 roof slope. Alternatively or in addition, basements can be built with preserved wood foundations that use 30 percent less embodied energy than concrete and can be finished with more ease by the homeowner (Figure 5.10).

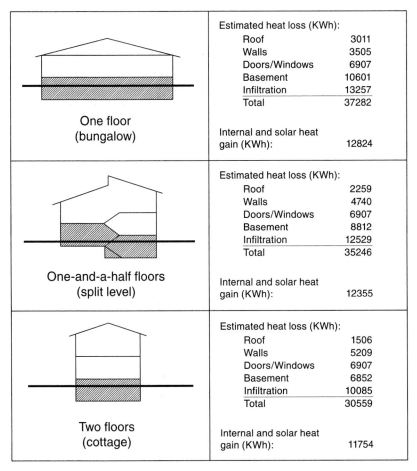

One floor (bungalow)	Estimated heat loss (KWh):	
	Roof	3011
	Walls	3505
	Doors/Windows	6907
	Basement	10601
	Infiltration	13257
	Total	37282
	Internal and solar heat gain (KWh):	12824
One-and-a-half floors (split level)	Estimated heat loss (KWh):	
	Roof	2259
	Walls	4740
	Doors/Windows	6907
	Basement	8812
	Infiltration	12529
	Total	35246
	Internal and solar heat gain (KWh):	12355
Two floors (cottage)	Estimated heat loss (KWh):	
	Roof	1506
	Walls	5209
	Doors/Windows	6907
	Basement	6852
	Infiltration	10085
	Total	30559
	Internal and solar heat gain (KWh):	11754

Figure 5.10: Vertical stacking reduces excavation, foundation requirements, and basement and roof sizes. It also improves energy efficiency as lower levels heat the upper ones.

Grouping and joining units also promotes savings in both construction and energy, as repetition of design reduces construction time and sheathing requirements. Heat loss is reduced by 21 percent when two dwellings are attached and a further 26 percent for a middle unit when three or more units are joined (Figure 5.11). The usable floor area can be increased without any exterior additions to the home by avoiding basements with *slab-on-grade* and crawlspace construction and making attic space usable. In addition, clustering spaces with pipe and duct requirements and utilizing an open plan that minimizes hallways and little-used circulation paths will more efficiently use the available interior space.

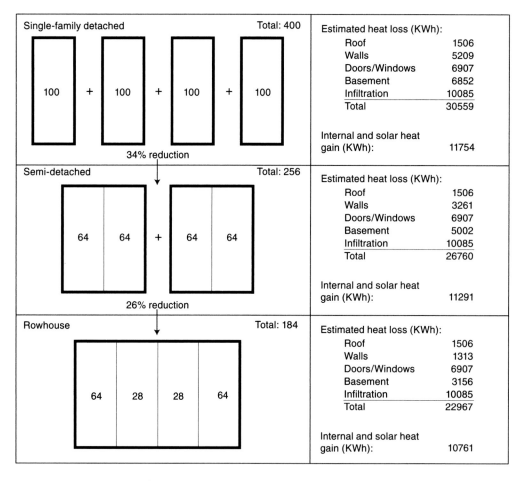

Figure 5.11: Reduction of exterior wall area, and heat loss, is achieved by joining single-detached units into semi-detached units or rowhouses.

Savings in construction materials can be achieved through efficient planning at the onset of the design process. Simplification, stacking, and dimensioning reduce waste, can reduce the environmental impact without affecting the occupants' living comfort.

Building Materials

In examining a building's environmental impacts, designers need to consider the energy and resources required to produce, use, and dispose of building materials. A *lifecycle analysis*, also referred to as *cradle to grave*, of each product examines energy efficiency, waste generation, natural resource pollution, recycled content or recyclable capabilities, sustainability, and costs during acquisition. Building materials require energy to be extracted as a raw resource, processed and manufactured, packed and distributed, constructed and assembled, used, renovated, and demolished (Figure 5.12).

Lifecycle investigation often involves some compromise, as illustrated in the analysis of aluminum. This highly durable and appealing building material is lightweight and versatile and requires little maintenance. Some aluminum products are made from recycled scraps, which can be recovered and recycled endlessly if the design and detailing of a home does not use mixed-material assemblies. However, the extraction of alumina found in bauxite ore requires a large amount of energy and generally involves strip mining. Although strictly

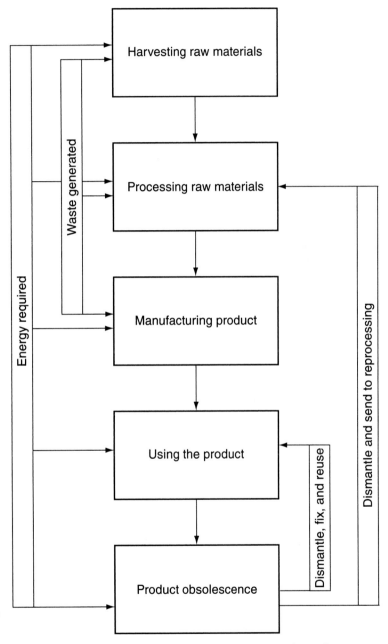

Figure 5.12: During design and product selection, analysis of energy invested and waste generated needs to be done from "cradle to grave."

monitored, the manufacturing process of aluminum also generates hazardous waste containing fluoride and cyanide in large amounts of waste water. Therefore, while aluminum may be an optimum material for some building applications, materials containing less embodied energy than aluminum can be used where its advantages are not required.

Minimizing waste of non-recyclable, non-renewable, or toxic building materials and replacing them with natural, healthier materials is an effective way of reducing the environmental impacts of construction. Toxic materials include sealants, which often contain plastic resins and harmful chemicals; vinyl, which contains high-waste producing polyvinyl chloride (PVC); and carpets and paint, which can off-gas toxic air pollutants and incorporated petrochemical products. Many healthier building materials consume less energy within their lifecycles. In a 1500-square-foot (140-square-meter) dwelling, for example, replacing plywood floors, walls, and roof sheathing with oriented strand board reduces embodied energy, or sum of all energy requirements, for those components by 59 percent; replacing fiberglass insulation in walls and roofs with cellulose reduces embodied energy by 64 percent. Similarly, replacing carpet and vinyl flooring with parquetry and ceramic tile, replacing vinyl siding and asphalt with cedar boards and shingles, and replacing clay brick with concrete also lowers the embodied energy (Figure 5.13).

Such improvements illustrate the potential savings and reduction of environmental impact that a carefully designed and efficient home can achieve using alternative building products such as linoleum, stone, low–volatile organic compound (VOC) paints, and recycled wallboard (sheetrock). As a greater number of alternative, healthier, and low-embodied energy products enter the market, "greening" the home is becoming more accessible and profitable for the average builder.

Water Efficiency

Water is a staple in our daily requirements, and concern for water and its safety has existed in society for millennia. Although fresh water sources seem plentiful, the rising demand for potable water is resulting in regional water withdrawals at higher rates than natural aquifer discharges. The volume of wastewater is also increasing, as are the costs and facilities needed to provide sewage treatment and water purification. Currently, water rates charged to the user often do not cover the cost of supply, distribution, water collection, and wastewater treatment, and considered options of applying water surcharges or raising water rates to homeowners leads to the conclusion that water efficiency makes both economic and environmental sense.

Water efficiency in the home can be achieved by installing hardware that reduces water requirements and/or by reusing water within the home. However,

Building Material	Environmental impact [1]	Waste generation [2]	Resource conservation [3]	Embodied energy	Operating energy	Indoor air quality
Structure						
Concrete foundation	•	•	••	••	••	•
Solid wood studs*	•••	•••	••	•••	••	•••
Manufactured I-joists	•••	•••	•••	•••	••	•••
OSB subfloor	•••	•••	•••	•••	••	•••
Insulative sheathing	•••	••	••	•••	•••	••
Raised heel roof trusses*	•••	•••	•••	•••	•••	•••
Thermal/moisture protection						
Cellulose insulation	•••	•••	•••	•••	•••	••
Polyethylene vapor barrier	••	••	•	•	••	••
Polyolefin weather barrier	••	••	•	••	•••	••
Metal flashing	••	••	••	•	N/A	••
Silicone sealants	••	••	•	•	•••	•••
Windows						
Wood frame/casement	••	•••	••	••	•••	N/A
Low-E glass; argon filled	••	••	••	•	•••	N/A
Exterior finishes						
Brick masonry	••	••	••	•	••	N/A
Wood fiber siding	•••	•••	•••	•••	••	N/A
Aluminum soffits	•	••	••	•	••	N/A
Wood fiber shingles	•••	•••	•••	•••	••	N/A
Interior finishes						
Fiberbond wall board	•••	••	•••	•••	••	•••
Eco-logo paints/coatings	••	•••	••	••	••	••
Parquet floors	••	•••	•••	•••	N/A	•••
Recycled carpeting	•••	•	•••	•••	N/A	•
Ceramic tile	••	••	••	•	N/A	•••
Solid wood cabinets*	••	•••	••	•••	N/A	•••
Services						
Copper plumbing	••	••	••	•	N/A	N/A
Water-efficient fixtures	•••	••	•••	••	•••	N/A
Heat recovery ventilator	••	•••	•••	••	•••	•••
Electric baseboard heaters	•	••	•••	••	•	•

[1] Exploitation of endangered species, ozone layer depletion, loss of land, water or habitat
[2] Release of toxic/hazardous pollutants; volume of waste generated; biodegradability
[3] Recyclable/recycled content; based on renewable resources; efficient use of existing resources
* Assumes that sustainable forestry principles are in effect

• Poor
•• Fair
••• Good

Figure 5.13: Environmental quality of various building materials

an awareness of responsible water usage will also have a large effect on the water requirements of a community. Planting local flora, for example, requires the use of less water from the municipal system, and reducing the footprint of and paving around a home will allow for water to infiltrate naturally into the earth via swales and gullies, therefore reducing the load on municipal sewage systems. Domestic water use accounts for 44 percent of total municipal water consumption, and of that, the bathroom accounts for 75 percent.

An effective and easy way to reduce personal water consumption is to install water-efficient fixtures that add little to the construction costs. Aerators in faucets and ultra–low-volume toilets can reduce water consumption, while water-efficient household appliances also require less electricity to operate, resulting in a financial payback within the appliance's lifetime. Similarly, the cost of heating water for these appliances is reduced by initially lowering water consumption, and additional savings of 25 percent can be achieved simply by turning the water heater thermostat down from 140ºF (60ºC) to 122ºF (50ºC) and by insulating the heater and pipes to reduce heat loss in transit (Environment Canada, 1991). Figure 5.14 illustrates the water savings accomplished with the installation of water-efficient fixtures with no change to occupants' water usage habits.

In addition, modifications to the main intake and output water pipes will reduce the volume of required water loads and generated wastewater. Because water pressure is higher than necessary in many water distribution systems, pressure-reducing valves can be used to curb water use. Water intake can be supplemented by the collection of rainwater from roofs in cisterns. Water discharge is reduced by the installation or redirection of graywater pipes that carry used water (that does not contain sewage) from showers, sinks, and laundry rooms. This system presents the option for water reuse in gardens or toilets, although many municipalities have strict restrictions on graywater usage.

Construction Details

A basic consideration of an energy-efficient home is the effectiveness of its building envelope. In addition to protection from the elements, a building envelope must also provide structural support. In a typical home, about one-half of the total indoor air is replaced every hour through leaks in the house membrane, accounting for about 25 percent of the dwelling's heat loss. While it was once thought that this leakage provided fresh exterior air, it is now recognized that no beneficial reason exists for air exchange in this uncontrolled manner. Warm exfiltrating air carries moisture into the envelope, which may condense as it cools, causing moisture damage and mold growth. Infiltrating exterior air will adjust the indoor air temperature and may bring with it harmful exterior pollutants and emissions from the building materials. Although most leakage occurs at areas where building materials are joined—such as around windows or doors or at intersections of walls, floors, and roofs—energy savings can be assured by using proper insulation on either side of the structural framing members.

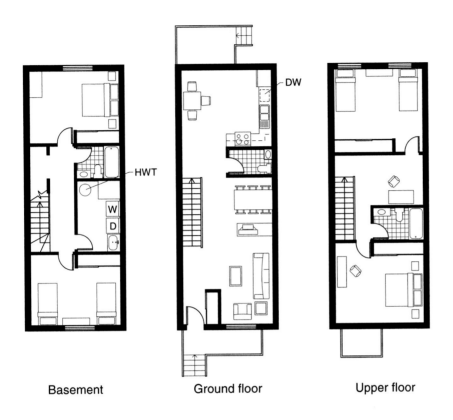

Basement   Ground floor   Upper floor

	Fixture	Conventional fixture	Water-efficient fixture	Water savings
Basement	Toilet	5.2 gal (20L) / flush	1.6 gal (6L) / flush	3.6 gal (14L) / flush
	Shower	5.2 gal (20L) / min	2.5 gal (9.5L) / min	2.8 gal (10.5L) / min
	Bathroom faucet	3.6 gal (13.5L) / min	0.5 gal (2L) / min	3.1 gal (11.5L) / min
	Washing machine	60 gal (225L) / load	46 gal (175L) / load	14 gal (50L) / load
	Laundry faucet	3.6 gal (13.5L) / min	2 gal (7.5L) / min	1.6 gal (6L) / min
Ground floor	Kitchen faucet	3.6 gal (13.5L) / min	2 gal (7.5L) / min	1.6 gal (6L) / min
	Dishwasher	9.7 gal (37L) / load	5.5 gal (21L) / load	4.2 gal (16L) / load
	Toilet	5.2 gal (20L) / flush	1.6 gal (6L) / flush	3.6 gal (14L) / flush
	Bathroom faucet	3.6 gal (13.5L) / min	0.5 gal (2L) / min	3.1 gal (11.5L) / min
Upper floor	Toilet	5.2 gal (20L) / flush	1.6 gal (6L) / flush	3.6 gal (14L) / flush
	Shower	5.2 gal (20L) / min	2.5 gal (9.5L) / min	2.8 gal (10.5L) / min
	Bathroom faucet	3.6 gal (13.5L) / min	0.5 gal (2L) / min	3.1 gal (11.5L) / min

Figure 5.14: Water consumption comparison between a conventional home and a home using water-efficient fixtures shows that substantial water can be saved.

Insulating walls will reduce heat flow through leakage, infiltration/exfiltration, and *thermal bridging*, a process by which as much as 10 percent of the total heat lost through the envelope is lost via conduction. The most basic way to upgrade the thermal performance of a wall is to replace commonplace exterior sheathing such as plywood or waferboard with rigid or semi-rigid insulation (sometimes called boardstock insulation). This can increase *thermal resistance values* of the wall from R20 (RSI 3.5) to R28 (RSI 4.9), a 40 percent improvement over conventional walls. The installation of interior horizontal strapping creates additional space for insulation, reduces thermal bridging across wall studs, and allows for insulation of plumbing and electrical devices in the strapping space, minimizing penetrations in the air/vapor barrier that are responsible for air leakage. When interior strapping is combined with exterior insulative sheathing, an 80 percent improvement of thermal resistance values over conventional walls can be achieved, raising the R-value from R20 (RSI 3.5) to R36 (RSI of 6.3).

Additional energy savings can be achieved with the construction of a double-stud wall consisting of one load-bearing wall (either interior or exterior) and a second non-bearing wall, both filled with and separated by insulation usually 3.5 inches (89 millimeters) wide. Thermal performance can be raised to R36 (RSI 6.3) or higher if a greater width of insulation is added, and additional energy savings occur because the structure becomes airtight, as no plumbing or electrical equipment pierces the envelope. However, the double-stud wall requires more material, space, and labor to install, sometimes rendering it unfeasible for smaller, more affordable homes. A variant on the double-stud wall is the standoff wall in which non-load–bearing trusses are added to the exterior of a standard stud wall to accommodate varying widths of insulation. A continuous polyethylene vapor barrier is installed from roof to foundation wall over existing exterior sheathing. Figure 5.15 illustrates several variations on wall construction and insulation. Maximum insulation should be used according to budget, unit type, and space limitations.

The challenge to controlling heat, vapor, air, and water flow from the exterior to interior of a building occurs where the building envelope is interrupted—around joints, windows, doors, and service openings. *Thermal resistance* in a wall can be as low as R1.9 (RSI 0.33) where no insulation exists, particularly where the joists intersect the foundation wall and the concrete provides a direct thermal bridge from the interior to the exterior. Several methods of eliminating thermal bridges at corners and joist-joist or joist-wall intersections by reducing framing members, and therefore mass, of the structure are illustrated in Figure 5.15.

The location and continuity of the vapor barrier is essential in keeping moisture from deteriorating insulation material or causing rot in framing members. Although water vapor will be diffused through the materials of a properly insulated wall with a 4 mil (0.1 millimeter) polyethylene vapor barrier, the effect is a

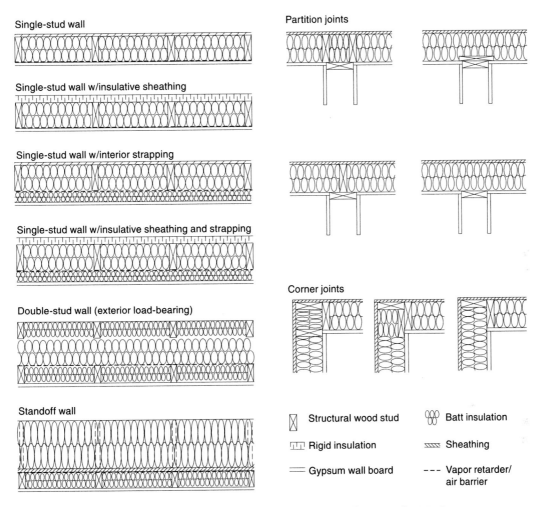

Single-stud wall

Single-stud wall w/insulative sheathing

Single-stud wall w/interior strapping

Single-stud wall w/insulative sheathing and strapping

Double-stud wall (exterior load-bearing)

Standoff wall

Partition joints

Corner joints

▨ Structural wood stud	⊗⊗ Batt insulation
⊞ Rigid insulation	⌇⌇ Sheathing
═ Gypsum wall board	- - - Vapor retarder/ air barrier

Figure 5.15: Energy-efficient wall alternatives that maximize insulation and minimize thermal bridging (left), and alternative corner and partition details that can eliminate thermal bridges (right)

thin layer of frost or condensation on the inside surface of the exterior sheathing. Continuity and rigidity of air barriers are also essential to reducing uncontrolled leakage throughout the gaps and cracks in a building's skin to a negligible amount. This can be done by using a membrane of polyethylene that is wrapped around header joists and window and door openings. The same continuity can be achieved with a rigid air-barrier method that uses the structural framing components and sheetrock by applying gaskets and sealants between the plates, header joists, and subflooring (Figure 5.16).

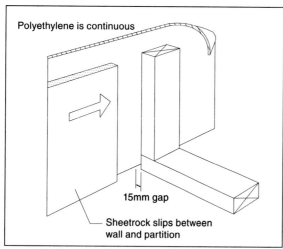

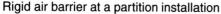

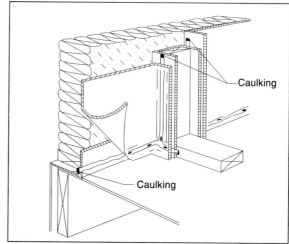

Rigid air barrier at a partition installation

Membrane air barrier at partition installation

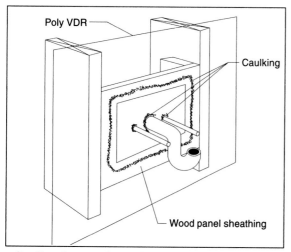

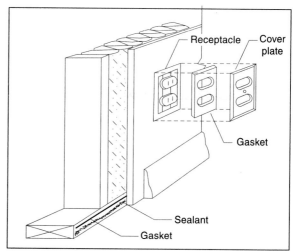

Sealing the envelope after plumbing penetration

Sealing the envelope at an electrical outlet

Figure 5.16: Measures that can reduce heat loss by sealing the building envelope

Basements, common in urban and colder suburban municipalities, account for 20 to 30 percent of energy loss through the building envelope and are particularly susceptible to moisture penetration and cracking. With proper insulation and waterproofing, basements can provide an added 30 to 50 percent more usable floor area to a house at a modest additional construction cost. Figure 5.17 illustrates two basic approaches for basement wall insulation and outlines their advantages and disadvantages. However, replacing the basement with either a crawlspace or slab-on-grade reduces unused space, materials, costs, and energy consumption for those who do not need the space. In addition, a concrete slab-on-grade can act as a thermal storage device for solar energy and can easily incorporate piping for radiant floor heating (Marbek Resource Consultants, Ltd., 1987).

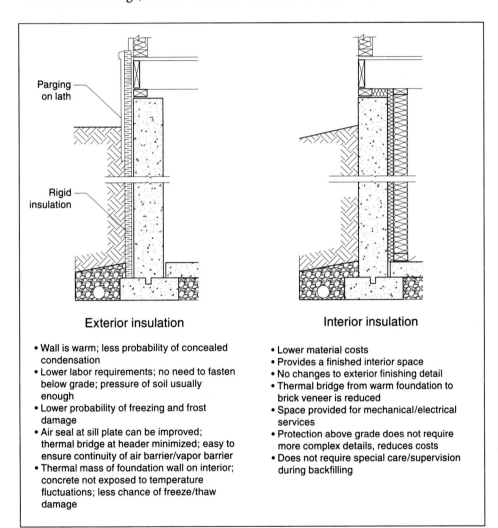

Exterior insulation

- Wall is warm; less probability of concealed condensation
- Lower labor requirements; no need to fasten below grade; pressure of soil usually enough
- Lower probability of freezing and frost damage
- Air seal at sill plate can be improved; thermal bridge at header minimized; easy to ensure continuity of air barrier/vapor barrier
- Thermal mass of foundation wall on interior; concrete not exposed to temperature fluctuations; less chance of freeze/thaw damage

Interior insulation

- Lower material costs
- Provides a finished interior space
- No changes to exterior finishing detail
- Thermal bridge from warm foundation to brick veneer is reduced
- Space provided for mechanical/electrical services
- Protection above grade does not require more complex details, reduces costs
- Does not require special care/supervision during backfilling

Figure 5.17: Two options for insulating basement walls and their advantages

Insulation in the attic and roof space is also essential for an airtight assembly—roof trusses should accommodate consistent insulation beyond the top plates of exterior walls. Several roof truss options that allow greater amounts of insulation, especially over the exterior wall's top plates where heat loss is typically the highest, are illustrated in Figure 5.18.

157

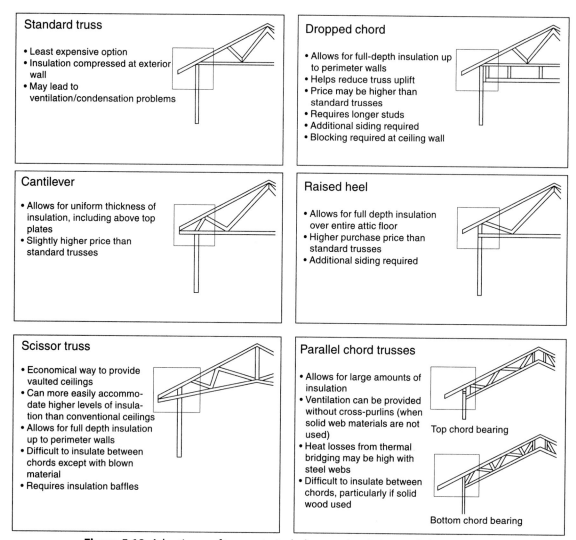

Figure 5.18: Adapting roof trusses to include more insulation and eliminate thermal bridges reduces heat loss through the envelope.

Prefabricated Wall Systems

Prefabrication methods can offer many advantages over conventional construction methods. The assembly of units, panels, or components under factory-controlled conditions yields a higher quality product that generally results in more energy-efficient homes. Due to the quick and efficient assembly that takes place in the factory, the effect of poor weather conditions, particularly in cold climates, is reduced, as is the potential for damage due to inadequate material storage and vandalism. Cleanup time and material costs are also reduced with less waste (Figure 5.19).

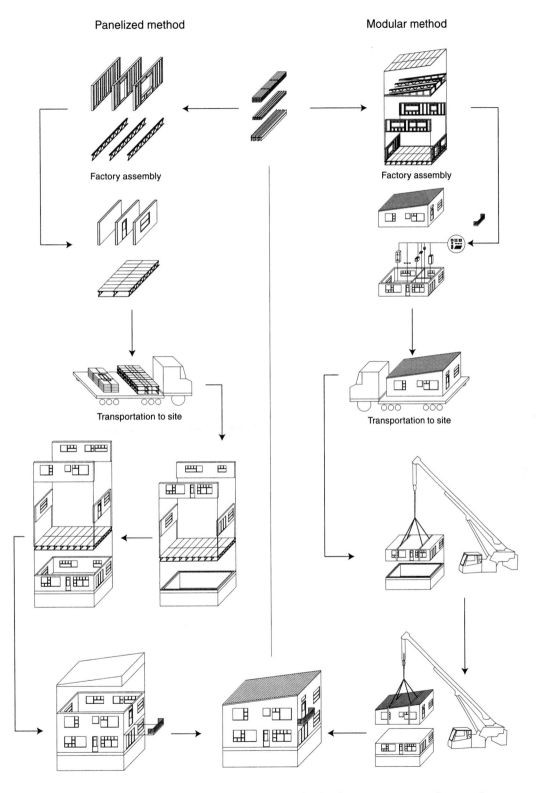

Panelized method

Modular method

Factory assembly

Factory assembly

Transportation to site

Transportation to site

Figure 5.19: Panelized and modular prefabricated methods of construction are often used.

Panel Systems

Numerous types of prefabricated systems, subsystems, and components can be combined at various levels to provide a complete system package. Nine types of panel systems are applicable to woodframe residential construction, which can be divided into three categories (Figure 5.20):

- Open-sheathed panels (using conventional construction methods)
- Structural sandwich panels
- Unsheathed structural panels

Open-Sheathed Panels (OSP) OSPs are available in many variations. The most common systems are built either with 1.5 by 5.5 inch (38 by 140 millimeter) studs with plywood or waferboard sheathing, or with 1.5 by 3.5 inch (38 by 89 millimeter) studs and extruded polystyrene sheathing. In either case, the panels are delivered open on the interior to facilitate the installation of electrical and/or plumbing services. Batt insulation is usually installed on site and is sometimes supplied by the manufacturer.

Structural Sandwich Panels (SSP) Also known as *foam core panels*, SSPs consist of a core of rigid foam insulation that is laminated between two facing materials. In its most basic form, the sheathing materials may be plywood or waferboard. More complete options offer exterior and/or interior finishes that replace the basic facing material and become an integral structural part of the panel.

The core material contains precut electrical chases and may be either one of four different types of insulation: molded bead expanded polystyrene, extruded polystyrene, polyurethane, or polyisocyanurate (PIR). A variety of options are available for the joints between the panels.

Unsheathed Structural Panels (USP) USPs, or *composite panels*, are built using a combination of wood or metal structural elements combined with rigid foam insulation infill, usually expanded polystyrene. Four basic variations of these systems are available with different configurations for their structural elements, which provide a continuous thermal break and/or an airspace on the interior of the panel. Horizontal chases for electrical wiring are often cut into the insulation.

For each of the systems, it is possible to add value to the panel by integrating a larger portion of the building envelope during fabrication. Added components vary from air barriers to exterior and/or interior finishes. The extent to which the panels are finished has different implications for the builder and the worker who will select and install the system.

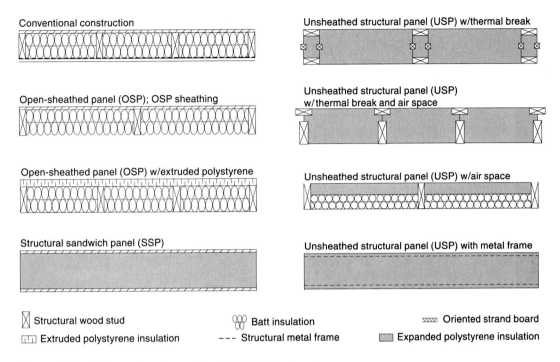

Conventional construction

Open-sheathed panel (OSP); OSP sheathing

Open-sheathed panel (OSP) w/extruded polystyrene

Structural sandwich panel (SSP)

Unsheathed structural panel (USP) w/thermal break

Unsheathed structural panel (USP) w/thermal break and air space

Unsheathed structural panel (USP) w/air space

Unsheathed structural panel (USP) with metal frame

Structural wood stud   Batt insulation   Oriented strand board

Extruded polystyrene insulation   Structural metal frame   Expanded polystyrene insulation

Figure 5.20: Horizontal sections of prefabricated wall systems

Quality and Energy Efficiency

One of the biggest advantages of prefabricated panel systems is the superior level of quality that can be achieved through the manufacturing process. The quality of prefabricated wall systems can be evaluated in terms of three interrelated characteristics: craftsmanship, technical performance, and durability. The system's craftsmanship governs its potential to achieve consistent levels of performance from one application to another. The wall's technical performance, particularly with respect to its airtightness, will affect the rate of deterioration due to condensation. Fire and sound resistance, critical for dividing walls, will contribute to the quality of the unit's interior environment. The panel's durability depends on the various materials' resistance to elements and on the probability of exposure to these given the panels' design.

Prefabricated panel systems are generally capable of technically outperforming walls built using conventional construction methods. SSP systems, particularly those with urethane or isocyanurate foam, provide excellent insulation value for their thickness. This is due partly to their continuous thermal break across the joints, particularly with the double-spline variation (Figure 5.21). These panels also result in the tightest assemblies, due to their exceptionally well-fitted joint systems and the possibility of extending the exterior skin below the floor level, allowing for a continuous barrier across the end of the floor section. The inherent simplicity of the design makes these panels high performing. The critical nature of the lamination process, however, requires a relatively high level of quality control. Among the questionable characteristics is a susceptibility for these systems to ridge at the joints because of inadequate allowance for thermal expansion and a possibility of panels delaminating (Andrews, 1992).

USPs appear to provide good performance in all respects, but they benefit from a few extraordinary characteristics. The panels' biggest advantage is that they can overcome the inadequate workmanship that can be found in conventional construction without requiring unfamiliar building techniques. The use of expanded polystyrene foam between the structural elements significantly improves the performance of the wall in that area, which is a key failure point in conventionally built walls: discontinuous insulation and air barrier caused by improper insulation. Tight friction-fit joints and the ability to accommodate electrical boxes without interrupting the continuity of the insulation provides an attractive advantage over conventional construction methods. Furthermore, the relatively simple manufacturing techniques (some make no use of adhesives) to provide continuous thermal breaks and adequate air barriers make USPs likely to achieve consistent performance levels.

Conventional construction and OSPs are considered to have the lowest overall technical performance potential, due to the lower thermal resistance of batt insulation, thermal bridging caused by the framing members, and the unsealed joints that occur between the insulation and the studs. The biggest advantage of conventional panels appears to be their durability, due not as much to the material's ability to resist deterioration as to the panel's ability to retain its structural integrity. Due to their lack of dependence on the insulation material for structural stability, temperature variations, rodents (which have been known to burrow through rigid foams), and chemicals have less of a damaging potential on OSPs. While their susceptibility to moisture damage remains higher than that of other systems, OSPs benefit from the fact that the interior of the wall can be relatively easily inspected and repaired. Stick-built structures are the least preferable option due to the high variability of craftsmanship and susceptibility of materials to damage from inadequate site storage.

Wall system	Thermal resistance R-value (RSI) [1]	Conductive heat loss (W)	Energy consumption (KWh) [2]
Conventional construction	18 (3.177)	1139	3379
Open-sheathed panels			
• w/ OSP sheathing	18 (3.177)	1139	2254
• w/ XEPS sheathing	19 (3.420)	1058	2134
Structural sandwich panels			
• w/ MEPS core	22 (3.925)	922	1932
• w/ XEPS core	28 (5.017)	722	1634
• w/ PUR/ISO core	40 (7.091)	510	1320
Unsheathed structural panels			
• w/ thermal bridge	20 (3.546)	1021	2078
• w/ thermal bridge and air space	19 (3.385)	1069	2150
• w/ air space	18 (3.223)	1123	2230
• w/ metal frame	21 (3.738)	968	2000

[1] Adjusted for thermal bridging
[2] Includes infiltration losses, assuming 0.1 ACH for prefabricated systems and 0.3 ACH for conventional construction

Figure 5.21: Energy performance of various prefabricated wall systems

Material Wastage

As is the case with any manufactured component, waste generation from pre-fabrication of panel systems is less than what would be expected from on-site construction. Assembly of the wall system in closed, controlled environments ensures that materials are used efficiently and that "scrap" pieces are more easily recovered and reused. Furthermore, the fact that the panels can be erected quickly and the dwelling unit can be assembled within a short period of time reduces delays due to bad weather. The probability of vandalism and theft is reduced because less material is stored on site, and the cost of replacing materials damaged by inadequate storage and exposure is also reduced. Since less material is wasted, the costs of clearing and removing debris are less. Considering that the construction of an average house produces some 2.5 tons of waste, 25 percent of which is dimensional lumber and an additional 15 percent manufactured wood products, the savings realized by using OSPs could be substantial, particularly in large developments (CMHC, 1991).

Windows

Heat losses through the building envelope can occur via conduction, convection, and radiation. In all three cases, windows are the weakest link, and, as such, they represent the most important investment in the construction or renovation of any dwelling. Considering that an average window has a thermal resistance value of R1.8 (RSI 0.32) as compared to R20 (RSI 3.5) for a wall, 1 square foot (0.1 square meter) of window loses as much heat as 10 square feet (1 square meter) of wall. Three factors should be considered in selecting window units: the frame type and material, the glazing unit, and the spacer bar.

Coupled with edge losses from the glazing unit, conductive heat losses through the window frame can account for up to 20 percent of the total heat losses from the window unit. The selection of an appropriate framing material is, therefore, not simply a question of appearance. Wood, for instance, is a good insulator, but it is easily damaged and requires higher maintenance. Metal (aluminum) requires much less maintenance but is a good conductor. Plastic (vinyl) frames are maintenance free but, like metal frames, are susceptible to temperature changes. Combining these materials takes advantage of the thermal qualities of wood while protecting it with either vinyl or aluminum and reducing maintenance requirements (Figure 5.22).

Infiltration losses between the frame and the sash (the moving part) depend on the number and type of operable components and on the type of gasket used. Several types of windows can be categorized by the type of operation: fixed, awning, hopper, casement, sliding, single-hung, double-hung, pivoted (vertical), and multiple (for cleaning and ventilation). It is also possible to manufacture window units with combinations of these.

Generally, windows with fewer operable parts are more energy-efficient. The more linear feet of joint, the more heat loss occurs. Fixed windows are the best in this regard. As far as the type of operation is concerned, pivotal components (as in awnings and casements) are more energy-efficient, since they make use of compression seals. Sliding parts are least effective in terms of air leakage.

All three types of heat losses mentioned occur across the glazing unit. These losses are controlled by the type and number of layers present in a glazing unit, the type of space that separates them, the type of coating (if any) applied to the surface, and the type of gas that fills the cavity between them. Conductive losses can be reduced by using a *low-conductivity gas* such as argon, sulphur hexafluoride, or carbon dioxide, which can increase the thermal resistance of the unit by 12 to 18

Frame material	Thermal resistance R-value (RSI)	Heat loss (W)	Energy consumption (KWh)
• Thermally broken aluminum	2.8 (0.49)	1307	1909
• Wood or wood clad	3.4 (0.59)	1093	1597
• Vinyl	3.9 (0.69)	442	646
• Glazing assumed to be double, with Low-E coating, argon, and insulative spacer			

Figure 5.22: Effect of frame material on energy consumption

percent while reducing sound transmission. Since argon is heavier than air, it does not circulate as easily, reducing the transfer of heat from cold to warm through circulation/convection.

The problem that remains is one of radiative heat transfer, both across the airspace and through the glass to the interior. The addition of a low-emittance (Low-E) coating reflects heat back outside in summer and back inside in winter. The result of combining a Low-E coating with argon gas is a thermal resistance close to that of a triple-glazed unit, which tends to be heavy, cumbersome, and expensive, not only because of the extra glazing, but because of the heavy-duty operating mechanisms that are required (Figure 5.23).

Glazing type	Thermal resistance R-value (RSI)	Heat loss (W)	Energy consumption (KWh)
Double, air, alum. spacer	2.0 (0.36)	1780	2599
+ Low-E coating	2.7 (0.47)	1363	1991
+ argon gas	3.0 (0.52)	1232	1799
+ insulative spacer	3.4 (0.59)	1093	1597
• Window frame assumed to be wood			

Figure 5.23: Effect of type of glazing on energy consumption

The function of the spacer bar is to seal the glazing unit so that no air or moisture enters the airspace. It consists of a hollow metal section sealed with an organic compound. To ensure that no moisture is allowed in, a chemical drying agent is added into the spacer bar and small holes are drilled so that any moisture that gets into the airspace can be absorbed. Since much of a window's heat loss occurs at the edges, insulative spacer bars, such at those made of butyl metal, can be used to reduce conductive heat loss along the glazing unit's perimeter.

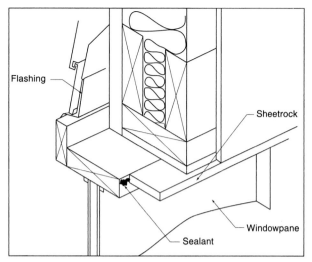

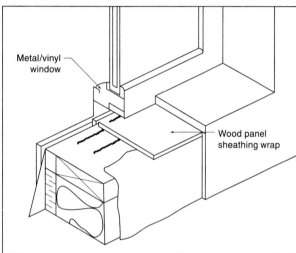

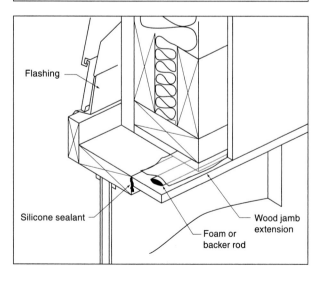

Size, type, location, and orientation of windows all affect the energy performance of the home, and thus their careful selection and installation is critical in reducing the energy and costs required for heating, cooling, and lighting. High-performance windows with tight and water-absorbing seals between frames, sashes, and layers of glass increase thermal resistance but also increase costs. Finally, proper installation of windows will also affect energy consumption (Figure 5.24).

Mechanical Systems

Recent technological advancements have rendered well-built houses more energy-efficient and airtight. Heating and cooling systems include consideration of energy loads, cost efficiency, types of structure, and climatic data. In addition, concern for proper ventilation within airtight homes is of greater concern, not only because of infiltration of pollutants but also because of off-gassing toxins within the home from building materials.

Heating, ventilating, and air-conditioning alternatives in modern homes vary according to efficiency, the system's ability to transform a power source into usable energy, or how much of the energy produced is actually used to condition the environment. Electrical and oil and gas systems are the most widely used but, depending on the source of the electricity,

Figure 5.24: Proper installation practices of windows in the building envelope can significantly reduce heat loss.

can be unhealthy for the environment. Options that use renewable energy, such as heat pumps and solar heat collectors for radiant floor heating, are becoming more popular and economical to install. Electrical systems transform electricity into heat distributed via either forced air, baseboard heaters, or fan-assisted room heaters. Baseboard heaters are widely popular and have a 100-percent gross efficiency, but only a portion of the heat delivered actually heats the air, and they require a lot of power to operate. A time delay often occurs between thermostat temperature readings and baseboard compensation, resulting in further energy inefficiency.

Gas and oil systems, although exhibiting increased efficiency in recent years, are expensive to install and are not designed to operate at a heating capacity of less than 10,000 watts. Heat pumps are designed to transfer energy from one location to the next while providing comfort and efficiency. The two types of heat sinks commonly used are an air or a ground source. Air-air heat pumps draw hot and cold air from the outdoors as needed using outdoor heat exchangers, forcing the air through ducts or pipes attached to wall-mounted units. Geothermal heat pumps use the ambient temperature of the ground as a heat source or heat sink to heat or cool the home. Loops of pipes containing thermodynamic liquids exchange energy from the ground to the building interior via forced air (Figure 5.25).

Ventilation systems provide air exchanges in different parts of the home to ensure that stale and humid air is replaced with fresh air, currently regulated at one-third of an air exchange every hour. Because a substantial amount of heat can be lost in the process, most energy efficient homes use a heat recovery ventilation (HRV) system. An HRV recycles up to 80 percent of that heat with minimal extra cost and infrastructure such as a duct network.

Energy requirements to provide a comfortable indoor environment need not be extensive if adequate natural ventilation is designed in the home and off-gassing of building materials is negligible or kept to a minimum. The size and power source of a mechanical system will vary according to location and availability, but in the interest of the environment, systems that use renewable energy are always preferable.

Indoor Air Quality

Significant changes in building materials have led to more efficient and cost-effective construction alternatives. The introduction of composite wood products, for instance, such as hardwood plywood, fiberboard, and particleboard, have provided cost-effective alternatives with reasonable performance and durability. These products make more efficient use of natural resources, since a higher percentage of the tree can be used and the potential for using recycled materials, scrap wood

Ground coupled heat pumps (GCHP)
a.k.a closed loop heat pumps

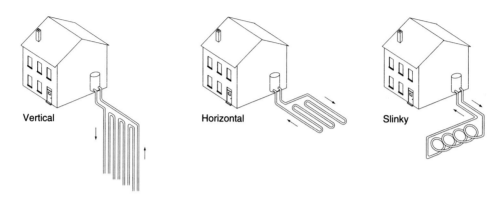

Vertical   Horizontal   Slinky

Groundwater heat pumps (GWHP)
a.k.a open loop heat pumps

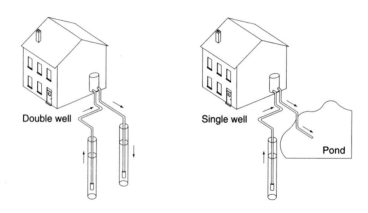

Double well   Single well   Pond

Surface water heat pumps (SWHP)
a.k.a lake or pond loop heat pumps

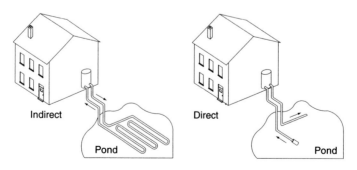

Indirect   Direct

Pond   Pond

Figure 5.25: Vertical loops for a geothermal heat pump

chips, and sawdust can be exploited. Similarly, stain-resistant carpets of synthetic fibers, thermally efficient rigid insulation boards, and a variety of coatings, cleaning agents, and furnishings have increased the design options and facilitated the assembly, operation, and maintenance of buildings.

Unfortunately, many of these innovations have a tendency to emit odorous, irritating, or in some cases toxic compounds into the surrounding air. If effective ventilation is not provided, the concentration of harmful pollutants can compromise the physical and psychological well-being of the home's occupants. The degree to which individuals may be affected depends on personal susceptibility, concentration of pollutants, and duration of exposure. The symptoms of exposure to poor indoor air quality (IAQ) are varied, and the result can range from mild discomfort to total disability (Figures 5.26 and 5.27).

Principal pollutant [1]	Building product	Timing/duration
Formaldehyde	Hardwood plywood, particleboard, and other glue-bonded wood products (structural products made with waterproof adhesives such as softwood, plywood, and waferboard have negligible emissions)	Highest emissions when new; may continue for up to a year; emissions increase with temperature and humidity
Toluene, xylene hexane, aliphatic hydrocarbons	Styrene butadiene rubber (SB-R) sealants, butyl rubber (BR) or solvent-based acrylic sealants [2]	May vary from 56 to 4,932 hours, depending on drying time
4-phenylcyclohexane (4-PC), styrene	Styrene butadiene (SB) latex-backed carpets	Low emissions, but may persist due to the high sink potential of carpeting
Multiple volatile organic compounds (VOCs)	Vinyl tile and sheet flooring	Decreases substantially after 24 hours if well ventilated; lower emissions can continue for years
	Traditional, multi-purpose carpet adhesives, both organic solvent– and water-based	Highest for the first 3–6 weeks; may persist depending on sink performance
	Latex (water- or organic solvent–based) and acrylic paints	During application and drying; lower emissions may persist for months
Fibers/particulates	Fiberglass and mineral wool insulation	Most pronounced when insulation is being installed or disturbed; airtight construction keeps fibers from blowing to the interior

[1] Many other building materials not included here also emit VOCs in negligible quantities
[2] Emissions may be acceptable when used in limited quantities or under special precautions

Figure 5.26: Indoor air pollutants from building materials

While the diagnoses and prevention of problems associated with poor indoor air quality is not an exact science, the need to address the issue has become a topic of great concern. Ventilation standards are being revised and product emissions monitored to promote "healthy," "safe," or "clean" environments. Achieving

Type of pollutant	Examples	Effect on occupant health	Source of contamination
Biological growth			
Fungi	Mold, mildew	Allergic reaction and aggravation of asthma symptoms in high concentrations; irreversible lung damage (with inhalation of mold spores)	High humidity levels caused by washing, bathing, cooking, unvented clothes dryers, etc.
Chemicals			
Inorganic gases	Carbon monoxide	Reduces endurance, worsens symptoms of heart disease, nausea, headache, dizziness, death (in very high concentrations)	Gas stoves, kerosene heaters, tobacco smoke, vehicle exhausts
	Carbon dioxide	Unlikely to affect health in low quantities that are generally found in houses	People, gas stoves, furnaces, kerosene heaters, combustion devices
	Nitrogen dioxide	Breathing difficulty in high concentrations; respiratory illness with prolonged exposure	Vehicle exhausts, industrial emissions, gas stoves, kerosene heaters
	Sulphur dioxide	Aggravates asthma symptoms and existing lung disease; breathing discomfort; lung disease with prolonged exposure	Mainly outdoor sources, unless sulphur containing fuels are burned indoors in unvented appliances
	Chlorine	Irritation in susceptible occupants	Household cleaning and laundry products; municipal water sources
	Ammonia	Irritation in susceptible occupants	Household cleaning products
	Ozone	Coughing; chest discomfort; nose, throat and windpipe irritation	Electrostatic air cleaners, arcing electric motors, photocopiers, outside air
Volatile organic compounds (VOCs)	Formaldehyde and other aldehydes, hydrocarbons, alcohols, phenols, ketones	Unpleasant odors; eye, nose and throat irritation; central nervous system depressant; possible carcinogens; prolonged exposure may cause sensitization	Building materials; furniture, carpets, synthetic floor coverings, wallpapers, plastics; household products, bedding, toiletries, etc; tobacco smoke; gas stoves, space heaters; pesticides
Particulates			
Biological particles	Viruses, bacteria, spores, pollen, cell debris, dust mites	Few health problems at levels normally found in house; high concentrations of pollen grains may cause allergic reactions or aggravate asthma symptoms; bacteria growth in stagnant water may case serious disease	Stagnant water, dust, water droplets
Non-biological particles	Dust, smoke, etc.	Effects may vary from mild discomfort to lung cancer	Tobacco smoke, woodstoves, open fireplaces, combustion operations; construction materials
	Fibers	Temporary eye and skin irritation; lung disease with prolonged exposure; glass fibers may be carcinogenic; asbestos causes lung cancer	Construction materials; fiberglass and mineral wool insulation
Natural soil gas			
Radon		May contribute to incidence of lung cancer with prolonged high exposure	Soil; improperly sealed basement floor slab

Figure 5.27: Types of effects and sources of indoor air pollutants

good air quality is quickly becoming an integral and essential part of the design of comfortable and healthy interior building environments, along with the control of temperature, humidity, lighting, and acoustics.

Poor indoor air quality has two basic causes: inadequate ventilation and excessive contamination. Deficiencies in ventilation may be due to inadequate design; improper insulation; or negligent operation or maintenance of heating, ventilation, and air conditioning (HVAC) systems. Excessive contamination is caused by harmful emissions from products that come into direct exposure with the indoor air or from polluted outdoor air that is somehow allowed to enter the building. The process of designing for IAQ is based mostly on the identification and avoidance of materials that are known to be strong sources of odors, irritants, or toxins, and on ensuring that adequate measures are taken to provide sufficient ventilation to occupied spaces. Accordingly, the two general objectives of improving the dwelling's ventilation and clearing the air of contaminants should be followed in designing for a healthy indoor environment.

Emissions

Emissions from building materials and products are produced at all phases of building's lifecycle. Most, however, can be controlled by careful consideration during the design phase. Emissions from a building material can originate from three sources: the product itself, the surrounding air, and products used to clean and maintain it.

Nature of the Product Emissions that come directly from the building material can be either wet or dry. Wet emissions can come from solvents, water, paints, sealants, adhesives, caulks, and sealers both during and after application. While most of these substances form an integral part of the product, some may be emitted from solvents used to clean products during application. In either case, emissions are usually highest while the material is drying, which usually takes a few hours or days. Many products can continue to emit substances at lower concentrations for weeks, months, and even years.

Dry product emissions come from products that do not involve a wet process on site but emit harmful substances nevertheless. Solvents that were used in manufacturing the product or its constituents are emitted, usually in an initial outburst when the product is first exposed. This is most noticeable when the product was packaged soon after its manufacture so volatile emissions had no chance to escape. The high initial concentration of emissions may also be due to changes in the product during transportation, storage, and handling. Examples of dry product emissions include those from carpets backed with styrene-butadiene rubber latex (SBR) and composite wood products, such as particleboard, made with formaldehyde-based resins.

Surrounding Air Building surfaces may also emit substances and particles that they have absorbed from the surrounding air. While all surfaces absorb molecules of chemical substances and compounds from the air, the process may be permanent or reversible. The degree to which a substance is absorbed depends on the chemical characteristics of the compound and on the virtual surface area (texture) of the surface (sink material). The sink material becomes loaded partially in proportion to the concentration of pollutants in the air. It can store pollutants during periods of high concentration that are later emitted when concentration is low.

Cleaning and Maintenance Products Substances used to maintain building surfaces and equipment could be strong sources of pollutants. Although these materials are not generally part of the original construction, their use is determined to a large extent by decisions made at the design stage. Proper material selection that accounts for required cleaning agents and durability (that will determine the rate of necessary replacement) can significantly reduce emissions from maintenance. Maintenance products with strong odors or irritating constituents should be avoided when possible.

Ventilation

Ventilation removes and dilutes pollutant concentration. The amount of ventilation required depends on pollutant source strength, types of contaminants, and occupant characteristics. Increasing the rate of fresh air intake alone, however, does not guarantee that a healthy indoor air quality will result. Design, installation, operation, and maintenance of the entire HVAC system must be considered, whether it is integrated or a system of baseboard heating complemented with a heat-recovery ventilator (HRV). Even with high ventilation rates, for instance, buildings may suffer from poor IAQ if an uneven distribution of air or insufficient exhaust mechanism is present. Several factors merit careful consideration, as they are common causes of indoor air problems (American Institute of Architects, 1992b).

Dilution of indoor pollutants is achieved, first and foremost, by increasing the rate at which outdoor air is supplied to the home. Whatever air is brought in, however, needs to be heated and/or conditioned to provide comfortable thermal and humidity conditions, which in turn requires energy. Minimum ventilation rates should not be determined solely by the thermal conditioning needs of a building. Systems that operate at reduced or interrupted flow during certain portions of the day, as in the case with variable air volume systems, may elevate indoor contaminant levels and impair their removal. Minimum ventilation rates should therefore be defined by air cleanliness and distribution, as well as temperature and humidity.

Uneven air distribution may result in variable temperature and humidity conditions in different parts of the building. Not only would this compromise the general quality of the indoor air, but it could result in the occupants' interfering with the operation of the mechanical ventilation system. Areas that have uncomfortable drafts, for instance, may tempt the users of the space to block the air registers if they emit uncomfortable hot or cold air. Ensuring adequate and even air distribution requires that the placement of barriers that disrupt airflow, such as partitions and furnishings, be anticipated.

The placement of supply and return registers too close to one another may lead to uneven fresh air distribution and inefficient removal of contaminants. On the exterior of the building, air supply vents that are installed too close to the exhaust vents may redirect contaminated air into the building. Similarly, the placement of supply vents near other sources of outdoor air pollution, such as loading docks, parking and heavy traffic areas, chimneys, and trash depots, can provide a pathway for contaminants to enter the building's ventilation system.

Improper maintenance of a mechanical system can cause the system itself to become a source of harmful pollutants. Lack of periodic cleaning may cause the system to become clogged and reduce or eliminate airflow. Particular attention should be given to the possible accumulation of water anywhere in the system, which may foster harmful biological growth such as fungi and bacteria that can be distributed throughout the building.

Air Cleaners

Air cleaners are an important part of any HVAC system, but they cannot in themselves adequately remove all the pollutants found in indoor air. They are generally effective in removing airborne particles, but special filter systems are required to remove specific contaminants. It is possible, for example, to reduce gaseous pollutants if the cleaner contains special material, such as activated charcoal. While these materials are usually effective in removing specific pollutants, none is expected to remove all gaseous pollutants typically found in indoor air. As is the case with all filters, they require periodic cleaning and filter replacement to function properly.

Green Roofs

A green roof is a roofing system made of vegetation and plant material as an alternative to conventional roofs made of shingles, tiles, gravel, or membrane. The basic components of a green roof include a waterproofing membrane, a root barrier, insulation, a drainage layer and filter fabric, and growing medium and plants (Scholz-Barth, 2005).

The first layer required for construction is a waterproof membrane, which safeguards the home from leaks and protects the roof's inner structure. Next is the root barrier, which is unique to green roofs. It protects the waterproof membrane from puncture or damage from stray roots. Membranes made of Polyvinyl Chloride (PVC) or other synthetic materials, however, do not usually require a root barrier. The next component is commonly some form of insulation, which is not a necessary element for the roof's structure but is usually needed by most building codes and is beneficial in reducing heating requirements in winter and air-conditioning in summer. It can be located between the roof deck and the waterproofing membrane or below the deck. Next is the drainage and retention layer, which is essential in preventing oversaturation of the soil and ensures that roots get enough ventilation and ample space to grow (Figure 5.28). Sloped green roofs do not require the drainage layer unless extra water retention is desired. The drainage layer can be synthetic or it can be composed of a granular aggregate, and the retention layer can be made of either felt or any absorbent material able to store or retain water in case of drought (Scholz-Barth). The next component is a filter fabric that keeps the growing medium in place. It is usually a polyester or non-woven polypropylene geotextile filter.

Once all the layers are in place, the growing medium can be applied, in which the vegetation itself is planted, providing it with nutrients as well as space for roots to grow. The growing medium used in rooftop gardens is different from ground soil and is called *substrate*. Rooftop substrate should be lightweight to reduce loads and be composed of a mixture of grain sizes to retain water and nutrients, all the

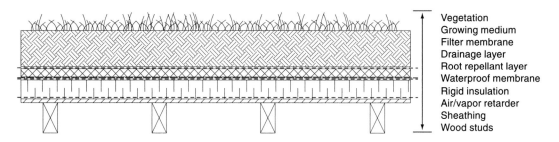

Vegetation
Growing medium
Filter membrane
Drainage layer
Root repellant layer
Waterproof membrane
Rigid insulation
Air/vapor retarder
Sheathing
Wood studs

Figure 5.28: The various materials that make a green roof section

while providing ample aeration for the roots of the plants. Commonly used substrates include expanded shale and clay.

When selecting plant species for a green roof, a variety of particulars must be considered. In addition to regional climate, the altitude, sun, shade, and wind patterns at elevation must be considered. Depending on the heights and locations of surrounding buildings, wind tunnels could affect the planting area (Scholz-Barth). Plants should be durable and low-maintenance, and vegetation weight must also be considered and roof loads determined. Lightweight, low-maintenance perennial plant material should be chosen, preferably of species that are conducive to maintenance-free growth in the local climate zone and with little to no requirement for irrigation.

Green roofs can be grouped into two categories: extensive and intensive. *Extensive green roofs* consist of a continuous layer of low-growing vegetation such as different varieties of grasses and herbs (Stromberg, 2005). The substrate's depth is between 2 and 6 inches (50 and 150 millimeters). Due to the small scale of extensive green roofs, they commonly do not require additional reinforcement on pre-existing roofs, and they rarely require irrigation. Due to the constraints in substrate depth, however, the variety of plant choices is limited (Landreville, 2005). *Intensive green roofs* are designed for a more complex planting system. They may contain several feet of substrate and can support a wide variety of vegetation, such as large shrubs or small trees.

The benefits of green roofs range from the various ecological considerations, to economic paybacks, as well as their contribution to the general well-being of users and the community. In terms of ecological benefits, green spaces contribute to air quality, climate mediation, and stormwater retention—to name a few. In urban and suburban communities, the area of green space lost to the construction of roads, buildings, parking lots, and other paved surfaces has significant consequences on the quality of the environment. The concept of greening rooftops is logical in the sense that whatever footprint of green space was lost to the construction of the building can be replaced on its roof.

Although green roofs are widely used in commercial and institutional sectors, they are making their way onto home rooftops as well. For single-family homes, since extensive green roofs can be installed on slopes of up to 30 degrees (Landreville), pitched roofs can be accommodated, plus lightweight, low-maintenance roof materials are usually more feasible for small homes. For example, a family home on the Lafayette River in Norfolk, Virginia, had an extensive green roof installed. With an old, leaky roof in need of replacement, the homeowners opted for a solution that would aid in stormwater management. A lightweight sedum plant material was chosen and the original structure of the roof did not need to be reinforced. The 600-square-foot (55-square-meter) roof was deemed a success, retaining 80 percent of annual rainfall and reducing the amount of runoff that eventually reaches the Lafayette River (Greenroofs Projects Database, 2006).

For multifamily housing complexes with larger roof areas, extensive green roofs are more feasible. For residents who do not have access to private backyards, a rooftop garden can be used and enjoyed communally and is often a major selling point. Church Street Station, a multifamily housing complex in Evanston, Illinois, installed an 8500-square-foot (790-square-meter) intensive green roof for exactly that purpose. With 8 inches (20 centimeters) of growing medium and an 18-inch (46-centimeter) perimeter parapet depth, the vegetation chosen has ample room to flourish. Irrigation is achieved through a drainage system that retains moisture and irrigates the vegetation from the underside (Greenroofs Projects Database).

Domestic Recycling and Its Outcome

The growing awareness of recycling is also reducing the burden of waste accumulation on the environment. Ideally, 32 percent of residential waste can be recycled, which includes materials such as paper, glass, metals, and plastic. Promotion and ease of recycling can be increased by integrating storage into the kitchen design (Goldbeck, 1989) (Figure 5.29). Recycling centers can then be established in common outdoor areas. Alternatively, curbside collection of recyclables can be established, requiring less effort by the homeowner and therefore increasing the rate of resident participation. Successful recycling of the average estimated volume from each home translates to approximately 0.22 ton per year (0.20 tonne per year) of diverted waste, or approximately 11 percent of the total municipal solid waste (Tchobanoglous, et al., 1993)

In construction, a visit to a conscientious builder's residential construction site shows how successful recycling programs can be. It also demonstrates that builders can help to keep the planet clean, even though switching to environmentally friendly building products has not been an easy process. Products must meet building standards regarding fire-rating, strength, and durability, yet they must be financially competitive with traditional products to be adopted by tradesmen and buyers alike. These products have gradually found their way into different parts of the home and their numbers are steadily growing.

Exterior wall insulation is another area in which recycled products have been making significant inroads. One of the chief products used is paper, which accounts for 21 percent of domestic waste. The most common type of recycled

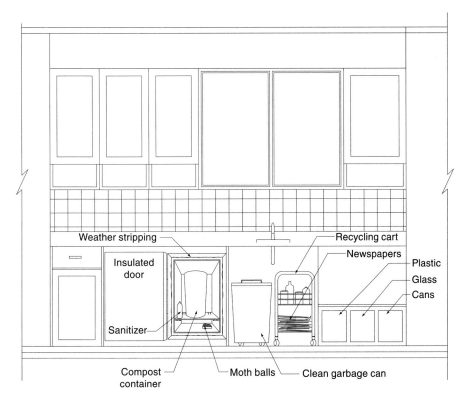

Figure 5.29: Special compartments can be arranged in the kitchen for the sorting and storage of recyclable household items.

paper is newsprint. Recycling newsprint not only decreases air pollution emissions up to 74 percent but also uses 58 percent less water than converting virgin wood pulp to paper. It also uses up to 50 percent less energy and saves millions of trees each year. The newsprint is chopped into small pieces, mixed with a bonding agent, and blown into the wall cavity to become an insulation buffer. Known as *cellulose insulation,* recycled newsprint can replace fiberglass insulation in the roof, where it's easier to handle and install. Recycled paper can also be found in roofing paper, shingles, and gypsum wallboard (sheetrock).

Some 50 to 100 percent of new steel products contain scrap metal. This scrap was traditionally recovered from industrial waste, automobiles, and the demolition of old steel structures, but in recent years, it's begun to include products from municipal solid waste. Empty cans put in recycling boxes are turned into light-gauge steel studs that are becoming common for use in interior partitions. They are light and will not warp, and electricians like them because, unlike wood studs, steel studs mean they do not need to drill holes in them when passing wires through.

The wallboard that covers the studs is, in turn, made of recycled gypsum mixed with fibers that strengthen the board. And the boards do not need a paper facing, which makes for a smoother finishing process and appearance.

Plastics, which account for 5 percent of domestic waste and 21 percent of total landfill volume, are also being sought after as a construction product. Reusing plastic containers for the food industry is too expensive, but they can be used for manufacturing building products. For example, interior or exterior carpets made from plastic are indistinguishable from conventional carpets, come in a range of shades and patterns, and are cost-competitive. Recycled plastic is also being converted into decking boards, outdoor handrails, street benches, planter boxes, and outdoor stairs.

The more than 300 million car tires that are discarded each year in North America have also become the target of intense recycling. Discarded tires are breeding grounds for disease carriers such as mosquitoes and rodents, and they constitute a serious safety hazard, especially if they catch fire, as extinguishing tire fires is extremely difficult. Recycled tires have already found their way into driveways, sidewalks, and paths in the form of interlocking pavers, and into living rooms as carpet underpads.

EcoVillage at Ithaca

Growing concerns about the environment, occupant health, and lack of social interaction has altered development practices in a number of communities worldwide. Those who have made a commitment to healthier and environmentally conscious lifestyles within their homes and neighborhoods are reaping the benefits of green design and building. One such community is the EcoVillage at Ithaca (EVI), a cohousing community in the Finger Lakes region of upstate New York.

EVI began in 1991 when founders Liz Walker and Joan Bokaer collaborated in a vision of creating ecological cohousing for families in Bokaer's hometown of Ithaca, New York. They began to channel the interest of approximately 100 adults and children who came to meetings to hear about this future community. The vision was to create neighborhoods in which responsibilities were shared as cohousing dictated and which treaded lightly on the land, creating a smaller ecological footprint than typical modern developments and promoting energy-saving measures through active and passive methods.

Two neighborhoods now exist, each comprising 30 units and providing homes to approximately 160 members. A third neighborhood of equal size is in the planning stages. The First Residents Group (FROG) was one of the earliest green cohousing developments in the United States. When planning began in 1991, codirectors Walker and Bokaer had many decisions to make about how such a community should be planned. Although FROG residents were involved in the decision-making process, architects and development managers Jerry and Claudia Weisburd of Housecraft Builders in Ithaca were clear leaders in the design and construction processes. The small, modular homes, finished in 1996, feature solar design and focus on the use of energy-efficient and healthy building materials (Figure 5.30).

Figure 5.30: A view of the western portion of the first neighborhood in EcoVillage at Ithaca

The Second Neighborhood Group (SONG) broke ground in 2001 following five years of planning headed by development managers Walker and Rod Lambert. After failed attempts at receiving affordable housing grants from urban and rural groups, all but three of the original SONG families backed out of the process. Lambert then took on the formidable task of site planning refinement. While the first neighborhood was based on identical patterns and building materials, the second neighborhood adopted a separate design/build process for each unit. Many homeowners contributed considerable sweat equity to achieve a personalized approach to the "green-ness" and style of their homes.

As many residents attested, some individuals joined the community for the *Eco* in EcoVillage because of concern for the environment and the desire to lead a more energy-efficient, ecologically conscious lifestyle; other residents were attracted by the *Village*, wishing for more social cohesion and contact with their neighbors. The product of all residents' work and beliefs is a community in which adults and children are socially supported and aware of their effects on the surrounding environment.

A general set of guidelines summarizing the key points that direct design and construction of green homes is presented here. These principles, which were largely implemented at EVI, address issues that are often altered or ignored in typical modern construction but that can reduce a development's impact on the land it inhabits.

Planning the EcoVillage

The guidelines for designing a sustainable community may be interpreted and enacted in a multitude of ways depending on the people and places involved. In fact, the innovative ways in which sustainability can be achieved are what makes green design and construction so unique and inviting.

Two main principles were employed in the planning of EVI to reduce its footprint on the environment. First, homes were small, efficient, well-insulated, and constructed with recycled, recyclable, and/or local materials. Architects and residents truly considered what was needed in a typical home, what size it should be to meet these needs, and how it could be constructed for reduced energy and material requirements. This design and building method is evident from site planning to each house's utility selection. Second, EVI residents are part of a community that shares resources. Intangibly, social services, support networks, child-minders, and a wide variety of talents help reduce the need to commute and the weight on public services in the town of Ithaca (Walker, 2005).

The EVI site was chosen after participants in the early planning stages weighed the options of three possible locations. The chosen site, a largely treeless parcel of land that was formerly a dairy farm, is located 1.5 miles (2.4 kilometers) from the town of Ithaca. This 176-acre (71-hectare) site, called West Hill, offered housing and farming along with attractive views and was purchased in 1991. At that time, EVI members flocked to the site to learn the literal "lay of the land." Although they hoped that EVI would have a small footprint, the best ways to achieve this were not apparent at first. Many residents wanted to build away from the main road, and an analysis of the soils for agricultural purposes determined that the worst farming soil, and therefore the most likely building area, was a half mile (1 kilometer) south of the road.

Although efforts were made to reduce dependency on public electrical, water, and sewage systems, EVI homes are all connected to the municipal grid. The clustering of homes and the forethought devoted to site design and home energy requirements created a community that uses one-third of the infrastructure necessary for traditional housing estates. Normally, the town would have to take over maintenance of roads and utilities on the site, but EVI residents maintain their own road while paying the same municipal tax rates as other town citizens. In addition, less strain is placed on many of the townwide public services such as social services and health care because of the close social network and desire to hire those who work within the community.

The first neighborhood (FROG) was placed along an east-west axis crossing a downward slope to the south. Being a hillside site, views from the homes were a high priority for almost all residents both in FROG and the future second neighborhood. Privacy, an initial concern for many residents new to clustered living, was carefully considered to afford individual space while simultaneously allowing a sense of visual proximity between neighbors and for community events. The units were staggered and structures positioned to allow vistas and establish private backyards. Home windows were placed to avoid overlooking a neighbor's backyard (Figure 5.31).

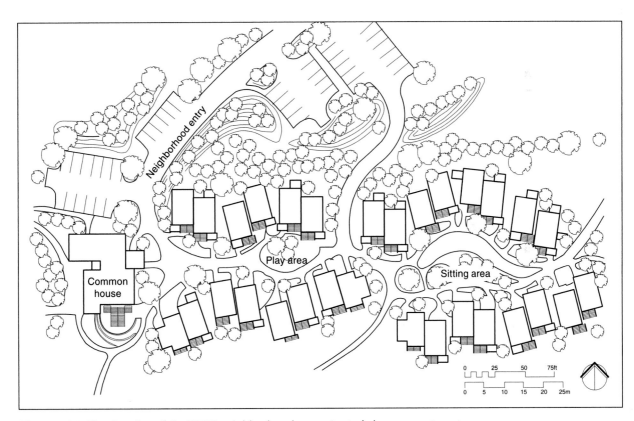

Figure 5.31: The site plan of the FROG neighborhood was oriented along an east-west axis for passive solar gain.

The common house, a structure prevalent in cohousing communities, contains facilities such as a kitchen, dining area, meeting spaces, children's playrooms, and a guest room. It is situated at the head of the site and is passed by many residents as they enter the neighborhood. This building, also designed by the Weisburds, capitalizes on passive solar gain with a view of a pond. The pond was constructed first as a water source for fire regulations and later became a habitat for wildlife and a swimming hole for residents (Figure 5.32).

Figure 5.32: The southern elevation of the common house to which the dining and meeting areas open.

The first neighborhood site planning followed a typical cohousing procedure. The architects designed five models from which residents could choose, ranging from one-bedroom, 900-square-foot (84-square-meter) models, to five-bedroom, 1650-square-foot (152-square-meter) models. FROG houses are 16-feet (4.9-meters), 20-feet (6.1-meters), or 24-feet (7.3-meters) wide and 32-feet (9.8-meters) deep. Duplexes are oriented east-west for passive solar gain from the southern façade (Figure 5.33). Despite the standardization, creative combinations of dwellings within duplexes created a varied and pleasant roofline in the neighborhood that avoided uniformity.

Because EVI residents are conscious of the waste they create, they made an effort to reduce waste not only through recycling and composting, but also through the purchase of goods with less or no packaging. Walker estimates that most of the kitchen waste goes to one of two compost piles. A maintenance crew is responsible for turning these piles twice yearly. A centrally located enclosed shed at the end of one carport holds recycling bins for every material used that can be recycled, which the town empties every two weeks. Waste that cannot be recycled, reused, or composted is put in a central, 108-cubic-foot (3-cubic-meter) dumpster

Figure 5.33: A southern façade of a FROG home with large windows and roof overhang for passive solar gain

that is emptied once a week. According to Walker, the town of Ithaca has informed EVI that residents there generate approximately one-quarter the garbage that a typical development of 160 people would throw away.

Although the lush, green countryside of New York State does not suggest thoughts of drought and water rationing, EVI water consumption is far lower than typical households, and most residents take pride in noting how little water is used in their homes. Dwellings in both neighborhoods include basic water-saving hardware such as low-flow faucets and shower heads. Conventional toilets are also low-flow, using 1.5 gallons (5.7 liters) per flush, and other homes feature composting toilets that are gravity-fed or operate from micro-flush toilets that direct waste to a prefabricated, self-containing unit in the basement. In the second neighborhood, residents use energy-efficient dishwashers, refrigerators, and other water- and energy-saving devices, such as a drain heat recovery that preheats incoming shower water with draining water from the tub.

The homes are also plumbed for future graywater reclamation as soon as funds become available to build reed beds and treatment ponds. Pathways and swales in the first neighborhood direct rainwater to underground pipes that feed the on-site pond, although problems have arisen such as pipe blockage and ice on paths. Some FROG residents have directed runoff from gutters into water-storage barrels for personal gardens. Others have installed underground cisterns consisting of three,

1000-gallon (3785-liter) standard septic tanks for rainwater from rooftops that is directed downhill to the community garden for watering.

EVI residents are responsible for their own front and back gardens. Although there is little formal community landscaping, most flora requiring greater amounts of water are planted near the home, often by the roofline where water drains naturally. Many plants and trees were chosen for a multitude of uses. A ridge of trees may act, for example, as a windbreak, a habitat for birds, and as providers of fruit for wildlife and/or human consumption. Some EVI residents are pursuing principles of *permaculture*, the multidimensional approach to creating diverse, stable, and sustainable ecosystems that meet human needs while emulating nature and keeping with natural processes.

House Design and Construction

Many green aspects of EVI home design were largely based on the desire to reduce environmental impacts by recycling and managing water usage. The use of technology in each home further helped EVI to fulfill many of the principles necessary to create a sustainable community. Additional environmental concerns related to the construction of the homes are discussed next.

Modularity

Dwellings in the first neighborhood made use of modular building materials to minimize waste and increase construction efficiency. At the time of construction, many advanced green technologies were unavailable or too costly for the cohousing community. Considerations were therefore made in site planning to ensure orientation for passive solar gain, and the decision to design clustered duplexes further reduced needs for heating, cooling, and infrastructure for utilities (Figure 5.34).

Traditional stick-framing was used in FROG housing but ensured super-insulation with double walls filled with dense-packed cellulose insulation made from recycled newspaper. Builders placed 2 by 6 inch (51 by 152 millimeter) studs 2 feet (0.61 meters) on center as opposed to the traditional 16 inches (406 millimeters) on center, thereby reducing required framing material; studs are lined with 2 by 3 inch (51 by 76 millimeter) horizontal cross strapping that reduces thermal bridging by approximately 75 percent, as the heat (or cold) must now bridge the stud, perpendicular strapping, and sheetrock. Although dense-pack cellulose is a good air barrier, a vapor barrier interwoven with the cross strapping was installed to restrict air infiltration. Special care was taken to fill cracks and holes around plumbing and electrical devices where leakage can occur. All light fixtures were wall-mounted to eliminate any punctures in the ceiling where moist, warm air could escape.

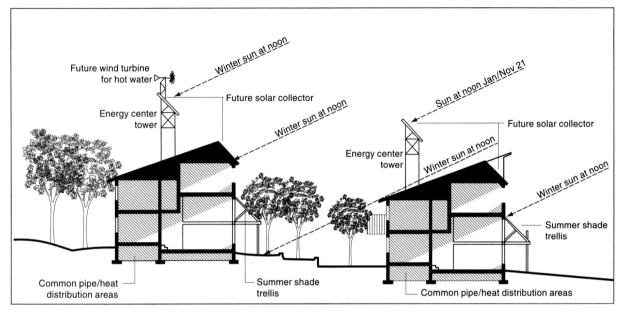

Figure 5.34: Solar access for two model homes in EVI

The foundations were made of insulated concrete forms (ICFs) that reduced the amount of concrete needed by half and a layer of expanded polystyrene insulation was added on either side of the concrete to reduce thermal bridging and create a uniform R20 (RSI 3.5) wall. Windows were modular, single-hung, and triple-paned to help create an efficient building envelope. At construction time, heat-recovery ventilators were expensive and it was deemed that the 30-year payback period was not feasible for residents. Indoor air quality was assured through the choice of low–off-gassing paints, varnishes, and building materials and through manually operated, fan-assisted air exchangers located in the bathrooms and kitchen (Figure 5.35).

The second neighborhood is more personalized and its homes serve as examples of ecologically sensitive buildings. Although homeowners considered independent needs and desires, general continuity exists within the neighborhood based on recommendations provided by a self-formed architecture review committee. As with the FROG homes, roofs are steel, a recyclable material with a 100-year lifespan. The cladding is largely raw, untreated hemlock from a local source.

The Building's Envelope

Most homes were constructed of 4 by 8 foot (1.2 by 2.4 meter) structurally insulated panels (SIPs) that combine structure and insulation in an efficient,

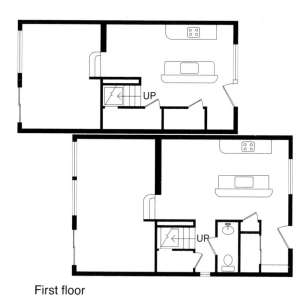

First floor

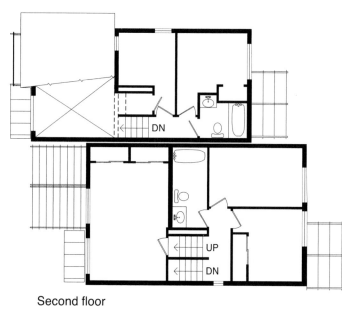

Second floor

Figure 5.35: First- and second-floor plans of a south-side duplex in the first neighborhood illustrate the proximity of the kitchen to the home entrance.

quick-assembled design. The SIP boards consist of expanded polystyrene insulation sandwiched between chipboard of poplar or aspen. SIP panels are not a natural building material, and they contain a low-emission formaldehyde glue that differs from the glue used in particleboard. The expanded polystyrene center is a petroleum derivative containing no CFCs. However, SIPs provide better thermal insulation than stud walls of the same thickness, and waste during fabrication is kept to a minimum as pieces are used efficiently, scrap is easily recovered and reused, and units are enclosed within a short time, reducing exposure to the elements or vandalism. Basements of SONG homes also use insulated concrete forms, but many homeowners chose either to turn the basement into living space or build a slab-on-grade floor instead of a crawlspace.

The individuality of homes in the SONG neighborhood also shines through where eco-decisions are concerned. Two homes experimented with straw bale construction, one home has a solar collector for water heating, and other homes contain no toxic substances such as glues (including those in SIPs), cabinet materials, or gas stoves. Windows, while generally being Low-E argon-filled, double-paned and R3 (RSI 0.53), have been upgraded to R10 (RSI 1.76) or better in one resident's home with the addition of homemade exterior thermal shutters. Approximately half the SONG homes have photovoltaic panels on the roof.

Heating and Cooling

The mechanical systems used in the homes provide high levels of heating comfort largely through hot water. Four energy towers, chimney-like structures attached to the side of four duplexes, house two high-efficiency natural gas furnaces that heat water, which circulates in a large diameter tube to eight homes. At each unit, an exchanger heats municipal water for hot water and radiant floor heating pipes on lower floors and for the hydronic air-handler system housed in an upstairs closet. Air from the house is blown over warm water and forced through ductwork into individual rooms, providing warm air. This heating system fulfils the desire of residents to exclude any combustible fuels from the home.

The redundancy of two furnaces is advantageous for experimentation with alternative fuel sources such as solar hot water heaters, fuel cells, or biomass, and their presence in the energy tower allows for easy retrofitting and potential technology alterations. However, about one-quarter to one-third of the background heat is lost through the pipes as they circulate from furnace to home, and the heating system is occasionally criticized as being too high-tech and difficult to repair. In addition, although meters were set up to monitor individual unit hot-water consumption, the readings have not been accurate and efficiency has been difficult to monitor.

Currently, all units in EVI are attached to the municipal electrical grid via buried cable. Dials are attached to the energy towers that monitor electrical use for each unit in FROG. Towers are capped with south-facing, tilted roofs that will host solar panels when budgets allow. SONG duplexes share "midget heaters," 95-percent efficient, natural gas condensing furnaces that hold latent heat in moisture. Hot water is circulated in a closed loop to radiant floor heating and hot water radiators, and furnaces also provide hot water for taps. One home features a solar water heater on the roof amid photovoltaic panels (Figure 5.36).

Fourteen of the thirty units in the second neighborhood also use photovoltaic panels on south-facing roofs to generate electricity. These units, however, do not have batteries to store electricity, so when the house consumes less electricity than is made, the electricity meters connected to the municipal grid run backward, feeding electricity into the system. One resident's photovoltaic panels were generating 1.005 BTUs per second (1060 watts) out of a listed potential of 1.327

Figure 5.36: The array of solar systems on SONG rooftops provide electricity and pre-heated water for residents.

BTUs per second (1400 watts) on an almost clear day, and in approximately one month of operation had generated 788,300 BTUs (231kWh). A second resident generated up to 1.706 BTUs per second (1800 watts) of a listed 2.085 BTUs per second (2200 watt) potential.

Conscious design and use of construction methods, water usage, and electrical systems in the EVI homes have resulted in significant reduction of environmental and economic impacts. FROG homes use approximately 40 percent less gas and electricity than typical northeast homes. SONG houses, which differ widely in environmental features, consume 25 to 75 percent less electricity and water than homes within the same area (Walker).

The Sustainable Factor

EVI's planning and construction process involved evaluation and exploration of various options and possibilities for building a green community. The commitment of the cofounders, research teams, architects, builders, benefactors, and residents resulted in a modern development that considered and remedied many environmental issues currently facing human habitats. By choosing building designs and materials that were appropriate and efficient for the northeastern American climate, such as siting for passive solar gain, the path of *least negative impact* was observed. Waste is composted and recycled, and new resources are saved by sharing and reusing maintenance tools and personal items. Homes are compact and efficient, are the envelope and layout are designed to buffer both hot, humid summers and cold winters through extensive insulation, continuous vapor barriers, and minimal thermal bridging. Low amounts of energy and water are used without compromising the residents' quality of life, and plans and infrastructure are in place to incorporate future technologies that use renewable energy and waste recycling. By building on a small portion of the available land, all EVI residents and visitors can appreciate and preserve the surrounding natural landscape, a pleasure often ignored in conventional suburban developments.

Homes not only sustain residents' needs within the community but also reduce or eliminate reliance on municipal systems. For example, existing photovoltaic panels generate surplus electricity that is fed to the municipal grid. The roof direction of homes and power stations already provide the structures necessary to mount additional panels. Rainwater falling on homes and pathways is channeled to gardens or a pond to return resources back to the land. In addition, integrated graywater plumbing, rainwater catchment systems, and composting toilets could one day render the homes independent from city water and septic systems. Currently, EVI not only provides comfortable and environmentally innovative housing to 160 residents, but it also services the Ithaca community, educating groups on the benefits of environmentally conscious housing. The on-site farm supplies organic vegetables to 1000 people per week in the summer, using only 10 acres (0.1 hectare) of land, and the remaining open space left untouched offers a green corridor for flora and fauna as well as parkland for residents and neighbors. These factors create a *self-sustaining* community that reduces the project's impact on the environment throughout its lifespan.

Socially, EVI has also considered many sustainable principles that create *supporting relations* within the community. Home offices and businesses in the common house allow residents to reduce or prevent commuting time and vehicle-derived pollution while also remaining close to family during the daytime. Informal carshare arrangements transport children to and from school. The interdependency of neighbors is beneficial when childcare or other services are bought, exchanged, or donated, and when a resident needs more care during illness or other times of need. The dense configuration of the homes makes security everybody's business, keeping crime and vandalism in check and, more importantly, creating a trusting social environment in which residents will want to remain.

The implementation of ecological initiatives, self-sustaining processes, and supporting relationships at EVI have enhanced the community's initial ideals of environmental and social awareness throughout the *project's lifecycle*. As residents notice the low energy and water bills and appreciate the benefits of living next to nature, they also reap the rewards of choosing to live as a village that prides itself on mutually advantageous relationships. EVI and other similar communities will become more attractive real estate for those desiring the "eco" aspects and those looking for the "village." As the community evolves, some duplexes may be converted into apartments, and some residents have made accessibility a priority for elderly family members who may join the household. In these ways, the community will last longer than the initial generation of dedicated residents.

The design of the first and second neighborhood homes were the outcome of a community's efforts to reduce their impact on the environment and the money and time available to do so. Many struggles occurred for long, exhausting periods of time between those who were interested in building a green community and those who monitored regulations and codes. The result of years of work by dedicated individuals is a community that is a viable alternative to the conventional suburb, incorporating sustainable ecological, social, and economic principles.

Urban and Dwelling Renewal 6

Despite a millennia of extensive urban transformations, the construction of new buildings has not always begun with massive clearance of old ones. Clearing a site for land development is a relatively modern phenomenon. Urban form can and should be regarded as a reflection of cultural identity, continuity, and heritage. *Heritage* is the notion that the built environment is a dynamic place where processes are ongoing and where past and present are linked to the future. Design for change and, therefore, renewal, should be an integral part of any urban process's lifecycle. Rehabilitating old homes can be viewed as a large recycling effort. Rather than discarding or destroying an older structure, it can be retooled and returned to use. The same analogy can apply to some neighborhoods, where the passage of time or unfortunate circumstances have led to a state of neglect or abandonment.

This chapter relates the concepts of *rehabilitation* and *heritage* of communities and dwellings to *sustainability*, where social, economic, and environmental issues are all present. It first explores the evolution of heritage conservation, then lists principles of renewal, and finally recalls the rehabilitation of a large neighborhood using sustainable strategies.

Urban Evolution and Heritage Conservation

The idea that old buildings should be considered important and should be preserved has been transformed with successive eras. Historically, people perceived ancient structures as reflections of human continuity. Heritage was understood as an enduring extension of the past, and relics were symbols to be retained. Old civilizations were consciously conserved and old structures were incorporated into urban developments. In contrast, perception in later centuries regarded older structures as having no connection with contemporary design, which meant that developers would need to start with a clean slate: they razed old buildings and neighborhoods to erect contemporary edifices. In recent decades, however, the latent cultural and economic values offered by heritage structures have been recognized, and as a result these structures are being conserved. To understand and appreciate the increasing return to the values of heritage, you need to understand when and how historic conservation of buildings and communities was introduced.

Materials, form, ornamentation, and design were conscious extensions of established urban and architectural frameworks. As a result, cities created cultural continuity through heritage integration. In the first century B.C., Roman architect Marcus Vitruvius Pollio (Vitruvius) compiled a manual of guiding principles for building and maintenance practices. *De Architectura* delineated guidelines that aimed at ensuring that new constructions were harmoniously integrated within the existing built environment. The manual emphasized that appropriate design depended on the education of the architect. It also stipulated that without an extensive knowledge of local history, designers would lose the symbolic meaning of urban and architectural elements during building and development (Jokilehto, 1999). Harmony among edifices founded both a historic identity and community consciousness, and heritage created a simultaneous sense of continuity and uniqueness that defined a place (Ouf, 2001).

Vitruvius's legacy continued about 400 years later, as the Roman Emperors Constantine I and Valentinian III began the restoration of Rome. The two rulers rehabilitated the city's dilapidated urban form and reinstalled dignity into public buildings. The emperors not only conserved historically significant structures, but they restored the structures' former uses. Later, in the eighth century A.D., medieval leaders such as Charlemagne sought to reinstate classical architectural traditions, and by the tenth century a civic consciousness of such magnitude existed that cities competed against one another to become cultural hubs. Centers such as Florence and Siena produced monumental classical works of art and architecture that expanded the medieval principles of design. The buildings around the Piazza del

Campo in Siena, for example, were designed according to guidelines established in 1297 (Hollister, 1994) (Figure 6.1).

Figure 6.1: The buildings enclosing the Piazza del Campo in Siena were designed in accordance with guidelines established in 1297.

During the eighteenth century, the Age of Enlightenment brought the advent of new scientific, spiritual, economic, and political ideas. As a result, history was no longer regarded as a particular extension of humanity but rather became a scientific inquiry.

New nomenclature generated value judgments that disassociated the past from the present. However, historic preservation was not altogether abolished. Instead, the Romantic Movement of the nineteenth century spurred an ideology of stewardship, which recognized that a balance could exist between progress and the inherited landscape. From stewardship, the notion of *custodianship* evolved, which was a social concept implying civic responsibility toward built heritage (Earl, 1996). Custodianship, however, still conceptualized heritage as an isolated phenomenon. Therefore, despite concerns over human destruction, built heritage traditions were not integrated into new design ideas. Only a few buildings were conserved, and those that remained often stood alone. One of these approaches is represented by Berthault's 1812 plan for the Roman Forum archaeological area (Figure 6.2). According to Jokilehto, ancient monuments became the focal points of the scheme, with the rest of the design otherwise continuing without regard to the old structures.

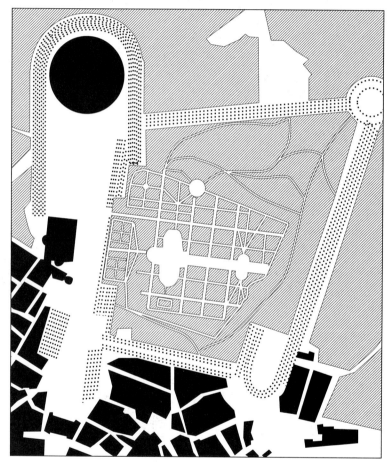

Figure 6.2: In Berthault's 1812 plan for the Roman Forum archaeological area, ancient monuments were restored and became the focal points.

One architectural example of historic detachment was the nineteenth-century endeavor of Stylistic Restoration. First defined by Merimée and Viollet-le-Duc, this movement aspired to make use of and preserve old architectural elements. As a result, buildings recaptured their economic importance, and restoration to a stylistic unity increased an area's prestige. In tune with the economic climates that defined the nineteenth and twentieth centuries, private interests helped create and capitalize on a new market niche. Entrepreneurs discovered that history could be sold. Still, this stylistic movement was short-lived as tastes rapidly changed (Boyer, 1995; Jokilehto). In its place, post–World War II technological advancements, economic affluence, and generous fiscal housing policies had a dominant influence on urban development. Respect for historic harmony was largely ignored, and attention was directed to the construction of mass-produced new projects rather than the renovation of old ones.

The 1950s saw the introduction of modernism. The Modernist Movement was an ideological reaction to nineteenth-century design and emphasized efficiency and the creation of a new social order and style (Knox and Marston, 2001). Modern concrete buildings bore no resemblance to old structures. Designers of North American neighborhoods, at times, failed to take advantage of the richness that the surrounding old buildings provided in favor of a *tabula rasa* (clean slate) approach.

Old Dwellings, New Life

Every home reaches a point at which renovations are needed to extend its useful life. Lack of owner interest, a result of declining economic fortunes, for example, can also cause an entire neighborhood to fall into a state of disrepair. Residential rehabilitation is a manifestation of sustainable development. Rather than demolish and discard infrastructure and building materials, a home can be retooled and restored to use. In addition to environmental issues, the regeneration of neighborhoods involves a number of social and economic interventions aimed at sustaining their existence, some of which are outlined here.

Motives and Processes

Physical, social, and economic causes can trigger deterioration within a community. Poor initial construction practices can lead to structural problems in homes in later years. When a dwelling's value is low and no economic justification exists for its repair, a downward spiral can result—for example, the departure of residents to a more affluent part of town and the replacement of a more permanent community by a lower income rental population that may lack incentive to maintain or restore homes. Absentee landlords are less likely to renovate, as anticipated returns will not justify such investment. This deterioration can be increased by local economic situations as well, such as the departure of a major employer, which causes large-scale unemployment in the area and lack of means to care for homes.

Rehabilitation can be driven by individual homeowners, an association formed by community residents, or municipal or state authorities (Figure 6.3). Strategies adopted for neighborhood renewal can also be diverse and the sources of funding varied. It might be financed by the owners or via a renovation assistance program initiated by a municipality or state. It can also involve loans or grants to residents that are managed by a lending authority. Home repair could be the responsibility of the owners or a government authority. The government might contribute only to the repair of public infrastructure such as roads and parks, leaving renovation of homes to the occupants. The level of intervention can also be varied and involve social, physical, and economic assistance. In all cases, issues rooted in the past must be addressed while preparing the community infrastructure for the future. Forecasting evolution in a neighborhood will contribute to the extension of its life for years to come.

Reasons for decline	Drivers of renewal	Funding source	Area of intervention
• Economic downturn • Poor initial construction • High level of low-income renters • Absentee landlords	• Individual homeowners • Non-profit local association • Governments	• Homeowners own funds • Government grants to homeowners • Government investment in infrastructure	• Physical (homes, infrastructure) • Social (education) • Communal (image, safety) • Environmental (clear brownfields)

Figure 6.3: A renewal process may involve various participants, funding sources, and areas of intervention.

Social Factors

A sustainable renewal process must have few negative effects on the surroundings, including the built environment as well as the residents' social environment. Some past projects that aimed at rehabilitating a community's physical state inflicted unwelcome consequences. Whether a result of an organized or natural processes, as the neighborhood's condition "improved," low-cost homes were sold at higher prices to outsiders, pushing out low-income renters and leading to gentrification. A process meant to offer physical benefits to a community often resulted in the creation of new social problems.

Mechanisms must be initiated from the start of the project to prevent such situations from occurring. Structural and infrastructural renovation can include the neighborhood's social infrastructure as well as the buildings that make up the area. By taking a "community pulse" to measure what attributes may be affected by a rehabilitation, several societal aspects can be studied early on and considered while creating sustainable strategies (Figure 6.4).

Factor		Effect
Demographic makeup	⟶	Ability to participate in a renewal process
Age of population	⟶	Interest in near- or far-sighted goals
Housing tenure	⟶	Interest in a long-term process
Level of income	⟶	Ability of residents to contribute financially
Level of education	⟶	Ability to obtain well-paying jobs
Public safety	⟶	Long-term residence within the community
Community leadership	⟶	Capacity to participate and see the process through

Figure 6.4: Social factors and their effects need to be considered in urban renewal.

Consideration of the demographic makeup and the age of the population is necessary to determine the long-term prospects for a community. A large number of elderly residents, for example, will be more interested in short-term goals and concerned with the adaptability of their homes' interior to meet their physical needs. On the other hand, younger populations will have a more long-term view of the effects of the rehabilitation. They may recognize and understand that such processes may take time and will require their ongoing participation at various stages.

The housing tenure of the population is also a crucial factor. Renters might be less inclined to get involved as their residency status may be uncertain. Landlords, primarily the absentee type, may lack motivation to contribute their own resources if tenants in the renovated homes continue to pay low rent. Therefore, an incentive—monetary or enforcement by local authorities—is required to make the renewal a success. For example, interest-free loans could be offered or bylaws could be created to ensure that the interior and exterior of buildings are properly maintained and comply with safety codes.

The residents' level of income and mortgages or rents paid are other key indicators that should be measured. This information provides a much-needed outlook of the occupants' ability to contribute financially to a renovation process. It will also determine whether external funding is required. Background studies must evaluate other social issues that may impede community renewal, such as education or public safety. At times, issues unrelated to the rehabilitation may cast a shadow on its possible successes. High crime levels, for example, may drive residents out and will require a greater level of policing. Lack of social infrastructure can also contribute to failure.

In addition, lack of pursuit of post-secondary education and low rates of school attendance in a community can severely limit present and future employment prospects for a large segment of the population. This can result in devastating repercussions on the economic viability of the community. Lack of public formal and informal education, health care, or social work support may cause additional communal strain. Once challenges in these areas are identified, measures to address them can be put in place before or in parallel with the physical rehabilitation.

Aspects related to community leadership, self-esteem, and cultural makeup can also be essential. They reflect the neighborhood's ability to participate in the process from beginning to end. Rehabilitation initiatives that do not involve residents tend to fail since they do not make residents' concerns part of the renewal. To help in this effort, local leadership should be identified and contacted early on. Weak leadership and lack of long-term objectives can bring a process to a halt, but long-term, enthusiastic support can make it a success. Therefore, consultation and goal setting with the community at large can be used to gauge the neighborhood's interest and to identify leaders.

Taking Urban Stock

Developing strategies for urban renewal begins by taking stock of the neighborhood's infrastructure. The fact that sufficient roads, sewage systems, and other infrastructures are in place is also a strong argument for rehabilitation, as utilities will not have to be constructed and the sprawl caused by new developments can be avoided (Figure 6.5). A study of the physical *urban morphology* (urban structure) and the historical evolution of the city and the neighborhood are also important, as this information provides an understanding of how the grid of streets and lots was formed.

Roads, parking, and public transit form parts of the community's infrastructure that often cannot be altered. Yet, at times, rerouting travel or integrating an existing lane system within the overall parking strategy can improve circulation in the neighborhood. Examining access to public transit is a necessary step in studying community needs. Additional bus stops and improved frequency will also reduce reliance on private cars.

Studying local zoning will help identify old bylaws that do not allow much-needed social and physical changes. Larger homes or complexes, for example, may be restructured to accommodate the needs of smaller households. Some activities that are not permitted in an area, such as home offices, can be reconsidered. And additions to existing dwellings can be restricted or updated via zoning ordinances to ensure safety and improve appearance.

Documenting and evaluating the status of public green spaces is also important. Often, these spaces are the first to fall into a state of disrepair as a result of

Factor		Effect
Infrastructure	⟶	Condition of roads, sewer networks
Urban morphology	⟶	Understanding urban structure and its possible future transformation
Local zoning	⟶	Ability to allow future land use changes
Roads and transit	⟶	Access to public transit and proper circulation
Public open space	⟶	Knowledge/existence of community meeting places
Curb appeal	⟶	A telling aspect of the locals' and visitors' first impression
Local history/heritage	⟶	Understanding of how the future can be built upon the past
Public institutions	⟶	A telling aspect of community's vitality

Figure 6.5: Physical factors need to be examined in urban renewal.

poor maintenance due to lack of funding. When a community lacks appropriate gathering places, the relationships among residents may also deteriorate.

The neighborhood's curb appeal is essential to its renewal as it projects the community image to its residents and its visitors. Street "furniture," such as light poles, planter boxes, benches, and signs, might be introduced. Even small improvements can send a renewal message, which can raise the residents' confidence in the seriousness of the process and can be considered by a municipal government in consultation with the community. Trees form an important part of the streetscape and help avoid sterile and barren environments. They are necessary to the creation of meeting places when benches under them are provided. Introducing human scale may involve the reduction of street widths, enlargement of sidewalks, and planting of trees. In addition, building local community pride by identifying notable buildings and celebrating local history and culture through plaques and dedications of civic spaces can help provide community enrichment.

Documenting and studying the neighborhood's public institutions and their level of vitality and physical state is another important part of urban infrastructure analysis. Centrally located and poorly maintained public buildings such as schools, churches, or medical clinics send negative signals to the community, and the rehabilitation process may begin with these structures.

Architectural Considerations

After the urban makeup of a community has been documented and analyzed, and rehabilitation strategies are tailored, the homes can be considered. Architectural observations have two objectives: They can aim at repairing the physical condition of old homes while preserving their heritage, and they can guide a renewal process that will see new dwellings constructed on empty lots or in place of dilapidated structures. These strategies are meant to ensure harmony between the old and the new.

When architectural heritage strategies are prepared for a large neighborhood, uniform rules are not usually applicable. The building of a large community takes many years to complete; during this time, several building types are likely to be used in construction, following different architectural styles and incorporating a range of materials and technologies. Some "detective" work to decipher the architectural language of a place is necessary; this will enable identification of styles and determination of the zones in which they have been constructed. After gathering the information, architects must reflect on the conclusions drawn during the urban investigation and overlap information gathered in all studies.

The process begins by tracing the "housing lifecycle." Familiarity with the date of construction leads to knowledge about their style and construction techniques. It is also of value to know who designed and built them. Homes constructed by a speculative building firm often use a limited number of plans. On the other hand, when homeowners initiate construction, they engage different architects or building firms. Such data is commonly available via local governmental offices and archives. Waves of economic upturn are often responsible for renovation cycles as well, as they provide the occupants with the means to renovate and are traceable.

The dwellings' original typology should also be traced, as this information can help with knowing whether some of the existing dwellings can be transformed from single-family to multifamily units, or vice versa, as needs arise. This step takes place in parallel with the recording of the dwellings' key features. Volumetric studies will examine the original structures and added components, such as roofs and porches. The homes' footprints, for example, will provide clues about future dwelling proportions, so when new homes are constructed in old neighborhoods they will fit in. Buildings of significant architectural importance need to be noted. They can be restored first or left unchanged, becoming markers of their period and educating those trusted with the preparation of guidelines about construction techniques or the way materials were used, for example.

Brand (1994) advocates studying buildings the way historians study the past: *diachronically* (with regard to changes over time), rather than simply *synchronically* (with regard to a single point in time) (Figure 6.6). Brand's observations of changes in buildings over time have led to a number of conclusions:

- Buildings are layered by various rates of change.
- Adaptation is easiest in lower cost buildings that few people care for.
- Adaptation is more sophisticated in buildings with sustained purposes.

- Designers and builders ignore adaptations.
- Flux in the real estate market severs continuity in buildings.
- The building preservation movement was founded to restore continuity and led to a new focus on maintenance.
- Respect for older buildings led to appreciation of their design by building historians.
- Backward perspective facilitates forward perspective.
- Buildings should be designed to facilitate adaptation.

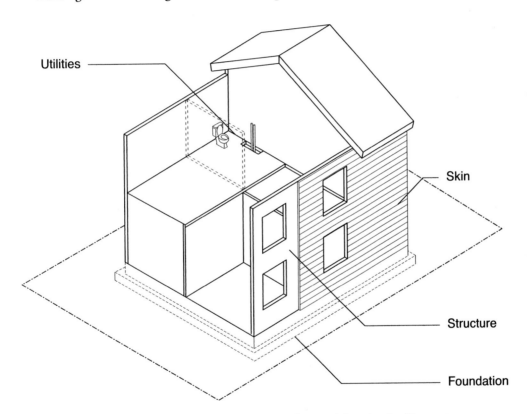

Figure 6.6: Since each component of a home has a different lifecycle, dwellings are undergoing constant change and transformation.

Brand's advice is to design and adapt with a sense of how a building originally looked and how it was adapted over time. He also emphasizes evolutionary design over visionary design.

A study of the building's exterior features can offer advice as to the range and type of components that should be respected as the rehabilitation begins. In addition, it can provide guidelines to the designers of new infill homes. The elements to be studied are cladding materials and color, decorative wood and brickwork, porch design, materials used, and window and door types, styles, and colors. Trees, flower beds, and shrub species might also be listed as well as driveways, pathway materials, fences, and garden structures.

Kalman (1979) urges repair rather than replacement in the rehabilitation of deteriorated houses. Similar to Brand, he recommends that a designer or renovator identify the basic house type and structure before commencing rehabilitation to understand why a house was built the way it was and which components should be preserved in rehabilitation. He also suggests that the location and key urban features of the neighborhood be considered in addition to the building itself. He proposes that attention be paid to architectural details to harmonize the old and the new. In his reference to windows, for example, he remarks that only a few types look appropriate on older houses (Figure 6.7).

To gauge the scope of a home's renewal and the necessary funding, designers must evaluate the dwelling's condition. The evaluation can categorize the home from "no intervention needed" to "serious renovation required." The condition of porches or decks may be indicative of other structural deficiencies of the house, such as failed interior bearing partitions or common walls. Since the lower floor is often the first to be damaged, wooden porches have a tendency to sag or be unstable. The surveys' outcome may help determine which structures can be demolished and which can be restored.

Heritage Preservation Strategies

Several strategies have been introduced to reconcile modern development with heritage preservation. The *conservationist* view of heritage preservation is based on the realization that well-preserved historical buildings can provide windows to the past and the society that built them. This view encourages the strict preservation of heritage structures so that they may not only serve educational needs, but also provide a certain sense of place while rooted in history. Earl (1996) suggests that buildings rapidly become obsolete because of reasons unrelated to their physical integrity, such as external economic shifts and technological and location demands. Adaptive reuse is often the only economically feasible option to save aesthetic and historic values.

A *functionalist* view, on the other hand, mediates heritage conflicts that arise between economic and cultural values. This perspective considers that buildings must be functional while being historically respectful (Feilden, 1982). For example,

	Reference	Observations	Guidelines
Massing	Area: 1200 sq. ft (111.5m²)	The common setback for houses is 115 ft. (35 m) or less. Most are two stories high. The average home size is 1200 ft² (112 m²). The average lot size is 17,500 ft² (1626 m²).	• New homes must maintain the average 115 ft. (35 m) setback by falling no more than 16 ft. (5 m) on either side. • The size of the homes and lots must maintain the average structure and lot sizes by falling within their standard deviations.
Exterior walls	Stone cladding Uniformly cut stone	A variety of cladding materials are used, the most prominent being brick (28%). Cladding colors are varied, white being predominant.	• Decorative colors must be limited to mild variations of white, brown, gray, and green. • Additions must be constructed of either wood or cement; vinyl, aluminum, or plywood is not allowed.
Porches		48% of the houses have a porch, most of wood or cement.	• New porches or porch additions must be constructed of either wood or cement; vinyl, aluminum, or plywood is not allowed. • Railings must be constructed of iron or wood.
Windows	2L 1.5L L L	There is no overwhelming majority of window type, though casement (34%) is the most prominent. More than half of the windows are made of wood.	• Vinyl is further restricted for additional window construction. • Wood-casement is encouraged for new window construction.
Doors	2.5L 2.5L L L	94% of the doors are single doors, predominantly wood (81%). Vinyl is the next most common (14%).	• New doors must be constructed of wood; a diversity of door colors (such as red, green, brown, white, or mild variations and combinations of these) is recommended.
Roofs		80% of the homes have either multigable or gable roofs. Half the homes have a roof angle of 45 degrees; the remaining have angles of less than 45. Nearly all have chimneys.	• Gable roofs are strongly recommended, with a series of variations permitted; roof slopes must have a standard deviation not exceeding 5 degrees. • Roof equipment may proliferate provided it is discreet (i.e., restricted from street view); chimneys are recommended.
Ancillary structures		Sheds (56%), garages (80%), and patios (62%) are common. Most structures are in close proximity to the main building.	• Sheds and garages should not be constructed with vinyl. • It is recommended that sheds, garages, and patios be adorned with neutral colors if they are not the same as the main building.
Landscape		The vegetation is often viewable from the street. Shrubs and flower beds are usually placed close to the house; fences and walls are often located on the border of the property.	• Vegetation in the form of trees, shrubs, and gardens is strongly advised, though it must not proliferate in such a way as to restrict street view.

Figure 6.7: Architectural guidelines for new infill homes can be based on components present in existing homes. This table demonstrates the quantitative analysis of key features.

the dwellings adjacent to the historic Ponte Vecchio in Florence were rebuilt using modern techniques after World War II devastated its riverside. The buildings' style and the relationships among them, however, kept the same rhythm and volume as those designed centuries ago (Figure 6.8).

Figure 6.8: The area bordering the historic Ponte Vecchio was rebuilt using modern techniques after destruction, while keeping the same rhythm and volume featured in the old structures.

The *sense of place* perspective of heritage combines the two preceding principles of preservation: uniformity and relationship. Instead of focusing on specific buildings, this view captures the uniqueness of the community as a whole. In other words, attractive communities are organic as they develop upon evolving social and built foundations. The significance of the sense of place view is evident in recent trends extending historic building legislation to the protection of entire areas. This reflects a growing awareness that standalone old buildings lose meaning when isolated among modern structures (Kain, 1981). Therefore, greater value is created by structures that are related to each other by replicating old buildings' style. Such an approach at the urban level denotes and creates a specific sense of place. New structures in Venice, for example, build upon heritage traditions to ensure that a sense of place is harmoniously maintained (Figure 6.9). Heritage building policies include the entire city and ensure that new designs respect traditions and reflect the town's historic identity. The continuous conservation throughout the historic center has resulted in a distinctive sense of place for both visitors and residents. In turn, this sense of place evokes awe, which drives further inquiry into Venice's past layers of development.

Figure 6.9: Venetian heritage policies ensure that new buildings adhere to old traditions and enhance the sense of place that defines the city.

Another sensible urban renewal that interweaves new with old and maintains a sense of place occurred in Birmingham, England. Lying northwest of England's second largest city center, the Birmingham Jewelry Quarter boasts a 200-year-old identity from the industrial era that dominated much of Birmingham's urban landscape (Figure 6.10). The urban form consisted primarily of three-story nineteenth-century brick buildings that housed small factories, workshops, and families. Middle-class population, which inhabited the area until the 1950s, was displaced as war damage and safety concerns condemned many buildings. In his investigation of Birmingham, Slater (1995) argues that in 1960, the Jewelry Quarter was one of the most intractable areas for planners and urban designers. It was an inner-city area, he continues, from which the population had been decanted, characterized by a declining industry occupying outdated premises. Successive 1950s and 1960s planning visions cleared Jewelry Quarter areas in favor of massive block redevelopment. As a result, the district remained undeveloped until the 1970s and 1980s.

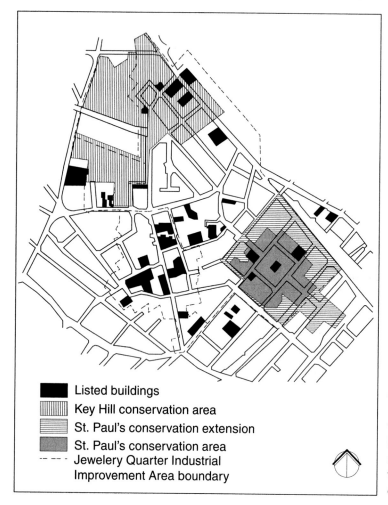

Listed buildings
Key Hill conservation area
St. Paul's conservation extension
St. Paul's conservation area
- - - **Jewelery Quarter Industrial Improvement Area boundary**

Figure 6.10: Massive block development caused Birmingham Jewelry Quarter to lose its inhabitants until heritage preservation bylaws restored the neighborhood to its original residential character.

A combination of events sparked interest in the city's architectural history as a backlash rejecting modernity propagated urban conservation. Also, the Victorian Society campaigned city officials to enact conservation legislation for the historic quarter. Through careful documentation of old structures, the society introduced strict planning regulations with the support of the city planning department. In 1980, Birmingham's city council legislated protection of the unique character of the Jewelry Quarter. Planning provisions prevented demolition and new development in the district while simultaneously encouraging restoration. Both private and public funding stimulated heritage rehabilitation within the delineated city district. The adaptive reuse of former workshops as commercial edifices reflects an awareness of the complex relationship between heritage and economic values. As a result, locals, tourists, and industry workers have moved back into the quarter.

Designing for Adaptability

The expected lifespan of many contemporary buildings is far less than those of masonry edifices in previous centuries. While some old stone structures lasted thousands of years, it is unlikely that many of today's homes will remain unchanged even within a 50-year time span from their building. Housing styles change, planning purposes are redefined, and poor construction renders buildings obsolete all too quickly. If such is the reality of modern construction, it is environmentally wise to consider what will happen to a building after it has served its useful life. Designing for disassembly at the outset greatly increases the chances that building components will be reused or recycled (Figure 6.11).

Several design and building methods can incorporate reuse and recycling of materials both before construction begins and when demolition occurs. During the planning phases, the architect can design the structure for adaptability to accommodate occupants as their needs change. Similarly, the designer can plan for disassembly to allow materials to be sorted out and reused with little or no damage. During construction, choices can be made to include recycled building materials and evaluate existing items such as doors, windows, or hardware for reuse.

Many components can be retained or enhanced, such as stonework or timber structures (Lowry, 1981). This will often require design flexibility to adapt the remaining or salvaged elements unknown in size and quality. Incorporating these principles can produce a building that not only saves energy, materials, and landfill space but also creates a unique architecture.

The design phase can also influence the home's reuse and recycling abilities. Designing for adaptability will diminish the environmental impact of future changes by reducing damage to existing components that do not need to be renovated or replaced. One major reason for renovation is the desire to change, repair, or upgrade old electrical and plumbing conduits. Brand recommends keeping these services separate from the building envelope. Burying wires and pipes in walls and ceilings makes it difficult to adapt or maintain these utilities in the

Item	Contribution to flexibility
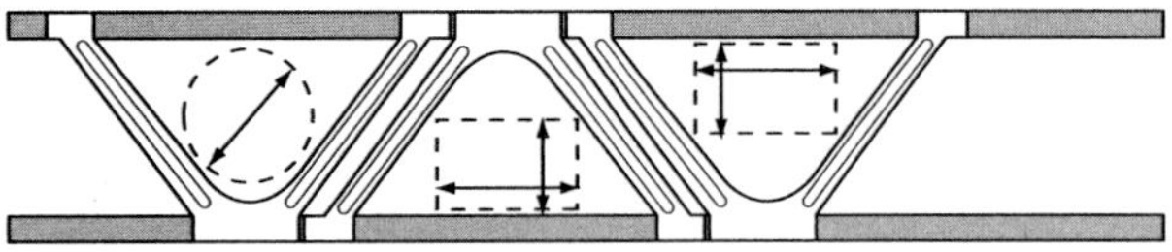 Space joist	• Allows wide spans and, as a result, eliminates the need for additional support walls • The open web allows for easy "fishing" of utility conduits
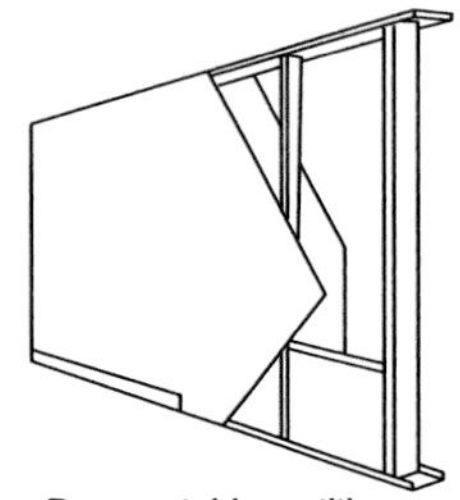 Demountable partitions	• Allows easy placement of partitions anywhere on a floor and ease of dismantling and reuse
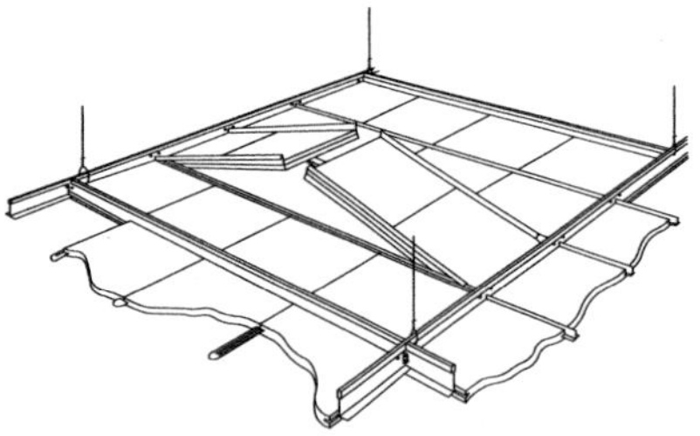 Suspended ceiling	• Allows quick covering of exposed joists and easy access to conduits for future alterations
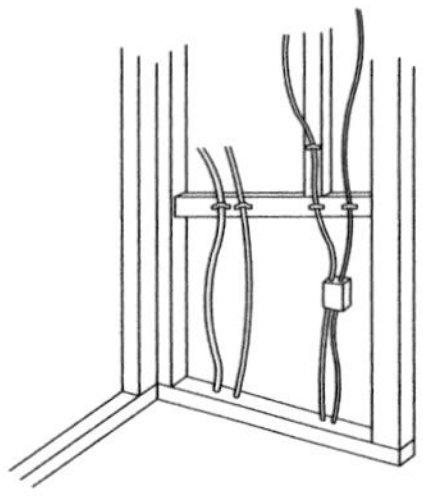 Flexible cold-water tubing	• Allows easier installation and replacement of plumbing fixtures
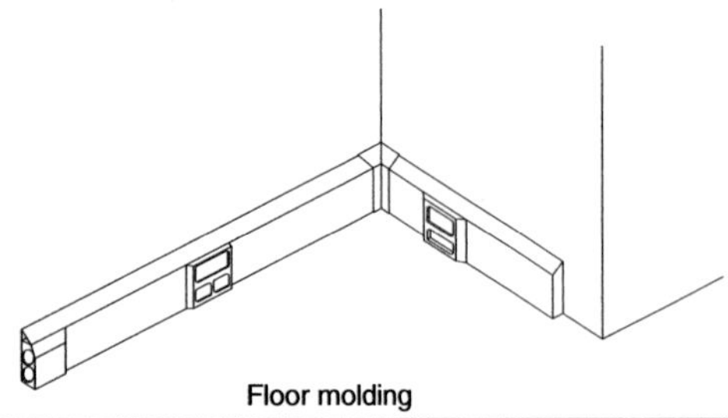 Floor molding	• Allows flexibility in installation of receptacles and avoids the need to pass wires through the wall

Figure 6.11: Contemporary construction methods and products permit adaptability, disassembly, and reuse of a home's components.

future. Currently, many baseboards and cable troughs can hide these wires, and many designers choose to keep the services exposed, lending a functional or even aesthetically pleasing appearance to the interior. Slightly oversizing electrical and plumbing also minimizes future needs for highly disruptive and damaging maintenance.

The advent of preformed metal in modern construction, such as light-gauge wall studs or steel beams, presents the option for recycling almost indefinitely the bulk of many housing envelopes and interior partitions. Separation of components built for longevity from those with a short lifespan follows a logical suggestion set forth by Francis Duffy (in Brand) that buildings be designed for deconstruction. By carefully ensuring that this principle is integrated into the design of a structure, long-lasting components will remain intact while other parts can be replaced. In addition, this process reduces a mixture of material types and encourages reuse and recycling of products as a building is reconfigured.

Reduce, Reuse, and Recycle

Renovation can be an environmentally responsible action as it extends the functional life of a building and keeps it working efficiently. According to the Environmental News Network (1999), construction and demolition in the United States creates 136 million tons of waste per year, only 8 percent of which is from new construction. Recycling used components can reduce waste by up to 75 percent. By reusing and recycling building products, designers and builders can be economical, environmentally sensitive, and often innovative.

Many materials used in construction can be altered in a recycling process to produce an identical building component or one with altered function. Demolition waste, such as lumber or masonry, can be reused, but often it is damaged so much during demolition that is has become structurally unsound. However, technology now exists to give otherwise useless pieces of concrete or masonry a new life. The average composition of demolition waste by weight in Western Europe, for example, is 45 percent masonry, 40 percent concrete, 8 percent wood, 4 percent metal, and 3 percent paper and plastic. The U.K. produces about 70 million tons of masonry and concrete waste per year. Four percent of this is processed to produce secondary aggregate, and 29 percent goes through low-level recycling on or near the site of origin. Bulk demolition waste, in some locations where facilities are available, are sorted. Lightweight materials such as wood and plastic are removed, and the rest is crushed. Steel is removed and sold for recycling, fine-grade crushed rock is sold for landscaping and topsoil, and larger pieces are slated for lower quality road and foundation aggregate (Golton, 1997).

While recycling a building material requires additional energy to extend its life, the reuse process can be as simple as installing a used component where you may have otherwise installed a new one. Although some materials may be difficult to remove intact, their value as a salvageable material must be considered. Steel structural members, sheet metal, piping, hardwood flooring, fireplaces, tiling, and old bricks or stones can be of a high monetary value (Reiner 1979). The biggest source for reusable materials is, however, the consumer. Old doors, light fixtures, sinks, and tubs are continually being discarded, rather than provided as a source of building materials with history and character that can be recovered from a salvage or recycling center, from an existing structure, or from another house or building slated for demolition.

Many found or purchased recycled products rarely come without problems. Often window sashes are broken, sinks lack necessary fixtures, or enamel tubs may be chipped—all of which take time and money to remedy. To use time and resources efficiently, Burnham (1998) suggests that the builder must be able to assess quickly whether recycling an object will be economical in terms of additional components and hours spent.

The repair and installation of several recycled windows, for example, may cost a fraction of the cost of a new window, and the reuse will save many windows from going to landfill. In fact, some people will be willing to give away materials instead of paying for them to be disposed of at a landfill. Many recycling centers stockpile wide varieties of building components. This provides an organized service for depositing and recovering discarded building materials and gives builders many options from which to choose without having to spend hours scavenging (Burnham). Environmentally, recycling and reuse centers can save useful materials but also educate the public on advantages of using "garbage" for building.

The process of considering a building's lifecycle is becoming increasingly important as society re-evaluates the way the built environment affects the natural environment. While designers and builders cannot re-create the past or predict the future, they can design buildings that incorporate recyclable and reusable materials that can withstand the test of time.

Building onto History: Le Village

The neighborhood of Le Village is located at the east end of Cornwall, a city in eastern Ontario, Canada, with a population of 47,403. The area was settled in 1784 and incorporated in 1834 (Figure 6.12). Le Village was founded in the middle of the nineteenth century with the establishment of the textile mill industry along the St. Lawrence River. Many homes were built in the vicinity to house mill workers, and businesses were launched to service the growing community. In 1924, the Courtaulds textile mill provided more industry jobs, pushing the boundary of Le Village further east. These mills allowed Le Village to survive the Depression years and expand steadily into the 1950s. The majority of the homes were built between 1880 and 1950, with a temporary halt in construction during both World Wars. The textile mills, one of which was once the third largest in Canada, closed in 1959 due to increased foreign market competition.

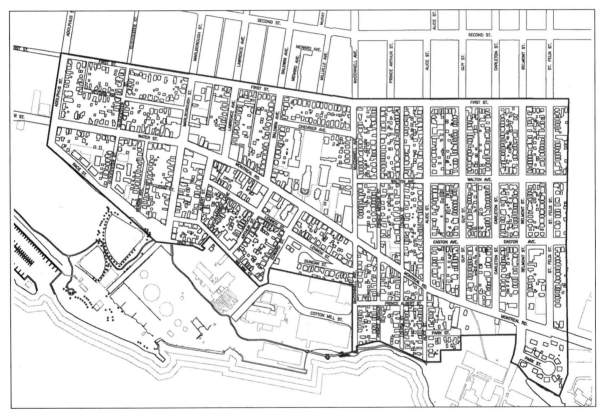

Figure 6.12: Map of Le Village and the area studied (bottom)

With the closing of the mills, many residents were forced into unemployment and welfare. With people moving out to find employment elsewhere, previously owner-occupied homes were bought by a few landlords who converted them into rental properties. Since the housing stock was old and the rents were lower than the rest of Cornwall due to high vacancy rates, Le Village attracted residents from lower income brackets. In the following decades, it became known as a seedy neighborhood (Figure 6.13). This negative image, combined with competition from other neighborhoods in Cornwall, further reduced the strength of the area's commercial district. The closing of the Courtaulds mill in 1992 exacerbated an already dire situation, both residentially and commercially (Courtaulds Fibres Canada, 1993; Kyte, 1983; McCullough, 1992).

Figure 6.13: The closing of Cornwall's textile mills in the late 1950s triggered an economic downward spiral that led to the departure of many homeowners. The homes were purchased by absentee landlords who failed to maintain them properly.

In conceiving the methodology for the rehabilitation of Le Village, the development team recognized that past events, present conditions, and future evolution must play a role in the process. An in-depth survey of the neighborhood provided an historical overview and a detailed assessment of current socioeconomic, urban, and architectural conditions (Friedman, 1999). Roads and public parks were documented, houses were visited, and their physical condition assessed. By the end of the process, the team had a comprehensive inventory and knew the magnitude of the problem as well as the steps that needed to be taken.

The next stage was to develop the conceptual framework and establish the objectives within which rehabilitation and new construction would occur. The team recognized that much in Le Village was valuable and worth preserving, so they focused their attention on tracing the existing urban fabric and architectural characteristics and on forecasting future transformations that might occur within this pattern. The team did not want to restrict change but to facilitate it within the context of existing conditions. The observations, guidelines, and strategies outlined here are a result of this approach and were meant to ensure that the original fabric of the community could be preserved yet allowed to evolve.

The Residents

A study of the population by age distribution revealed that Le Village fitted within the demographic fabric of greater Cornwall and had a healthy population with a sizeable segment of young people. According to Statistics Canada (1999), the total population of Le Village was approximately 5060 residents, representing 11 percent of Cornwall's overall residents. Seniors 65 and over constituted approximately 16 percent, while children 15 and under made up 19 percent. These figures show that the Le Village age distribution was fairly representative of Cornwall as a whole. Yet, unlike Cornwall, the 20 to 24 age range formed the largest group for Le Village. The percentages were also high for all ages between 20 and 39. This group included individuals typically in transition between school and the workforce and constituted potential homeowners. They would also be more likely to participate to a greater degree in renovation projects. A large youth segment stressed the importance of parks and other gathering and recreation facilities. Safety of children and seniors, though they represented a small percentage, could not be neglected in future planning (Figure 6.14).

The team found that approximately 2362 dwelling units in Le Village were inhabited by an average of 2.2 persons per household, representing 12 percent of Cornwall's total housing stock of 19,155 units. Le Village homes were not only smaller than other homes in Cornwall, but they were cheaper, with an average resale and rental value 14 percent lower than that of other Cornwall homes. Owner-occupied homes in Le Village represented only 27 percent of the total number of dwellings, while the remaining 73 percent were rental units (Figure 6.15). The tenants were more transient and were not engaged in proper maintenance or renovation which led to the deterioration of many homes.

Compared with the rest of Cornwall, the movement of the population within Le Village was judged problematic. Those who moved within the same census region accounted for 27 percent of the population, compared with 14 percent of the overall population of Cornwall, and they were mostly tenants who left their homes once their leases expired rather than undertake costly renovations (Figure 6.16).

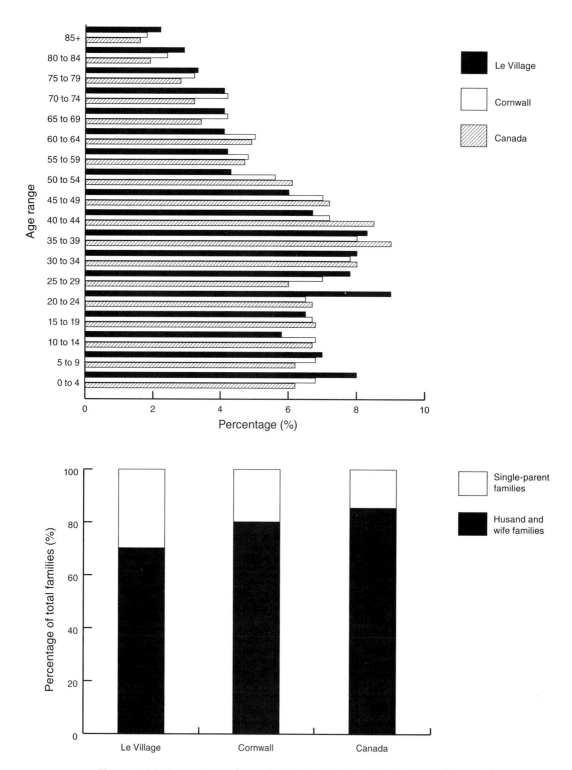

Figure 6.14: Comparison of age distribution (top) and family status (bottom) between Le Village, the City of Cornwall, and Canada

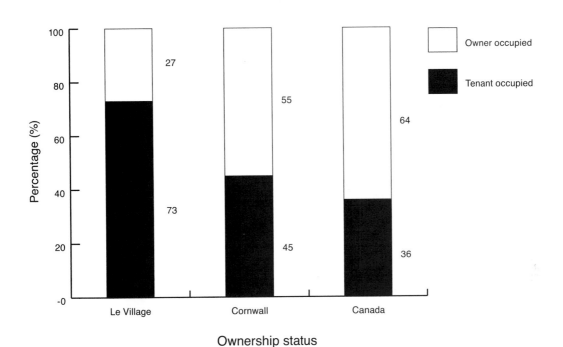

Figure 6.15: Ownership status of Le Village and Cornwall dwelling units

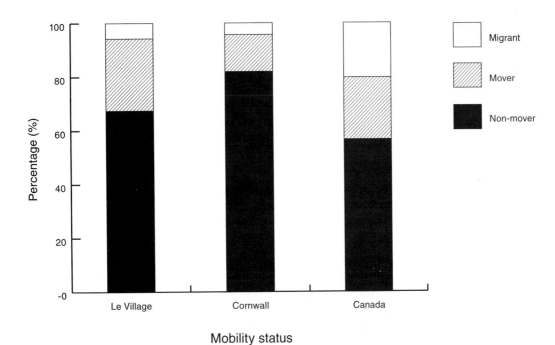

Figure 6.16: Mobility status of residents of Le Village, Cornwall, and Canada

The average income for a single person in Le Village fell short of Canada's average income. The team found an income disparity of 23 percent between residents of Le Village and all of Cornwall (Figure 6.17). The employed residents of Le Village had less disposable income for purchasing, renovating, or maintaining a home. Regardless of how inexpensive such investments might be, tenants did not renovate since such expenses would be lost upon moving. It was therefore decided that encouraging a shift from rental to ownership needed to be a priority in Le Village's renewal. Another telling economic statistic was the unemployment status, which for Le Village was high at about 23 percent, significantly higher than Cornwall's 14 percent and the national average of 8.1 percent. The low incomes of Le Village workers and its high unemployment rate could be interpreted as symptomatic of the education problem with which they were inextricably linked.

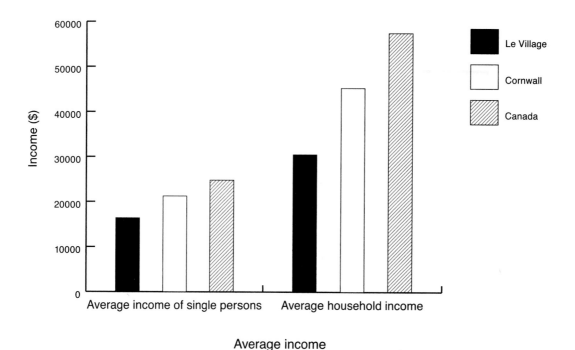

Figure 6.17: Average income of Le Village, Cornwall, and Canada

A study of the state of education in Le Village found that for those aged 15 to 24, the age bracket of high school and post-secondary attendance, 53 percent were not in school. The rest were in some form of school—43 percent full-time and 4 percent part-time. Of the Le Village population over 15 years of age, about

15 percent had graduated from high school, 26 percent had non-university post-secondary education, and only 4 percent had a university degree (Figure 6.18).

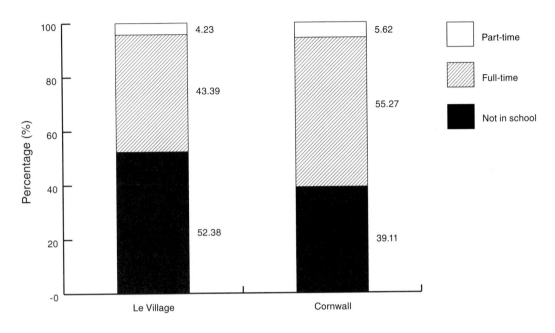

School attendance for residents aged 15 to 24

Figure 6.18: School attendance for Le Village and Cornwall residents aged 15 to 24

Urban Strategies

Conception of urban strategies for the rehabilitation of Le Village began by focusing on the neighborhood's lot layout, which originated when the initial square-mile plan was devised in 1783 (Figure 6.19). This square mile was intended to include the entire town and was divided into 81 blocks, each of which was further subdivided into squares that contained 24 lots around the perimeter (Figure 6.20). Streets alternating between 33 and 66 feet (10 and 20 meters) in width separated the blocks. In addition to this subdivision grid of the original square mile was farmland divided into a grid of long, narrow lots. The two grids together generated the overall pattern of Le Village's blocks, with an overlapping zone linking the two (Kyte, 1983; Wilson, 1995).

The zoning ordinances that governed the residential area in Le Village were also examined. They allowed a wide range of housing types, from single-detached homes to fourplexes. Institutions such as schools, churches, hospitals, and commu-

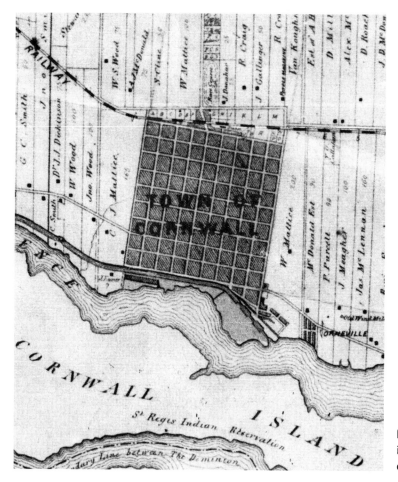

Figure 6.19: Cornwall's initial square-mile plan was devised in 1783.

nity centers, as well as home offices were permitted according to these ordinances. The main commercial zone, known as the business improvement area (BIA), extended the length of the main arterial road, Montreal Street, permitting a fairly comprehensive list of businesses. Parking typologies were also studied. Several parking types were found: those behind buildings, those with street access via a driveway, those next to buildings, those with direct access to the street, and corner parking in empty lots. Alleys in Le Village used as vehicular access to backyards had no clear boundaries and were bounded by high-density lots with no coherent circulation pattern.

Based on the lots' morphology, the roads, and the alleys, Le Village was divided into eight zones, each with a different lot width and length (Figure 6.21). An analysis of each zone yielded the general character and urban pattern of the

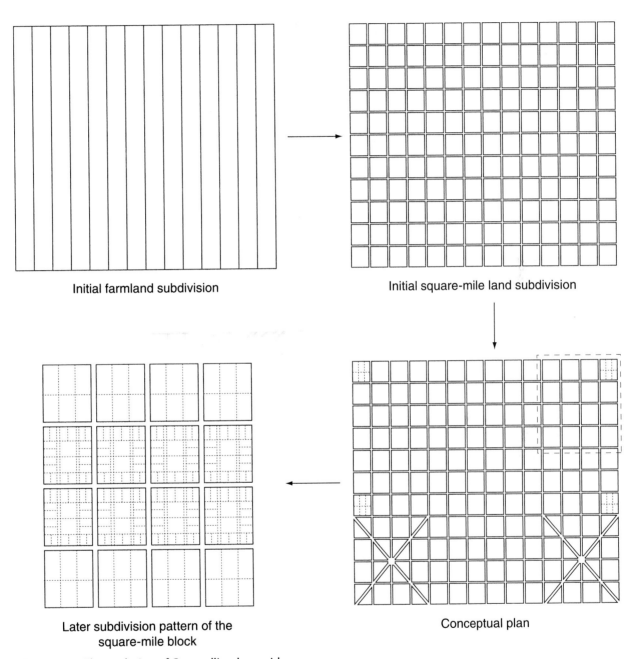

Initial farmland subdivision

Initial square-mile land subdivision

Later subdivision pattern of the
square-mile block

Conceptual plan

Figure 6.20: The evolution of Cornwall's urban grid

neighborhood, upon which foundation the team developed strategies to steer the macro aspects of the rehabilitation. A density analysis of all eight zones revealed that the lot density decreased from east to west, that the subdivision of lots was smaller in the east, and that the commercial area had the highest built density.

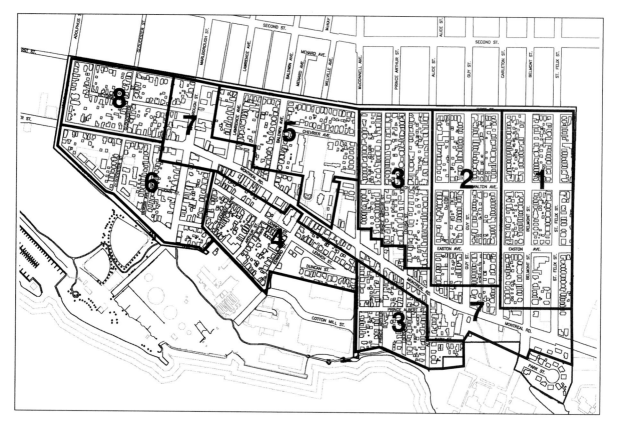

Figure 6.21: Based on Le Village's urban morphology and architectural character, the study area was divided into eight zones.

Following the division of Le Village into eight zones, the team analyzed a typical lot in each zone. By comparing and analyzing data such as land coverage and floor-area ratio, researchers obtained the general condition of land use and configuration in Le Village. An example of the lot analysis for one of the zones is displayed in Figure 6.22.

The next step was to synthesize the character of each zone, taking into account lot size and setback, parking, land use, additions, and building heights. Urban guidelines were then developed based on the synthesis of these features (Figure 6.23). To guide future construction, the team developed guidelines for two different lot types: typical inner lots and lots with alleys (Figure 6.24).

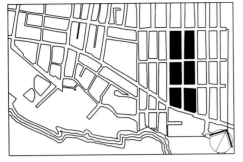

Zone locator

Data analysis

Site area	141,150 ft² (13,113 m²)
Land coverage	47,360 ft² (4400 m²)
Land coverage ratio	0.34
Floor area	87,800 ft² (8157 m²)
Floor area ratio	0.62

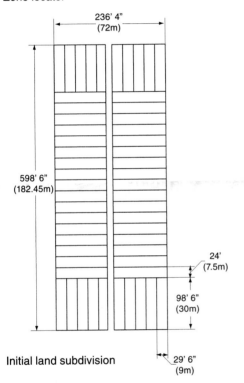

Initial land subdivision

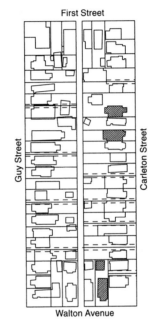

Existing land subdivision

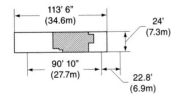

Typical plot analysis

Site area	2750 ft² (255.6 m²)
Land coverage	41,030 ft² (95.6 m²)
Land coverage ratio	0.37
Floor area	2059 ft² (191.3 m²)
Floor area ratio	0.75
Setback	22'8" (6.9 m)

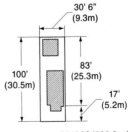

Site area	3015 ft² (280.8 m²)
Land coverage	1300 ft² (121 m²)
Land coverage ratio	0.43
Floor area	2250 ft² (209 m²)
Floor area ratio	0.74

Figure 6.22: Land coverage and floor-area ratio were some of the aspects studied, as shown in the lot analysis of zone 2.

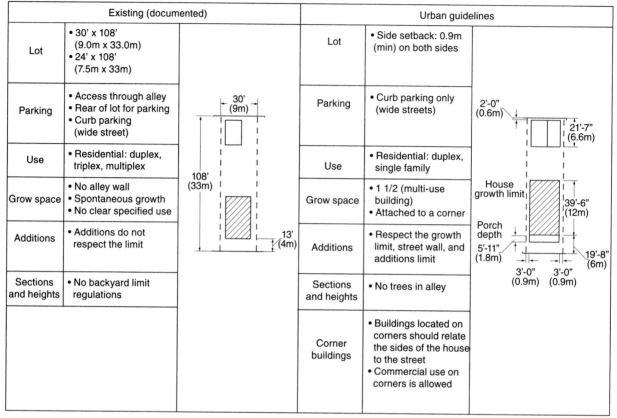

	Existing (documented)		Urban guidelines		
Lot	• 30' x 108' (9.0m x 33.0m) • 24' x 108' (7.5m x 33m)		Lot	• Side setback: 0.9m (min) on both sides	
Parking	• Access through alley • Rear of lot for parking • Curb parking (wide street)		Parking	• Curb parking only (wide streets)	
Use	• Residential: duplex, triplex, multiplex		Use	• Residential: duplex, single family	
Grow space	• No alley wall • Spontaneous growth • No clear specified use		Grow space	• 1 1/2 (multi-use building) • Attached to a corner	
Additions	• Additions do not respect the limit		Additions	• Respect the growth limit, street wall, and additions limit	
Sections and heights	• No backyard limit regulations		Sections and heights	• No trees in alley	
			Corner buildings	• Buildings located on corners should relate the sides of the house to the street • Commercial use on corners is allowed	

Figure 6.23: Example of synthesis and urban guidelines for zone 2

Architectural Strategies

In preparation for the development of architectural renewal strategies, the team studied the historical evolution of the dwellings. Documentation of types, construction dates, and the homes' lifecycles showed that only 112 homes built before 1900 remained in place, and many were unfortunately remodeled without consideration of their architectural heritage. The vast majority of the dwellings, 623 in all, were built between 1920 and 1939 (Figure 6.25). This boom in house construction correlates with the founding of the Courtaulds textile mill. The housing developed between 1900 and 1949 filled in most of the area near the old eastern limit of Le Village. These homes were built with wood-frame construction and the vast majority, 94 percent, were two stories. They were likely part of the same housing development and homogenous in design style.

With stable employment during the housing boom, both exteriors and interiors of homes were well-maintained. Wall insulation, fixtures, plumbing,

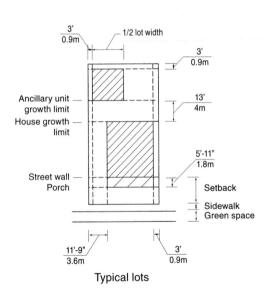

Corner lots

- Both front and side setback shall respect the street wall
- Minimum side setback shall not be less than 3' (0.9m)
- Maximum depth of the front porch is 5'-11" (1.8m)
- Ancillary units only permitted at the back corner off the street with a maximum width of 13' (4m) when lot width is less than 26' (8m) or 1/2 of the lot width when the lot width is greater than 26' (8m)
- Corner buildings should improve the façades of both sides of the street
- Distance between growth space and main building should be at least 13' (4m)
- Building height shall not exceed two stories or 27'-11" (8.5m)
- Architectural elements guidelines apply
- Home office guidelines apply with the following:
    - No more than 50% of unit may be used for light commercial
    - Acceptable uses may also include store, cafe, or hairdresser
    - No illuminated signs are permitted to advertise the home business; no sign may exceed 10.7 ft² (1 m²)

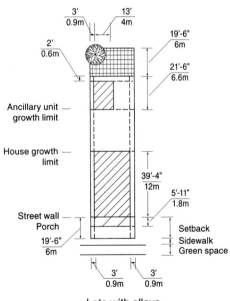

Typical lots

- Front setback shall respect the street wall
- Minimum site setback shall not be less than 3' (0.9m)
- Maximum depth of front porch is 5'-11" (1.8m)
- Ancillary units only permitted at the back corner off the street with a maximum width of 13' (4m) when lot width is less than 26' (8m) or 1/2 of the lot width when the lot width is greater than 26' (8m)
- Distance between growth space and main building should be at least 13' (4m)
- Building height shall not exceed two stories or 27'-11" (8.5m)
- Architectural elements guidelines apply
- Plot width less than 39'-4" (12m) shall leave 3' (0.9m) side setback on both sides

Lots with alleys

- Front setback shall respect the street wall
- Minimum site setback shall not be less than 3' (0.9m)
- Maximum depth of front porch is 5'-11" (1.8m)
- Ancillary units only permitted at the back corner off the street with a maximum width of 13' (4m) when lot width is less than 26' (8m) or 1/2 of the lot width when the lot width is greater than 26' (8m)
- Distance between growth space and main building should be at least 13' (4m)
- Building height shall not exceed two stories or 27'-11" (8.5m)
- Architectural elements guidelines apply
- Plot width less than 39'-4" (12m) shall leave 3' (0.9m) side setback on both sides
- Alley should have trees and pavement to improve condition

Figure 6.24: Urban guidelines for three different types of lots

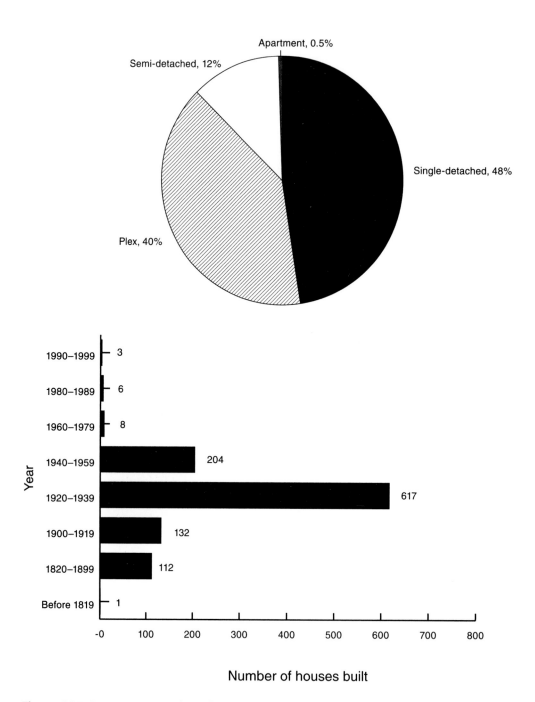

Figure 6.25: Documentation of Le Village's housing by type (top) and their date of construction (bottom)

mechanical services, and other elements had been upgraded when new technologies were introduced. Gradually, many dwellings underwent minor renovations and construction of small additions to suit the needs of growing families. These changes did not upset the urban fabric of the neighborhood and the architectural characteristics of the homes. Unfortunately, this era came to an end when the textile mills closed, leaving many residents unemployed and financially unable to carry out regular home maintenance. Weather and aging took their toll over the next few decades, and many homes fell into disrepair.

The closing of the mills also led to the collapse of the housing market, evidenced by a sharp drop in construction with only nine new homes built in 40 years. Many residents had also sold their homes and moved out of Le Village and Cornwall to find work elsewhere. As a result, a few individuals bought up many homes at low cost and converted them into rental properties. Many single-family homes were subdivided into multifamily units to maximize their rental income. With several households occupying the space where once only a single family resided, the homes' structure and utilities were severely overtaxed. Also, since many units were owned by absentee landlords, they had been poorly maintained.

One-story accessory buildings, functioning as sheds and storage garages, were also popular and sprang up in the backyards of many houses. Since they were not the principal living spaces, many of these accessory buildings were neglected and in worse condition than the residences. Having lasted many decades without maintenance, these structures posed a safety threat to occupants who still used them.

The research team also found that homes built in the 40 years prior to the study required minor renovations. These homes were built with advanced housing technology and durable materials. Of the homes built between 1820 and 1899, for example, 12.5 percent required serious renovations and 7.1 percent required moderate improvement. The upgrades included replacing windows, doors, flooring, or roofing since many of these components had exceeded their life spans (Figure 6.26).

The next phase included a survey of the form, style, and construction techniques of typical houses. They were divided into six types: single-detached narrow front, single-detached wide front, semi-detached, duplex, compoundplex, and fourplex (Figure 6.27). In addition, there were commercial buildings with residential use. Since most housing developers constructed the same types of home in a given area, many dwellings had been converted from their original type to form the diversity. Single-family detached homes that accounted for 48 percent of the

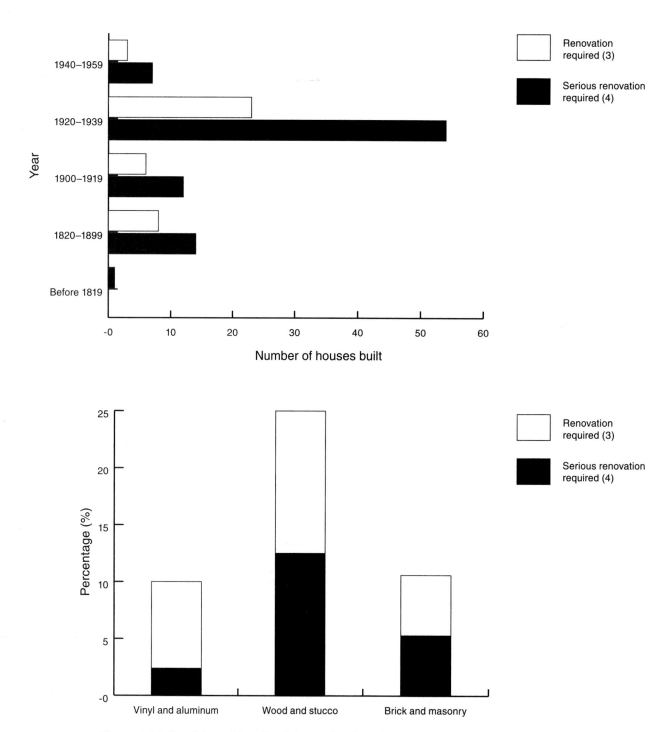

Figure 6.26: Conditions of Le Village's homes by date of construction (top) and exterior claddings used (bottom)

Type	Name	Form	Width	Height	Roof	Façade composition			
I	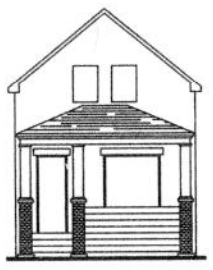 Single-detached, narrow front	Flat front with front porch	14'–20' (4.2m–6m)	1½–2 stories	Gable, hip, or flat with western front	2-bay first floor	2-bay second floor	2–4 steps up to near full-width front porch	Entry door in side bay of first floor
II	 Single-detached, wide front	Flat front with front porch	22'–28' (6.7m–8.5m)	1½–2½ stories	Gable, hip, or flat with western front	3-bay first floor	2–3 bay second floor	2–4 steps up to full-width front porch	Entry door in center of side bay of first floor
III	 Semi-detached	Flat front with front porch	30'–40' (9.1m–12.1m)	2–2½ stories	Gable, hip, or flat with western front	4-bay first floor	4-bay second floor	2–4 steps up to full-width front porch	Composed of two identical narrow-front units placed side by side
IV	 Duplex	Flat front with double-stacked front porch	22'–28' (6.7m–8.5m)	2–2½ stories	Gable or hip	3-bay façade with entry door in center bay, both floors	½ to ¾ width double front porch	2–4 steps up to lower porch aligned with lower entry door	Upper unit access via front stairs to upper front porch or via rear stairs to upper rear porch
V	 Compoundplex	Combination of narrow front types	35'–40' (10.6m–12.1m)	2 stories	Gable, hip, or flat with western front	Wrap-around front porch		Composed of narrow-front house with traverse wing to one side	
VI	 Fourplex	Flat front with double-stacked front porch	30'–40' (9.1m–12.1m)	2–2½ stories	Gable, hip, or flat with western front	Narrow type: similar to semi-detached but with double front porch and additional center door at lower floor for access to upper units		Wide types: composed of two duplexes placed side by side with central stairs to upper porch	

Figure 6.27: Le Village house types and their characteristics

227

houses varied in size depending on the number of family members that resided in them. Semi-detached wood-frame buildings formed only 12 percent of the housing in Le Village, and plexes housed a number of families on several floors.

The homogeneity of housing in the community was upset by the conversion of single or semi-detached houses into multifamily units. Though they constitute 40 percent of the housing in Le Village, only a few multifamily units were originally designed and built as such. These conversions involved the addition of external or internal stairwells and dividing walls, but their exteriors remained somewhat unchanged. Whether converted from another housing type or not, most of these plexes were rented and owned by absentee landlords.

Next to be documented were exterior architectural features that affected the public image. The elements surveyed included front and back porches, enclosures, doors and windows, additions, accessory buildings, decorative woodwork, awnings and shutters, landscaping, and fences. The synthesis of the data collected on homes began by studying building volumes and roofs. The houses were mostly rectangular boxes with porches at the front and back, and were one and a half to two and a half stories tall, with simple roof forms that included gable, hip, and flat roof with parapets (Figure 6.28).

Study of typical floor plans revealed that public areas were located on the lower floor and private spaces on the upper in two-story units, and both spaces were configured along the two deep sides. Additions to houses were built in the rear, on the side, and on upper floors and were used for storage, garages, and additional living space. Many Le Village houses had enclosures, generally front and rear porches, which were used as extensions of living space or for storage.

Though brick and masonry typify traditional architecture, these costly materials were not commonly used in the homes of Le Village. Vinyl and aluminum were the most common exterior cladding materials and covered 82.3 percent of the homes. As vinyl and aluminum siding are affordable and easy to install, many homes that were originally clad with masonry exterior were redressed when they were renovated or converted into plexes. Some blocks were composed almost entirely of vinyl or aluminum siding.

A large variety of window types were also identified and grouped in six categories. They were generally rectangular with a vertical orientation. Entry doors were similarly categorized, with eight main types. Roof details were noted, with attention paid to decorative work, fascia, and soffits. Particular mention was made of the elaborately detailed bargeboard (a board trim that is usually carved and projects from the gable line of a roof, used to hide the ends of the horizontal roof

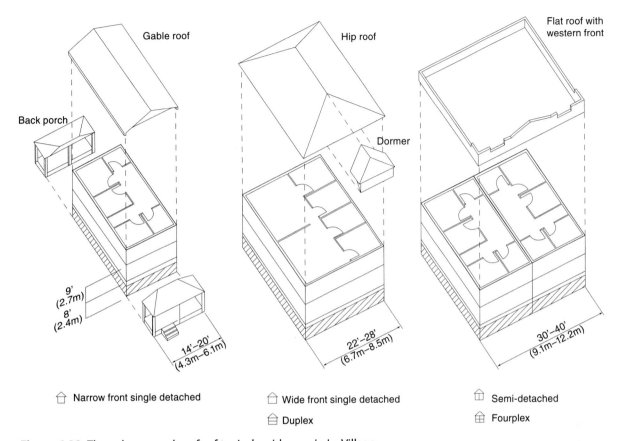

Figure 6.28: The volumes and roofs of typical residences in Le Village

timbers) with smooth paint finish on the houses with gable fronts. The porches of Le Village were valuable and significant architectural features; as such, the team carefully noted elements, such as posts, beams, balustrades, stairs, floors, and skirting (Figure 6.29). Most front and backyards had deciduous and coniferous trees as well as a variety of shrubs. The most common landscape features were plants and flowers in pots on porches. Front, side, and rear types and styles of fences were also analyzed.

Guidelines

The architectural guidelines for the rehabilitation and new construction of dwelling units were developed at two levels: first to provide the general requirements of the housing type and cover issues such as form and style of houses, and second to treat the technical requirements of architectural elements such as windows, cladding, and landscaping. Since all houses in Le Village were categorized according

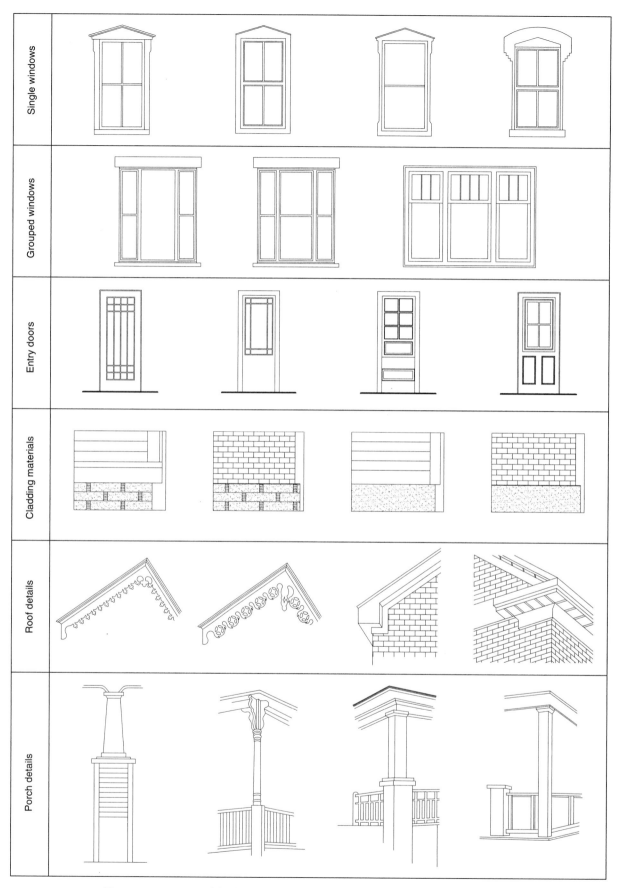

Figure 6.29: Many of the homes in Le Village had unique features with porches, cladding, and roofs.

to type, the guidelines were organized according to volume, unit height, width, and general floor area (Figure 6.30). In this manner, the guidelines would reduce arbitrary changes and expansions to homes and contribute to the rehabilitation of the traditional building pattern and eventual enhancement of the community.

Building type	I Single detached	II Semi-detached	III Duplex	IV Fourplex
Volume	All residential buildings shall have the following: • Front porch • Roof type of either hip or gable • Cantilevered walls and floors shall not be allowed along the wall facing the principal street • On rectangular sites, the wall facing the principal street shall be parallel to and along the front yard setback line, in order to respect and maintain the original character of the streetscape			
Height	• Minimum number of stories: 1½ • Maximum number of stories: 2½ • Upper half-story may be an attic space (unfinished) for future use • Maximum building height from ground level at fronting street to highest roof ridge or parapet: 25' (7.6m)	• Minimum number of stories: 2 • Maximum number of stories: 2½ • Upper half-story may be an attic space (unfinished) for future use • Maximum building height from ground level at fronting street to highest roof ridge or parapet: 25' (7.6m)		
Width	• Minimum width: 14' (4.2m) • Maximum width: 28' (8.5m)	• Minimum width: 30' (9.1m) [15' (4.5m) per unit] • Maximum width: 42' (12.8m) [21' (6.4m) per unit]	• Minimum width: 20' (6.1m) • Maximum width: 28' (8.5m)	• Minimum width: 30' (9.1m) • Maximum width: 42' (12.8m)
Floor area	• Minimum floor area: 1000 ft² (92.9 m²) • Maximum floor area: 2000 ft² (185.8 m²)	• Minimum floor area: 2000 ft² (185.8 m²) [1000 ft² (92.9 m²) per unit] • Maximum floor area: 3360 ft² (312.2 m²) [1680 ft² (156.1 m²) per unit]	• Minimum floor area: 1000 ft² (92.9 m²) [500 ft² (46.4 m²) per unit] • Maximum floor area: 2000 ft² (185.8 m²) [1000 ft² (92.9 m²) per unit]	• Minimum floor area: 2000 ft² (185.8 m²) [500 ft² (46.4 m²) per unit] • Maximum floor area: 3360 ft² (312.2 m²) [840 ft² (78 m²) per unit]
Illustrations				

Figure 6.30: Architectural guidelines for the various building types

The unit guidelines were meant to allow change without destroying the visual and functional integrity of the neighborhood. As such, the guidelines focused on materials, porch enclosures, unit additions, accessory buildings, and infill units (Figure 6.31). To prevent the replacement of windows and doors from degrading the architectural character of the homes, the guidelines that governed them also specified materials, details, proportions, and configuration (Figure 6.32). The cladding and roof guidelines focused on materials, construction details, and configuration (Figure 6.33).

Implementation

Once observations were made, a renewal process charted, and guidelines written, the rehabilitation of Le Village started. In addition to retooling the physical state, the beginning stages included social interventions. Several public meetings took place and a community association was formed. Group Renaissance was named and representatives elected, who voiced residents' concerns when common issues were raised. In addition to overseeing plans for the home rehabilitations, the group also began a dialogue with the City of Cornwall administration to address social issues. It became apparent that the neighborhood's safety was compromised. This sense of insecurity contributed to the ongoing departure of residents. Policing in the neighborhood street was, therefore, increased and other measures were taken by the citizens to provide an increased level of safety.

To improve community relations and foster a sense of place, a joint effort was undertaken by the city and citizens to ameliorate problems in public open spaces. Several "cleaning days" were announced in which city employees and citizens worked to improve public parks, play structures, signage, and street furniture. These small measures not only contributed to the appearance of Le Village, but they provided space for community gathering. To assist homeowners who wished to renovate, the City of Cornwall created a fund that lent money to residents. City assessors evaluated the condition of each home and determined the amount of a monetary grant. This initiative triggered a "renovation boom" that contributed to economic spin-offs in the form of job creation and prosperity of local businesses.

A superintendent was appointed by the city to help homeowners with technical issues and assure that the renovation would conform with the guidelines. As a result of the preliminary survey, several structures that could not be salvaged were demolished and lots freed for construction of new homes. The new homes inspired renovation and improvements of adjacent properties, leading to a "domino effect." Another outcome of the rehabilitation was the conversion of the abandoned textile mills' structures near the waterfront into affordable residences. Galvanizing com-

Type	Porch enclosures	Additions	Accessory buildings	Infill units
Materials	• Existing open porches that contain original elements of historical or heritage value shall be restored and maintained • Enclosures such as porches shall not be allowed • Porch enclosures shall be clad in horizontal wood or fiber cement siding as per the material requirements for exterior walls	• Additions shall be clad in wood, fiber cement siding, or brick as per the material requirements for exterior walls • The total number of cladding materials including that of additions shall not exceed two	• Accessory buildings shall be clad in wood, fiber cement siding, or brick as per the material requirements for exterior walls • The total number of cladding materials including that of accessory buildings shall not exceed two	• Infill units shall be clad in wood, fiber cement siding, or brick as per the material requirements for exterior walls • The total number of cladding materials including that of infill units shall not exceed two
Configuration	• Porch enclosures may be of another allowable material other than that of the main building • Windowsills in porch enclosures shall be located 2'-6" (750mm) to 3'-0" (900mm) above the porch floor	• In cases where additions continue or extend existing faces of exterior walls, the new cladding shall match that of the existing wall (including material, scale, color, finish, and texture) • Additions to the rear of the house are permitted up to the required rear yard setback. On lots 35' (10.6m) or more in width, additions are permitted to the side of the house up to the required side yard setback • The height of additions shall not exceed that of the principal building	• See Urban Guidelines for location, height, and use requirements of accessory buildings	• See Urban Guidelines for location, height, and use requirements of infill units
Details	• Windows and doors in porch enclosures and additions shall conform to the main building guidelines • All exterior walls of porch enclosures and additions shall conform to the main building detail guidelines		• Windows and doors in accessory buildings and infill units shall conform to the main building guidelines • All exterior walls of accessory buildings and infill units shall conform to the main building detail guidelines	
Illustrations				

Figure 6.31: Architectural guidelines for porch enclosures, additions, accessory buildings, and infill units

Type	Entry door	Entry storm door	Other exterior door
Materials	• Doors should be made of wood, metal, or vinyl cladding • Vinyl or vinyl clad doors are not recommended • Doors shall be glazed in clear glass with no more than 10% daylight reduction • Frame material: Wood or ESP white aluminum • Wood: recessed ladder-back; French doors (true divided glass)		• Doors shall be made of wood, metal, or vinyl cladding • Metal door shall be used in store door only • Doors shall be glazed in clear glass with no more than 10% daylight reduction • Wood: recessed ladder-back; French door (true divided glass)
Configuration	• Door type shall be pivot door • The width of doors shall be 3'-0" (0.9m) to 4'-0" (1.2m) • The height of doors must be between 7'-0" (2.1m) to 7'-4" (2.2m) • The width of the trim must be between 2" (0.05m) and 5" (0.12m)		• No key in knobs allowed
Details	• All doors must be hinged except garage doors • Sliding doors are not permitted • Door hardware pattern: Schlage Plymouth; Baldwin 5030; Kwikset Standard; US Lock Plymouth, or similar • The total glazing area on the façade shall not exceed 30% of the façade area		• All doors must be hinged except garage doors • Sliding doors are not permitted • Door hardware pattern: Schlage Plymouth; Baldwin 5030; Kwikset Standard; US Lock Plymouth, or similar • Garage door shall be wood section, panel-type, overhead by Crawford, Overhead, or equal, 9' (2.7m) width • The total glazing area on the façade shall not exceed 30% of the façade area
Illustrations	Original Replacement	Original Replacement	Original Replacement

Figure 6.32: Architectural guidelines for exterior doors

munity leadership and infusing economic prosperity were indirect benefits that contributed to seeing Le Village retooled and put back on track to sustainable recovery. To illustrate the renovation of homes, application of the guidelines on several structures is demonstrated in the following paragraphs.

Two detached abandoned houses at 310 and 312 Prince Arthur Street were originally designed and built as single-family homes but had, over time, been converted to duplexes. Since neither structure had enough space for two independent

Type	Exterior walls	Roofs
Materials	• Wood framed walls shall be clad in one of the following: Horizontal wood siding, with bevel or clapboard profile Horizontal fiber cement siding Brick veneer • Chimneys shall be finished in brick • Existing buildings with horizontal wood siding of 6" (150mm) exposure or less shall be maintained or replaced with the same • Existing buildings with brick veneer throughout shall be maintained or replaced with the same	• Roofs shall be clad in one of the following: Composite asphalt shingles Painted aluminum (ribbed or with standing seams) Galvanized or painted galvanized steel (ribbed or with standing seams) • Eaves shall be constructed of wood framing with fascia boards of wood or metal clad wood • Gutters may be used, and shall be made of painted aluminum or galvanized steel • Dormers shall conform to the wall and roof material requirements as indicated above
Configuration	• No more than one material shall be used for walls, except the walls of a porch enclosure may be of another allowable material different from that of the main building walls	Principal building roofs shall conform to the following: • Gables fronting the street shall be symmetrical, pitched between 6:12 and 12:12 • Gables facing the side may be asymmetrical, pitched between 3:12 and 12:12 • Hip roofs shall be pitched between 4:12 and 8:12 • Flat roofs shall be pitched no less than ¼:12, and enclosed by a parapet wall no less than 42" (1m) in height Dormers shall conform to the following: • Dormers fronting the street shall be no wider than 35% of the building width, and centered horizontally within the roof of the building, with its front wall set flush to, or set back from, the main building walls • Dormers facing the side of the house shall be no wider than 50% of the building length, with its front wall set flush to, or set back from, the building wall below
Details	• Horizontal siding (wood or fiber cement) shall have a vertical exposure of 4" (100mm) to 6" (150mm) • Wood trim shall be used at outside corners and around openings in walls that are clad in siding. Trim shall be 4" (100mm) to 6" (150mm) in width, and painted • Wood board trim is encouraged at the top and bottom of walls that are clad in siding, and required at the top of brick walls • All siding and trim shall be painted • Bricks shall be of the common modular size (2-1/4"x3-5/8"x7-5/8" [57mmx92mmx193mm], of colors selected for their history of durability in the local region, and laid in running bond pattern • Bricks shall be installed to allow for proper ventilation (using an airspace between the brick and the wood framing) and drainage (using weep holes) of the unexposed surface • See sheet no. 3.09 for suggested colors	• Overhanging eaves shall be terminated with continuous wood fascia boards, and boxed-in, or covered with horizontal soffits, of either wood or vinyl • Overhangs shall be between 6" (150mm) and 12" (300mm), except in the case of gable roofs, where the overhang may be reduced to 4" (100mm) at the eaves • Owners of gable-front homes with existing decorative barge boards are highly encouraged to repair and maintain these valuable features
Illustrations		

Figure 6.33: Architectural guidelines for cladding and roofs

units, the design strategy was to convert them back to single-family residences (Figure 6.34). The valuable architectural features of these houses, such as window trim, porch columns, and railings, were considered in the design and proposed for repair and rehabilitation to ensure that the conversion would respect their original character. The porch, windows, and door proportions as well as details were kept the same for the house at 310. The deteriorating cladding was replaced with wood siding, and the existing windows were replaced with wood or vinyl windows of the same dimensions and style. The front door was replaced with a door of the same dimensions. The addition in the rear, deemed structurally unsound, was demolished and replaced with a large deck that could later be enclosed if desired. Interior characteristics—the arches and the simple layout plan—were also retained. The two new bedrooms of the upper floor were located in the area formerly occupied by the upper-unit living room, dining room, and kitchen.

The proportions of the windows, the layout plan, and many interior details were also incorporated into the design for the house at 312. As with 310, the siding, windows, and front door were replaced. The porch columns, skirting, and railing were also changed. To alleviate the barren appearance in the front, a tree was planted in the lawn. Inside, repairs were made to the substandard bathroom areas, and the ground floor was redesigned to allow for larger living and dining areas, while the upper floor was redesigned to provide three, instead of the existing five, bedrooms.

The house at 210 McConnell was also vacant, while all the other homes on the same side of the block were occupied. The dual intention of this rehabilitation project was to reconvert the duplex at 210 back into a single-family dwelling with three different renovation options, and to improve the other building exteriors from 210 to 230 and to recover the traditional urban language (Figure 6.35). Several modifications to 210 had been made over the years, many of them ill-advised: the single-family house was divided into two units, an interior layout was inefficiently interconnected, and the interior stairs were removed and replaced by an exterior stair tacked onto a back addition that did not allow proper ventilation and light into the back rooms. Also, the front porch was enclosed in a manner that damaged the traditional appearance, the vinyl cladding hid the original character of the house, and the Polyvinyl Chloride (PVC) windows were not energy-efficient. To remedy these problems, the traditional façade language of the house was recovered by re-establishing the integrity of the original open porch; wood was used to replace the materials of the siding, windows, doors, and front porch; the back porch was demolished; and the landscaping was improved to add vegetation to the barren yards.

Existing ground floor plans

Restored ground floor plans

Existing upper floor plans

Restored upper floor plans

312   310
Existing front elevations

312   310
Restored front elevations

Figure 6.34: Rehabilitation of the homes on 310 and 312 Prince Arthur Street

237

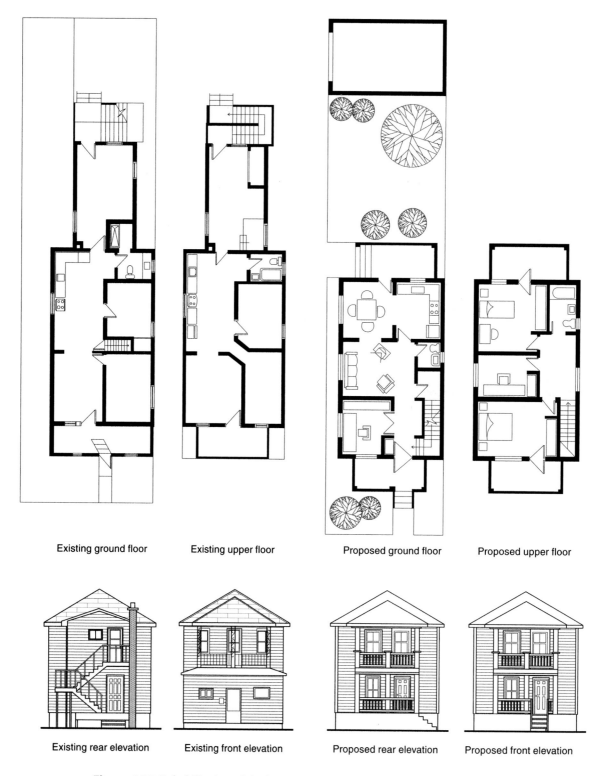

Existing ground floor   Existing upper floor   Proposed ground floor   Proposed upper floor

Existing rear elevation   Existing front elevation   Proposed rear elevation   Proposed front elevation

Figure 6.35: Rehabilitation of the home on 210 McConnell Street

The three interior options included plans for a home office in the rear that could be turned into a bachelor apartment by removing the door connecting the kitchen and office, the reintroduction of an interior stairway, and a home office at the front of the house. All three options were based on household scenarios that included a mother, father, and one or two children. To reduce construction costs, the positioning of the kitchen was retained in the rear to save on plumbing work, the second-floor bathroom was also not moved, the back doors were re-used, and the roof was repaired but not replaced. With regard to the urban design of the block, the plan was to recover the traditional shapes, styles, and colors on the façades and porches; plant vegetation in the front yards; replace vinyl and aluminum siding with wood; and replace windows and doors that did not match the traditional façade of the other structures on the street.

Assessing the Process

The urban and architectural renewal of Le Village offers several important lessons on community renewal along sustainable guidelines. One of the basic rules was the attempt to chart a course of *least negative impact.* By consulting and involving citizens and creating a grassroots process, gentrification, with low-income renters replaced by a higher-income population, was avoided.

Maintaining the original urban and architectural character of Le Village had a similar objective. Guidelines suggested by the design team were meant to limit the negative effects that a non-sensitive intervention would have on the area's appearance. By undertaking meticulous documentation, new rules and measures were taken to weave old and new. By paying attention to the 3 Rs—reduce, reuse, recycle—the negative environmental effects were minimized. More attention was therefore paid to renovation rather than demolition.

Rehabilitating physical aspects of a community must occur in parallel with other considerations when creating a *self-sustaining process.* Financial assistance provided to renovators has led to economic prosperity. Jobs have been created and local businesses are prospering. The building of new dwellings also helped transfer people from rental to ownership tenure. It helped keep residents in Le Village and infused much needed "new blood" into the older pool of residents, as young homeowners contribute to a continuous renewal process of the place. By converting the abandoned textile mill buildings to affordable units, future building activity and attraction of new residents is guaranteed.

By viewing the renewal process comprehensively and dealing with social as well as physical issues, a contribution to *supporting relations* between all aspects was made. Improving school attendance rates and encouraging local citizens to pursue higher education will result in higher incomes and the strengthening of the economic foundation of the community. It is likely that citizens with means will contribute to maintenance and improvement of homes. Residents also stand a greater chance of becoming homeowners. Work with local officials on improving safety and security of residents led to improving community pride and elimination of a poor public image.

Seeing future evolution beyond the present rehabilitation will thrust Le Village into future prosperity and a sound lifecycle approach. By renovating the homes to higher building standards and installing proper maintenance traditions, energy consumption can be reduced and the homes will last longer. A key lesson to learn from the Le Village renewal is that communities need to be designed for change, and when deterioration occurs, houses should be retooled rather than demolished.

Implementing Sustainability

Designing sustainable communities is a holistic process that regards the life of communities and homes from cradle to grave. Tasks are viewed as a continuous chain of events, from site selection to retrofitting residences as needs change and new technology requires. Another critical planning issue is the need to balance social, environmental, and economic aspects. Since developments in many countries are initiated and driven by a profit-motivated private sector, proposing ideas that ignore the priorities of the developer are destined to fail.

This chapter provides a discussion of the practical aspects of implementing sustainability. It covers general criteria for acceptance of new design methods, describes common standards and certification methods for identifying sustainable projects, and illustrates two projects that follow sustainable principles.

Ensuring Sustainable Solutions

The application of sustainable principles in residential development presents several challenges because the process often involves compromise between environmental/sustainable aspects, costs, and aesthetic considerations. Some tasks or products designed to improve a building's environmental quality may either be more expensive or require a change of traditional installation or construction procedures. The basic question is this: "How green can a project be before it becomes either unacceptable or unaffordable to the builder and/or the consumer?"

The design of a green housing development must consider factors other than environmental concerns. These include issues related to practicality and cost. Furthermore, the design of a sustainable residential development should not be restricted to preserving the natural outdoor environment. The provision of safe and healthy interiors, particularly in cold climates where residents spend much time indoors, also needs to be regarded.

In addition to consideration of the environment, the consumer's ability to afford and willingness to buy a product, and the builder's ability to make necessary changes without jeopardizing operations, are critical issues that must be investigated. When building a "green" project, the most common concerns of sustainable housing must be weighed against practicality, marketability, quality, and cost.

Practicality

An important requirement in sustainable developments is ensuring that a product or method does not disrupt the builder's operational efficiency. The organizational structures that characterize the construction industry are complex. In the housing sector, the building process has evolved into a concise, unique operation that has been streamlined over the years. The result is a highly efficient system with a complicated order and time schedule (Figure 7.1). Any major change or innovation that severely interferes with this process runs a high risk of being rejected. A traditional construction process consists of a sequence of tasks; each task affects the performance of the next, and each worker's task affects the tasks of another worker. Innovative changes may occur within the scope of a task, but acceptance of such changes will be problematic if they involve more than one type of trade, or if the change in the work accomplished by one tradesman affects the work of another tradesman. In other words, if a change creates more work for everyone, it translates to more money, more time, and more skill to implement, and is therefore likely to be unacceptable.

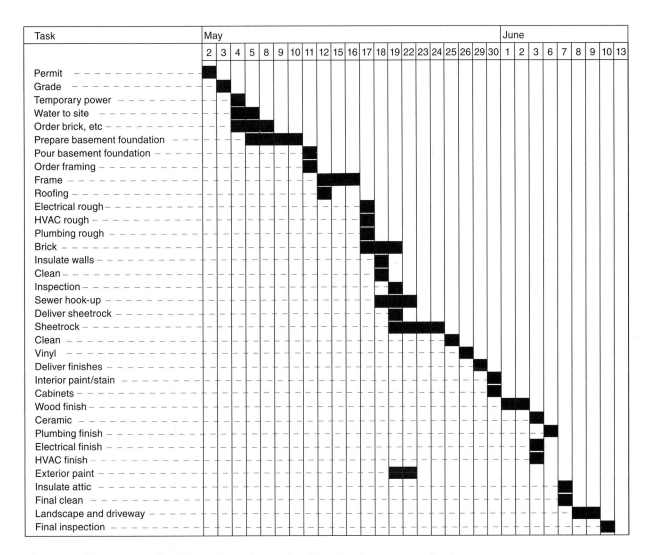

Figure 7.1: The process of building a home has evolved into a unique system of tasks.

If you divide a house into a hierarchical arrangement of systems (envelope), subsystems (walls), components (windows), and materials (glass), you'll realize that the larger the element, the greater the operational and physical interdependence exists among the levels of hierarchy. Therefore, the effect of changing an element lower in the hierarchy—window glass, for example—has less effect on other aspects of construction than changing an element higher up in the hierarchy—such as a wall or roofing system. Changes in higher level systems stand a better chance of being accepted if they come as a complete package that includes both material and labor, and therefore do not rely on the willingness or ability of everyone involved to accept the change. The practicality of the design is, therefore, critical. Any proposed change should not require extensive retraining of staff; nor should it significantly increase construction time. Products that require special tools and/or skills merit particular consideration before being approved for a project (Friedman, 1989).

Marketability

The purchase of a home represents the largest investment a person is likely to make in a lifetime. The decision to buy a particular house is influenced by a variety of factors, including culture, personal taste, cost, and popular trend. For many buyers, the potential resale value of the home is also of major concern, and, therefore, so is the house's mass appeal. The home builder must therefore consider the preferences and aspirations of any speculative home buyers. An innovative product may be rejected by a buyer who believes his or her aspirations will be compromised, even though the builder may be personally convinced that the innovative product itself is superior.

Several aspects contribute to a product's marketability, including cost, appearance, and quality. The degree to which the building systems, materials, and components can influence these requirements will vary from product to product. Because a dwelling's attractiveness is largely a function of personal taste, the builder's ability to offer a range of options to a prospective buyer is an important marketing tool. The ease with which a dwelling can be adapted to meet particular demands is therefore a critical factor in the decision to use a method or product that advances environmental concerns.

During occupancy, the ability of the buyers to customize their dwellings, be it through modification or decoration, is a primary consideration. Any method that will inhibit or restrict this freedom will be interpreted as a deficiency, regardless of any technical advantage that may be gained. For example, in a survey of 107 builders and architects conducted by the Structural Insulated Panel Association, the most commonly cited reason why respondents might not use structural insulated panels was concern about their design limitations, even though the panels are thermally and structurally efficient when used (Winter, 1991). The study suggests that new, untried products are not considered trustworthy. Figure 7.2 illustrates the adoption of the innovation process. Only 2.5% of all builders will try new products or technologies without prior experience. If they are proven successful, the rest of the industry will follow suit (Rogers, 1983).

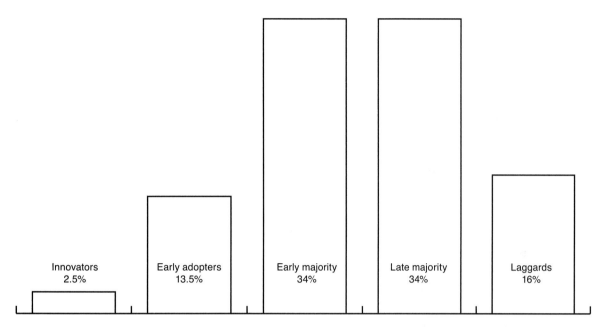

| Innovators 2.5% | Early adopters 13.5% | Early majority 34% | Late majority 34% | Laggards 16% |

Figure 7.2: According to the National Association of Home Building, only 2.5 percent of all builders will be willing to assume a risk by selecting an untried product.

Quality, Durability, and Maintenance

The fact that a product is new or innovative does not translate into an increase in sales volume, unless the product is perceived by the consumer as having a superior quality-price ratio (Figure 7.3). When building materials are subjected to lifecycle analysis, two essential considerations are how long the product or material can be expected to last, and how much effort is required to keep it in operational condition. The durability and maintenance requirements of a building material can have a substantial effect on the environment and will determine the actual value of the element. Less durable materials require frequent replacement, which translates to higher cost. Untreated materials based on natural, renewable resources may require more energy and harmful maintenance products to stay useful and acceptable in appearance. The environmental benefits associated with a particular product may lose their significance if the product has only one-half or one-third the useful lifespan of an alternative product. Energy consumption, waste generation, resource depletion, or ecosystem alterations associated with a particular quantity of material must be multiplied by an appropriate factor if it is to be compared with more durable alternatives.

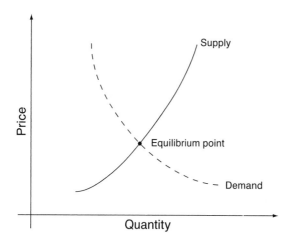

Figure 7.3: Increased demand leads to economy of scale, which moves a new, innovative product into the mainstream.

In addition to economic and environmental variables, a more practical reason exists for considering product durability. If a product/material is perceived by the buyer as being inferior in quality compared to the standard, its marketable value decreases and it stands a risk of being rejected by builders. Furthermore, a less durable product may represent a risk for the builder, who, in most countries, assumes responsibility for any defects arising from construction for the first five years after completion. The costs of any repairs or additional maintenance must be factored into the cost equation, since such repairs not only affect the builder's return on investment, but also his or her reputation.

The complexity of maintenance required is another consideration. Mechanical systems that require special skill to operate and maintain, for instance, may not be considered feasible by builders. The objective is to use environmentally sound materials without unnecessarily burdening the builder and the consumer.

Cost

For obvious reasons, cost is one of the most important factors in the sale of a home, particularly for first-time buyers. Both the unit's selling price and heating costs should be kept within reasonable limits. Interviews conducted by the author with real estate agents, builders, and suppliers concerning marketing trends revealed a consensus that all are concerned with energy efficiency, not in terms of conservation, but in terms of cost savings. The addition of insulation to reduce heat loss and, consequently, operating costs associated with heating requirements was identified as the primary marketable component in sustainable developments. The consumer, however, was found to be generally unaware of the energy and environmental costs involved in the construction of a house.

It is not certain how much more the average consumer would be willing to pay for an environmentally sound housing alternative. The extent to which a unit's cost could be increased and remain marketable would have to be traced back to reasons why an average consumer would prefer to own rather than rent. Because of limited funding, particularly for buyers with growing families, those buying a first or second home would likely prefer to pay for functional amenities rather than environmentally sound materials. Unlike household products, for which the decision to purchase a more "green" product over another might incur a fairly modest cost, an increase in the purchase price of a home due to its environmental soundness can make the difference between a consumer's owning and renting. Even if the added expense is due to some energy-saving product or amenity that would decrease operating costs in the long run, the expected occupancy period may not justify technologies that would pay for themselves in more than three to five years. No matter what the estimated annual savings, a substantially higher purchase price might put the home out of the consumer's price range altogether (Figure 7.4).

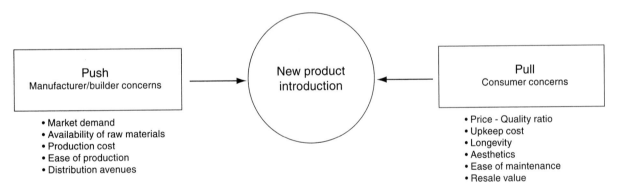

Figure 7.4: Factors other than environmental considerations can influence the introduction and acceptance of a product.

From Cradle to Grave

The development of environmentally sound housing involves a process that includes site planning, design, and construction, among other considerations. In examining the environmental impacts of a residential project and comparing alternatives, the entire lifecycle of the project should be taken into account, from the acquisition of raw materials, through production packaging, delivery, construction use, and disposal. At every stage of the process, resources are consumed and waste is generated. The efficiency with which natural resources, including energy, are used and the manner in which the waste is treated or disposed of will determine the overall environmental impact of the project.

For obvious reasons, not all the environmental aspects of construction can be solved in an absolute sense. They can be minimized, but they cannot be eliminated. The selection of materials based on lifecycle analysis often involves some compromise. The process is aimed at optimizing cost, durability, and sustainability. What may appear to be an environmentally sound product in one respect, for example, may exhibit compromising qualities in another. In the absence of reliable, quantitative data, many decisions are based on qualitative assessment, some of which are objective. Although lifecycle analysis of building alternatives is a complex process, a basic knowledge of what makes up a building product and how it is manufactured can be useful in selecting alternatives to minimize the environmental impact of building materials.

Acquisition of Raw Materials

The mining, harvesting, or extraction of raw materials to manufacture a building product may deplete existing natural resources or cause damage to land, water, air, and wildlife habitat. The sustainable builder must consider whether the resource is renewable or recyclable, and whether or not its use is detrimental to humans and/or animals and their habitats. Improper disposal of contaminated solid, liquid, or gaseous waste that is produced in the acquisition of raw materials can pollute the environment, while extensive mining and harvesting operations can disturb natural ecosystem cycles.

Processing/Manufacture

The processing and fabrication of materials and components requires energy and generates waste. Some manufacturing processes recover waste products, which are either reworked into the process or sold to other manufacturing industries. Contaminated waste may be treated prior to disposal or destroyed by incineration. When no recyclable use exists for a hazardous material, strictly regulated disposal procedures may reduce potential harm to the environment.

Packaging/Distribution

The type and amount of packaging used for a product and the energy required to distribute it to its point of use are important environmental considerations. In the construction of an average two-story house, up to 14 percent of the total waste volume is typically cardboard and other packaging (REIC Ltd. and Associates, 1991). The ability to recover, reuse, or recycle these containers can have a considerable impact on the solid waste stream. Availability of local raw materials and building products is also of concern. Imported products may be environmentally sound in many respects, but they may require more natural resources to transport them to their final destinations.

Construction/Assembly

Construction is responsible for some 16 percent of the total solid waste production, and approximately 20 percent of this comes from new homes. Some 80 percent of this waste ends up in a landfill, much of which could be avoided. A study conducted during a period of high building activity found that construction of an average home produced 2.5 tons of waste, and 20 tons in cases where demolition is required (REIC). Approximately 25 percent of the waste is dimensional lumber, and another 15 percent is attributed to manufactured wood products. The situation is not only wasteful in terms of embodied energy, but it also contributes to the problem of waste disposal. Waste disposal in landfills has led to a serious crisis, with a growing problem of toxic release, resulting in contaminated soils and groundwater.

Occupancy

Many of the factors to be considered in the occupancy phase of a building's lifecycle are dependent on the living habits of the occupants. The consumption of energy, for instance, can be controlled through energy-efficient envelopes and heating systems. For water, the provision of appropriate facilities through design can encourage more environmentally sound behaviors. If recycling and composting facilities are made available, less wasteful habits will likely result. Similarly, the promotion of energy-efficient appliances and lights, which are often beyond the builder's responsibility, can significantly reduce energy consumption. Consumer knowledge of the existence and availability of such amenities can be helpful in promoting environmentally sound living habits.

Demolition/Renovation

The fate of building materials when a house is partially or fully demolished is an important environmental concern. At the final stage of their lifecycle, some building materials can be reused for similar applications or recycled as raw materials for manufacturing other products. Other used materials have no useful purpose and must be discarded in landfills or incinerated. Disposal of concrete demolition debris accounts for approximately 67 percent by weight and 53 percent by volume of all demolition debris in North America according to the American Institute of Architects (1992a).

Certifications of Sustainable Practices

In recent decades, governments, construction associations, and non-governmental organizations around the world have set standards for sustainable building practices. In addition to national building codes, which established minimum requirements for energy performance, for example, the new offerings set stricter criteria that raised the bar to a higher efficiency level. These standards act as accreditation systems that qualify builders and projects according to the scope of their environmental and sustainable pursuits. Two such systems will be elaborated here: Leadership in Energy and Environmental Design (LEED) set by the U.S. Green Building Council (USGBC), and R-2000, which was founded by the Canadian Department of Energy, Mines and Resources (EMR) in collaboration with Canadian Home Builders' Association (CHBA).

Leadership in Energy and Environmental Design

Created by the USGBC and later adapted for Canada by the Canada Green Building Council, LEED is a rating system that recognizes environmental building design practice. According to the USGBC Web site, the system was created to be used as a tool by architects, engineers, and builders who want to develop sustainable design strategies. Various LEED standards define requirements for each sector of construction. LEED-NC for new commercial construction and major renovation projects is the most commonly used system; however, standards have been developed for Existing Building Operations, Commercial Interior Projects, Core and Shell Projects, and Homes and Neighborhood Development.

The LEED standard is divided into several categories with prerequisites and additional credits. Points are accumulated for each satisfied requirement, and certification is provided once a minimum specified number of points are acquired. Depending on how many points the building is awarded, it can be rated as LEED Platinum, Gold, Silver, or Certified.

LEED-ND: Neighborhood Development

LEED for Neighborhood Development (LEED-ND) is one of the newest standards. Still under development by the USGBC in conjunction with the Congress for New Urbanism (CNU) and the Natural Resources Defense Council (NRDC), LEED-ND seeks to create environmentally responsible communities that protect and enhance overall health, natural environment, and quality of life. Philosophies of *new urbanism* are employed, stressing a reduction of reliance on cars and use of alternative means of transportation, such as public transit, cycling, and walking. In addition to new urbanist city planning, LEED-ND seeks to aid in the design of neighborhoods that promote efficient use of energy and water (USGBC, 2007b).

The system functions with prerequisites in each category and points allotted for supplemental requirements that are satisfied. Categories include Location Efficiency; Environmental Preservation; Complete, Compact, and Connected Neighborhoods; and Resource Efficiency (Figure 7.5). With a total of 114 available points, a neighborhood will be considered Certified if points in the range of 46 to 56 are attained, Silver between 57 and 67 points, Gold if it accumulates 68 to 90 points, and Platinum if between 91 and 114 points are granted (USGBC, 2007c).

Location Efficiency

The Location Efficiency category examines the relationship between a proposed site and its surroundings. The first prerequisite requires access to efficient modes of transportation that promote pedestrian activity and use of public transit. Neighborhoods should be well-connected to reduce reliance on cars. The second prerequisite is proximity to existing water and stormwater necessary to conserve resources required for new infrastructure. Additional points are allotted for projects that plan to restore contaminated sties, or projects that situate themselves within existing communities. Further emphasis is placed on responsible transportation by granting points for communities located on sites with outstanding transit development, as well as to communities that offer vehicle- or bicycle-sharing facilities and programs. To limit the effects of transportation even more, communities are encouraged to offer mixed land use with diverse job opportunities, as well as children's schools and daycares, enabling residents to work, shop, and attend school close to home. Parks, plazas, and other public green spaces are also encouraged to promote community interaction.

Environmental Preservation

The Environmental Preservation section includes 13 points forming 11 percent of the document. Several prerequisites stipulate that public parkland and farmland must be preserved, the siting of the project may not be such that it poses a threat to animals on the endangered species list and does not threaten the presence of existing bodies of water or wetlands, and finally that an erosion and sedimentation control plan be drafted to protect existing soil, bodies of water, and air. The main goal of this category is to minimize disturbance on the project site. Ideally, the project should be located on a previously developed site; however, if this is not possible, impact on the existing habitat can be minimized by preserving the use of

Title	Points	Percentage of Total
Location Efficiency (2 prerequisites / 7 credits / 28 points / 25% of total points)		
Prerequisite: Transportation Efficiency	-	-
Prerequisite: Water and Stormwater Infrastructure Efficiency	-	-
Credit: Contaminated Brownfields Redevelopment	4	3.5%
Credit: High Cost Contaminated Brownfields Redevelopment	1	0.9%
Credit: Adjacent, Infill, or Redevelopment Site	3 to 10	8.8%
Credit: Reduced Automobile Dependence	2 to 6	5.3%
Credit: Contribution to Jobs-Housing Balance	4	3.5%
Credit: School Proximity	1	0.9%
Credit: Access to Public Space	2	1.8%
Environmental Preservation (5 prerequisites / 11 credits / 13 points / 11% of total points)		
Prerequisite: Imperiled Species and Ecological Communities	-	-
Prerequisite: Parkland Preservation	-	-
Prerequisite: Wetland & Water Body Protection	-	-
Prerequisite: Farmland Preservation	-	-
Prerequisite: Erosion & Sedimentation Control	-	-
Credit: Support Off-Site Land Conservation	2	1.8%
Credit: Site Design for Habitat or Wetlands Conservation	1	0.9%
Credit: Restoration of Habitat or Wetlands	1	0.9%
Credit: Conservation Management of Habitat or Wetlands	1	0.9%
Credit: Steep Slope Preservation	1	0.9%
Credit: Minimize Site Disturbance During Construction	1	0.9%
Credit: Minimize Site Disturbance Through Site Design	1	0.9%
Credit: Maintain Stormwater Runoff Rates	1	0.9%
Credit: Reduce Stormwater Runoff Rates	1	0.9%
Credit: Stormwater Treatment	2	1.8%
Credit: Outdoor Hazardous Waste Pollution Prevention	1	0.9%
Compact, Complete, & Connected Neighborhoods (3 prereq / 22 credits / 42 points / 37% of total points)		
Prerequisite: Open Community	-	-
Prerequisite: Compact Development	-	-
Prerequisite: Diversity of Uses	-	-
Credit: Compact Development	1 to 5	4.4%
Credit: Transit-Oriented Compactness	1	0.9%
Credit: Diversity of Uses	1 to 3	2.6%
Credit: Housing Diversity	4	3.5%
Credit: Affordable Rental Housing	1 to 2	1.8%
Credit: Affordable For-Sale Housing	1 to 2	1.8%
Credit: Reduced Parking Footprint	2	1.8%
Credit: Community Outreach and Involvement	1	0.9%
Credit: Block Perimeter	1 to 4	3.5%
Credit: Locating Buildings to Shape Walkable Streets	1	0.9%
Credit: Designing Building Access to Shape Walkable Streets	1	0.9%
Credit: Designing Buildings to Shape Walkable Streets	1	0.9%
Credit: Comprehensively Designed Walkable Streets	2	1.8%
Credit: Street Network	1	0.9%
Credit: Pedestrian Network	1	0.9%
Credit: Maximize Pedestrian Experience	1	0.9%
Credit: Superior Pedestrian Experience	1 to 2	1.8%
Credit: Applying Regional Precedents in Urbanism and Architecture	1	0.9%
Credit: Transit Subsidy	3	2.6%
Credit: Transit Amenities	1	0.9%
Credit: Access to Nearby Communities	1	0.9%
Credit: Adaptive Reuse of Historic Buildings	1 to 2	1.8%
Resource Efficiency (0 prerequisites / 17 credits / 25 points / 22% of total points)		
Credit: Certified Green Building	1 to 5	4.4%
Credit: Energy Efficiency in Buildings	1 to 3	2.6%
Credit: Water Efficiency in Buildings	1 to 2	1.8%
Credit: Heat Island Reduction	1	0.9%
Credit: Infrastructure Energy Efficiency	1	0.9%
Credit: On-Site Power Generation	1	0.9%
Credit: On-Site Renewable Energy Sources	1	0.9%
Credit: Efficient Irrigation	1	0.9%
Credit: Graywater & Stormwater Reuse	2	1.8%
Credit: Wastewater Management	1	0.9%
Credit: Reuse of Materials	1	0.9%
Credit: Recycled Content	1	0.9%
Credit: Regionally Provided Materials	1	0.9%
Credit: Construction Waste Management	1	0.9%
Credit: Comprehensive Waste Management	1	0.9%
Credit: Light Pollution Reduction	1	0.9%
Credit: Contaminant Reduction in Brownfields Remediation	1	0.9%
Other (0 prerequisites / 2 credits / 6 points / 5% of total points)		
Anticipated Accredited Professional Innovation Credit(s)	1 to 2	1.8%
Anticipated Innovation Credit(s)	1 to 4	3.5%
TOTAL	114	100%

Figure 7.5: Evaluation criteria for a LEED neighborhood development

native vegetation and by maintaining or reducing stormwater runoff rates. On-site stormwater treatment is encouraged to minimize the amount of pollutants that will eventually end up in bodies of water.

Complete, Compact, and Connected Neighborhoods

The most important category in LEED-ND is Complete, Compact, and Connected Neighborhoods, accounting for almost 40 percent of possible points. The category borrows from new urbanist principles and seeks to create dense communities with full sets of infrastructure that are easily accessible to neighboring communities. Projects must foster a sense of place, conserve land by promoting density, be transportation efficient and promote pedestrian movement, and attract diverse uses.

Credits can be accumulated for a variety of efforts. Diversity in building use and in housing type is encouraged to attract citizens from a range of economic levels and age groups. The footprint of outdoor parking should be reduced and the area between the front façade of a building and the street should be limited to one row of either parallel, perpendicular, or angled parking.

Block design and building access are important considerations. Building design can promote walkability by providing pedestrians with safer and more pleasant streetscapes. Points are awarded, for example, to buildings with fenestrated ground levels that promote safe walking. Safe travel for cyclists and pedestrians should be provided with frequent intersections and continuous sidewalks. On-street parking can include a buffer zone of trees between sidewalks and vehicles. And, finally, to enhance pedestrian experience, ground floor retail spaces in commercial or mixed-use buildings can be offered.

This category also encouraged design that reflects local conditions in material use, scale, local climate such as solar orientation, and consideration of prevailing wind patterns. Points are also awarded if existing historic buildings are adapted and/or rehabilitated rather than demolished.

Resource Efficiency

The Resource Efficiency category makes up 22 percent of the possible LEED points. The category recognizes green initiatives at the level of individual buildings as well as at the community level. Projects that plan to incorporate LEED-certified green buildings or other eco-friendly buildings that provide energy and/or water efficiency can also accumulate points. Plans should include designs that reduce urban heat effects by providing shade over paved surfaces, use of light-colored materials, placing parking underground, and/or providing green roofs. Infrastructure, such as street and traffic lights, should be energy-efficient, and additional points can be allotted where on-site power generation or renewable energy sources are installed. The use of native plants, high-efficiency irrigation systems, rainwater collection, and graywater systems can be implemented to reduce irrigation requirements by 50 percent compared to conventional means. Efficient use of materials is rewarded where reused, recycled, and/or local materials are used. Decontamination or remediation of contaminated or brownfield sites is also encouraged.

LEED for Homes

LEED for Homes (LEED-H) was developed to enable the home building industry to move toward sustainable construction. Initially, the standard focused on construction of new single-family homes but eventually expanded to include low-rise multifamily housing. Categories and credits were adapted to the residential sphere and concern construction, design, and site aspects specific to the house (USGBC, 2007b).

Location and Linkages

The Location and Linkages category recommends that the home be sited in a community that fulfills requirements similar to those of a LEED neighborhood. As in LEED-ND, the location should be served by existing or adjacent infrastructure, developments should be compact and efficient, and the community should be equipped with services such as banks, convenience stores, post offices, pharmacies, and schools to encourage walking.

Sustainable Sites

As with the Sustainable Sites category for new construction, the goal is responsible site development that reduces the site's ecological impacts as well as its effects on the environment as a whole. Landscape features that reduce the need for irrigation and synthetic chemicals should be used, and paved areas such as sidewalks, driveways, and patios should be shaded with trees and shrubs to reduce the effect of urban heat islands.

Water Efficiency

To reduce unnecessary consumption of potable water, rainwater collection and graywater reuse are recommended, and where the need for irrigation is necessary, highly efficient systems are a must. In terms of indoor water use, low-flow faucets and showerheads are recommended as are dual-flush toilets.

Indoor Environmental Quality

For desired indoor air quality, LEED-H recommends the use of the Energy Star Indoor Air Package, which includes ventilation systems, source control, and air removal. Other equivalent systems may also be used to regulate indoor humidity levels, air distribution, and air filtering. The USGBC also offers recommendations for local exhaust systems for kitchens and bathrooms.

Materials and Resources

The Materials and Resources section of LEED-H specifies minimization of construction materials and the use of recycled and native materials and environmentally preferable products. However, it goes a step further by providing guidelines for appropriate sizing for homes. Based on the number of bedrooms, usually a good indicator of the number of residents in a home, square footage recommendations are provided for the home's floor area.

Energy and Atmosphere

In the Energy and Atmosphere section, once again, the Energy Star package is recommended. The house should be well insulated, with efficient windows, minimal air leakage from ducts, highly efficient space heating and cooling, and an efficient water heating and distribution system. Outdoor lighting fixtures should have motion sensors to minimize use, and indoor lighting as well as appliances should be very efficient. Installation of renewable energy sources such as wind generators and photovoltaic panels is encouraged, and points are allocated for each 10 percent of annual electrical load met by the system. The use of HCFC refrigerants, usually emitted from air conditioning systems and are large contributors to ozone depletion, should be either eliminated or minimized.

Homeowner Awareness

Homeowners should receive a user manual and a 60-minute walk-through of their new home to provide them with the necessary information for proper operation. For the design of a green home to be effective, its features must be used correctly and efficiently. Therefore, the education of residents is an important factor.

R-2000

The R-2000 Program provides technical information to the industry as well as financial and marketing assistance to participating builders. The program is voluntary and open to different levels of involvement. Builders wanting to participate fully are offered a complete package of services including training, certification, and marketing. Alternatively, builders can familiarize themselves with the technology to improve the quality and energy efficiency of their homes.

Although certain planning options, construction methods, and building materials for R-2000 homes are suggested, the program is essentially based on a performance standard. The standard is in the form of an energy budget adjusted for house size and climate, and a set of technical criteria. Registered builders may meet the energy budget using designs and materials of their choice, suited to local conditions and market preferences. During construction, the home is inspected and tested to verify that it meets the design criteria, and an identification sticker and certificate are issued. Some of the program's principles are listed here (CHBA, 1989):

- **Energy Budget** The total energy budget from an R-2000 home is derived from an equation that provides a specified figure for non-space heating energy requirements and for building envelope losses per square foot or meter. The calculation allows for variations in climate (degree days) and house size, expressed in equivalent floor area (the heated volume of the house, including basement, divided by 2.5).

- **Technical Requirements**
  - *Air leakage* 1.5 air changes per hour at 50PA maximum.
  - *Ventilation* Continuous ventilation at a rate of 10 cfm (5 liters/second) for each room, plus 20 cfm (10 liters/second) for the master bedroom and basement. Exhaust capabilities must be supplied in the kitchen and bathroom.
  - *Replacement air* Must be provided for all appliances that exhaust air from the home, such as clothes dryers, power-ventilated hoods, and central vacuum systems.
  - *Combustion equipment* Specific requirements for gas or propane, oil-fired, and solid fuel-fired appliances.
  - *Windows* Double-glazed with 1/2 inch (12 mm) air space minimum.
  - *Walls* Insulated at R20 (3.5 RSI) minimum.
  - *Water heaters* Insulated at R10 (1.75 RSI); "heat trap" or insulation for the first 9.8 feet (3 m) of pipe; temperature normally set at 120°F (50°C) maximum.
  - *Appliances* Within the upper 35 percent of the EnerGuide rating (EMR).

Energy-Efficiency, Durability, and Occupant Comfort

The program also considers the whole house and accounts for how the various building systems, subsystems, and components—including the people using it—

interact and perform. It acknowledges the close relationship between the external environment, the building's envelope, and the building's mechanical systems. It also accounts for the effects of interior finishes, furnishings, lighting, and appliances on the house's total energy performance. It includes the migration of heat, moisture, air, sound, and radiation between the exterior and interior environment, and it provides recommendations for virtually every design and construction aspect, from site planning to envelope detailing. By concentrating on performance rather than construction specifications, the program ensures that the home is assembled using quality craftsmanship. By adopting an integrative approach to building construction, it helps builders provide a product that is not only more energy-efficient, but also more durable, comfortable, and healthy for occupants.

Principles

R-2000 technology addresses three general areas of building design and construction. The first deals with planning principles at the site, lot, and unit level. The use of proper landscaping and unit orientation helps reduce exposure to wind and snow, while attention to floor layout ensures that the appropriate spaces benefit from solar exposure. Solar heat gain is controlled through size and placement of window units and shading devices to reduce heating costs and prevent heat gains from reaching uncomfortable levels.

The second area deals with the design, detailing, and construction of the building envelope. Higher insulation standards, air-tight construction, and high-performance windows ensure that heat loss is minimized and that pollutants are not carried into the house. With proper detailing, water vapor and air migration are controlled to avoid penetration and condensation, which could rapidly deteriorate the building.

Finally, the use of efficient mechanical systems ensures that space conditioning, ventilation, and water heating requirements are fulfilled with minimal amounts of energy. Due to the airtight envelope, ventilation is given special attention, requiring that a constant and sufficient supply of fresh air is distributed to every room.

Potential for Improvement

R-2000 houses built to performance standards consume half of the energy of a typical house built in the 1980s and a quarter of the energy of post–World War II–built houses. While the cost of building such homes can vary widely depending on builder and location, significant reductions in heat loss can be achieved with relatively minor investment by simply applying some of the practices recommended by R-2000. With attention paid to frame detailing and stud spacing, for

257

instance, energy consumption related to heat loss can be reduced by as much as 10 percent. Replacing the exterior sheathing material with rigid board insulation can save an additional 8 percent, and the use of energy-efficient windows could save 15 percent of total energy costs.

Although attractive savings can be achieved by addressing individual components, energy efficiency can be applied successfully only through a systems approach, whereby the performance of all building systems, subsystems, and components are carefully considered. The high interdependence between heating and ventilation systems and the building envelope's performance require that all aspects of the building's interior environment and physical construction be considered. Misapplied R-2000 building technology can otherwise result in problems such as poor indoor air quality and moisture damage.

Building Envelope Alternatives

One of the most basic considerations in the design and construction of R-2000 energy-efficient housing is the amount of heat loss that occurs through the building envelope. While this heat loss could be reduced by adding insulation, the design and construction of an energy-efficient envelope involves much more.

In addition to providing structural support for the building, the basement, walls, and roof must perform several functions at once and be able to resist deterioration. As a basic form of shelter, the envelope must prevent the entry of water, snow, and ice that are propelled by wind, air, and hydrostatic pressures, as in the case with basement walls. Also, exterior noise and air pollutants need to be kept out, and vapor carried in the warm interior air must be kept in. Convective, radiative, and conductive heat flow must be minimized in both directions to reduce energy losses through convective currents, air space, and materials.

While it is beyond the scope of this section to study scientific principles of envelope design, a partial summary of the functions of the R-2000 building envelope is provided in Figure 7.6, along with the normal solutions and materials used. The alternatives presented here represent only some of the possibilities for upgrading the thermal performance of the envelope.

Setting Benchmarks

Implementing large-scale sustainable developments often requires participation of several stakeholders. Investments in such projects draws involvement of government agencies as well as the private sector. Successful outcome also depends on

Function		Mechanism	Solution	Materials/Processes
Control heat flow	Heat loss	Conduction	Insulate; avoid thermal bridges, particularly at foundation wall, floor/wall junctions, roof/wall junctions, and window frames	Batt, rigid board, blown or sprayed insulation; careful detailing to avoid thermal bridges
		Radiation	Reflective coatings (where air spaces are present); low emissivity coatings in glazing units	Aluminum-coated papers, proprietary coatings
		Convection	Keep air spaces narrow and/or interrupt convective currents with grid patterns; fill in wide air spaces with insulation	Use appropriate designs/processes—e.g. apply adhesives for rigid boards on foundation walls to form squares/rectangles
	Heat gain	Solar	Control heat gain for summer and winter conditions through appropriate design and window size, location, and orientation	Overhangs, solar shading devices, low-emissivity windows
Control air flow	Infiltration/ exfiltration	Diffusion	Provide continuous layer of sheet materials that are impervious to air	Air barriers: rigid sheet materials (sheetrock, plywood, etc.) or membranes (polyethylene, aluminum, etc.) or a combination of both
		Leakage	Seal all gaps to form a continuous airtight building envelope, particularly at windows, electrical boxes, and service penetrations	Sealants, caulking beads, tapes, and gaskets; polyurethane foams; airtight boxes and wraps for electrical fixtures
Control moisture flow	Water	Gravity	Slope exterior finishes and flashings away from wall at joints; slope grade away from foundation wall; use overhangs with drips (where applicable)	Weather barriers: olefin sheets, building paper, tar coatings, polyethylene, exterior finishes, waterproof paints, etc. Flashing materials: metal, plastic, etc: gaps sealed with sealants, caulks, and gaskets
		Capillary action	Keep exterior finishes away from soil; interrupt flow of water from soil with a weather/moisture barrier	
		Momentum	Keep exterior finishes away from soil; use appropriate flashing materials and details; provide roof overhangs	
		Pressure difference	Use rainscreen principle—i.e., provide sealed, drained air spaces between exterior finishes and wall to equalize pressure difference	
	Vapor	Diffusion	Provide a continuous layer of sheet materials that are impervious to vapor; located on the warm side of the insulation to control outgoing vapor	Vapor diffusion retarders (VDRs) or vapor barriers: aluminum-coated kraft paper, polyethylene, vapor-resistant paints, extruded polystyrene; multiple layers of building paper, and other materials may also act as VDRs

Figure 7.6: R-2000 principles of envelope design and construction

public participation, as homeowners have to bear the consequences of the design as well as contribute their own efforts to partake in recycling programs and other activities, for example.

Public Participation

Steps and processes have been proposed to achieve successful public participation in a project (CMHC, 2000). They include involving the public early on in the planning, since the earlier they are asked to contribute their opinions, the less likely future community members will believe that participation was "imposed" on them.

Providing people with information and setting up a mechanism for ongoing updates will keep participants well-informed. The material provided must be clear and easily understood. Welcoming the public and making people feel that they are an integral part of the decision-making process is another aspect of public involvement. Meetings at various levels of government—at municipal, state, or federal level—should include members of the public or should be open to them at the very least. Finally, to avoid frustration, the process needs to move fast and lengthy delay prevented.

Demonstration Projects

Creating a sustainable community requires an understanding of what makes a neighborhood affordable, socially supportive, and environmentally friendly. Two contemporary residential sustainable communities are featured here. These homes demonstrate alternative approaches to sustainability by being energy-efficient, flexibly constructed, and focused on environmentally friendly building methods and materials. They have also become desirable places to live, demonstrating what makes a healthy house, in fact, a home.

Ecolonia, Netherlands

The Ecolonia Development in Alphen aan den Rijn, Netherlands, applied creativity and environmental concern to the design of 101 semi-detached homes and rowhouses. The development is a demonstration center for many types of ecologically sound building techniques used throughout the units. Ecolonia was built between 1991 and 1993 by the Netherlands Agency for Energy and the Environment.

Situated between Amsterdam, The Hague, Rotterdam, and Utrecht, an area of the Netherlands known as the "green heart" was experiencing rapid growth with little experimentation of alternative construction methods. The National Environmental Policy Plan, however, began a major initiative to move the Dutch to higher standards of resource efficiency and quality of life by implementing a plan that stressed three major themes in sustainable building practices: energy conservation, integral lifecycle management, and quality control of building materials and methods (van Vliet and Jones, 2005). The ensuing Ecolonia project sought to increase public awareness, use ecological building materials and renewable resources, and to reduce energy and water consumption and construction waste (van Gerwen, 2005).

Nine architects designed the homes that were integrated into the town's master plan conceived by Lucien Kroll of Brussels. The architects focused on different themes of ecological building. Kroll envisioned dwellings created using non-toxic and energy-efficient features that responded to local site conditions and cultural considerations. The site imposed no strict geometry and was continuously altered as architects consulted each other and refined the layout of the homes (Figure 7.7).

Pedestrians were given priority in circulation design, as paved areas were not intended for high-speed travel. Pathways in the neighborhood weave through housing units of various themes, which in turn integrate with squares, gardens, and back lanes, creating a community that is both stimulating and educational for residents and visitors (Jones, 1992). Energy efficiency was the focus of 18 dwellings that use extra insulation with 4.7 inch (120 mm) thick limestone, 5.1 inches (130 mm) of thermal skin, and 0.6 inch (15 mm) of sheetrock on each wall (van Gerwen). Small windows to the north, solar hot water panels to the south, and heat recovery units produce hot air and water, minimizing energy loss and maximizing solar gain. Solar power also plays a key role in 10 of the dwellings, which are equipped with south-facing conservatories and use passive and active solar technology.

A heat recovery unit, sun protection, and ventilation reduces the energy needed to heat or cool each home, and a solar boiler supplies hot water. Similarly, the use of solar energy, this time for light, is essential for 10 dwellings designed by Architectenbureau Hopman. These bring daylight and passive solar energy into all areas of the home with a split-level floor plan. A heat recovery ventilation system and cold buffer control zones limit the need for space heating. Solar heaters provide hot water and underfloor heating, a low-temperature alternative to forced air.

Ten additional dwellings—four rowhouses and six semi-detached homes—also use passive and active solar energy systems. The homes also make use of natural raw materials such as wood, cellulose for insulation, and rainwater catchment tanks that provide water for toilets and gardens. Water-saving faucets are also included in each home (Figure 7.8).

To reduce waste, building materials were recycled. Concrete granulate was ground to use as flooring and efficient prefabricated timber frame construction was used. Organic architecture permeates 12 dwellings designed by Architectenbureau

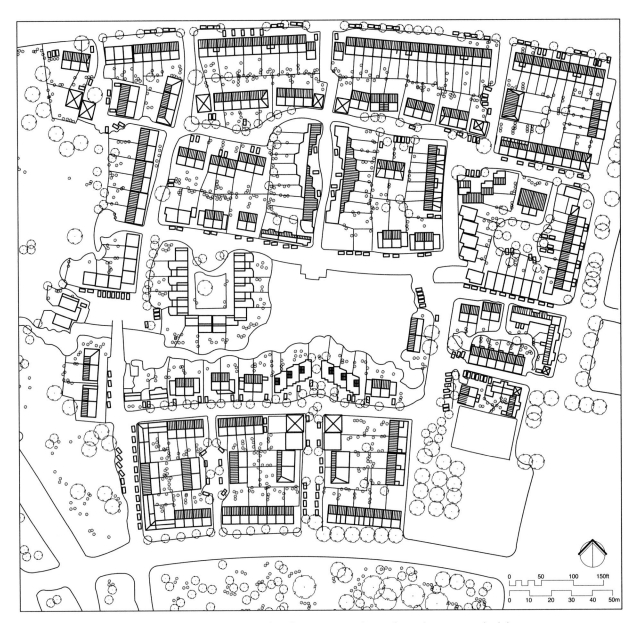

Figure 7.7: The master plan of Ecolonia centered on a formal square and a lake connected to a dyke.

Alberts and Van Huut and incorporates natural building materials that are durable and pleasing to the eye. Limestone and clay brick provide heavy mass for solar gain and require little maintenance, and local lumber was used for windows.

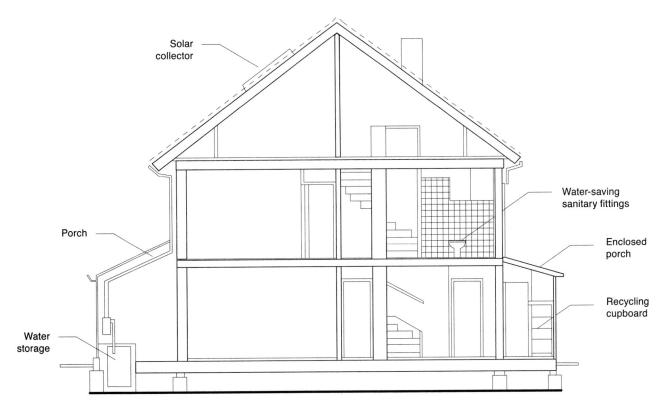

Figure 7.8: A section showing several environmental features included in the design of a home in Ecolonia

The flexibility of the home was explored in 10 dwellings designed by Lindeman Architects and Engineers, which featured moveable interior walls to allow for a wide variety of living arrangements depending on changing family needs. Lightweight dividers were used within floors and modifiable heating/ventilation in the roof, allowing rooms to change size and function easily. Evolving family and neighborhood needs led to 10 dwellings designed by the Technical University of Eindhoven as an experiment with noise reduction within and among units. The foundations were separated and the floor plans clustered noisy rooms, such as kitchens and bathrooms, away from quiet rooms such as bedrooms. Extra insulation was used, especially for the quiet rooms, which feature 5.9 inch (150 mm) limestone walls, insulated timber frame, and heavy doors (van Gerwen).

Twelve units designed by Peter van Gerwen Energy Design, Architecture and Urban Development Consultants, focused on health, safety, and quality control, taking into account the growing demand for dust- and allergen-free environments and adding safety considerations such as extra light. The prevalent air ventilation system includes extra filters and is easy to clean, and the subfloor heating system and non-toxic building materials allow for clean air. In these homes, solar collectors and window blinds add energy efficiency.

Finally, eight dwellings designed by Architectenbureau Archi Service feature what the designer describes as "bio-ecological building," or natural building that uses non-toxic and water-soluble paints and avoids negative electromagnetic fields. Unique three-bedroom homes were built with environmentally sound materials, green roofs, and rainwater catchment tanks. A lime-sandstone and brick exterior houses a new heating system of hot water pipes embedded in the walls. The effects of electromagnetic fields and radiation on occupants were mitigated with 0.8 inch (20 mm) cork flooring and natural paints and anhydrite sealants. A solar collector provides hot water (van Gerwen; van Vliet and Jones).

The community created in Ecolonia is varied in planning, design, and livability. A central pond collects rainwater and provides a green space, cars are parked in bordering ports to encourage walking, and a community house holds central facilities that save energy and increase social interaction. The result is a neighborhood that is well-used and safe, incorporating the three mandates originally set forth by the National Environmental Policy Plan at the project's inception and demonstrates energy efficiency, ecological building practices, and pathways to more sustainable lifestyles.

Village Homes, Davis, California

Although western Europe is generally acknowledged to be the leader in several fields of sustainability, including housing, the movement toward sustainable homes and communities has been taking shape in North America for several decades. In 1975 in the university town of Davis, California, Judy and Michael Corbett began directing construction of the then-controversial Village Homes, conceived from ideas gathered at meetings in the early 1970s with fellow students who were interested in obtaining a better quality of life while treading lightly on the land.

Village Homes is a community of 220 single-family homes, 20 apartments, business spaces, a common house, and a community center on 60 acres (24.28 hectares) (Figure 7.9). Although 60 percent of the homes were built by the Village Homes company, the remaining lots were bought and developed by individuals (Bainbridge, 2004), including one nine-bedroom housing cooperative designed by students (Corbett and Corbett, 2000). Diversity within the development created a more stimulating living environment while providing a test ground for different ecological techniques. The density of the homes is almost double compared to the surrounding area, but the incorporation of common gardens, park space, and pedestrian-oriented green belts creates a strong sense of community and a better quality of life. Completed in 1981, Village Homes is a popular neighborhood with a low turnover rate, high home value, and low food and utility bills (Bainbridge).

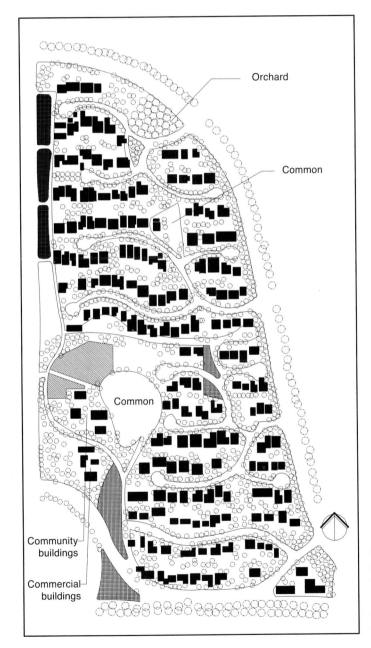

Figure 7.9: A site plan of Village Homes features curved streets, vegetation, and homes designed for passive solar gain.

Homes in the development were built with advanced energy-saving technologies. Although compact in general, designs were intentionally varied from 600 square feet (56 square meters) to 2800 square feet (260 square meters) to attract homeowners of different income levels. Cul-de-sac design, small lots, and two-story houses resulted in 15 percent more available land for other uses compared to conventional developments. According to Corbett and Corbett, this "liberated land" is now used for community orchards, vineyards, and gardens.

Emphasis on energy conservation was a key factor in Village Homes—in particular, the use of passive and active solar energy systems. The climate of Davis—hot summer days with cool nights, mild winters, and rare freezes—lent itself perfectly to simple solar strategies. Homes have insulated roofs, and edges of floor slabs, cracks, and joints to window and door frames are caulked. House lots are of varied shape and size to allow for north-south orientation, and calculated overhangs shade south-facing windows and deciduous vines and trees provide added protection (Corbett and Corbett). Narrow streets reduce the heat island effect 10 to 15°F (6 to 9.5°C) lower than nearby conventional streets during hot months (Browning and Hamilton, 1993), while lowering costs of infrastructure and amount of paved land.

Massive adobe walls and concrete floors absorb heat and coolness, bringing temperature extremes to a minimum inside the homes, and many houses feature solar greenhouses with pipes running under the floor surface through which a computer-controlled sensor pulls in warm air during the winter and cool night air in the summer (Corbett and Corbett). (A later study of one such "thermosiphon-loop" showed a lack of pressure in the tubes and, therefore, inadequate air flow for heating and cooling the sun space, suggesting that a hybrid system of fans may have been needed in the original design [Vital Signs Project, 1996].) According to Bainbridge, however, utility bills are 40 to 50 percent lower in these homes than in surrounding homes.

Almost every roof supports a solar water heater that provides 100 percent of each home's hot water requirements for seven months of the year, and 40 to 50 percent during the remaining months. Simple water-saving appliances within each home reduce hot water consumption by 20 to 25 percent. The importance of the sun in the everyday life of Village Home dwellers was emphasized and protected in the *Declaration of Covenants, Conditions and Restrictions* signed by all homeowners that prevents residents from building fences around greenbelts or in any way interfering with a neighbor's "solar rights" (Corbett and Corbett).

Nature-based landscaping provides multi-fold benefits for Village Homes residents. Instead of being graded toward the street as in conventional developments, land in Village Homes is graded away from the street and toward shallow swales and streambeds (Figure 7.10). Check dams slow surges and encourage infiltration, reducing watering needs of surrounding plants by a third (Browning and Hamilton). Although initially refused by the city as an approved drainage system, the system used in Village Homes has been one of the only developments in the area that has not flooded during unusually heavy rains (Bainbridge). Further retention basins and ponds have been added as a result of the system's success in water management and cost savings and have created habitat for the lush and edible landscape from which residents pick a wide variety of fruits, vegetables, and nuts (Browning and Hamilton).

Village Homes sets a precedent for modern housing communities in North America. Its dedication to common-sense principles found in nature are emulated in the design of homes, common areas, and neighborhoods. As solar technologies improve, the energy efficiency of each new home will change, but community sense and the sheer pleasure and pride experienced by those living in Village Homes need not change at all.

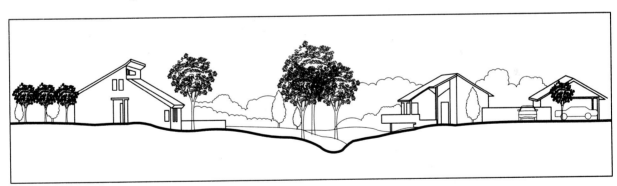

Figure 7.10: A section through Village Homes shows that shallow swales collect rainwater that then slowly percolates into the ground, reducing flooding and toxic run-off from streets.

Bibliography

Alexander, G. "Overview: The Context of Renewable Energy Technologies," in *Renewable Energy: Power for a Sustainable Future*. G. Boyle, ed. Oxford, NY: Oxford University Press, 1996.

American Institute of Architects. "Materials," in *Environmental Resource Guide*. Washington, DC, 1992a.

———. "Indoor Air Quality Facts," in *Environmental Resource Guide*. Washington, DC, 1992b.

Andrews, S. *Foam-Core Panels & Building Systems: Principles, Practice and Product Directory*. Arlington, MA: Cutter Information Corp., 1992.

Arendt, R. G. *Conservation Design for Subdivisions: A Practical Guide to Creating Open Space Networks*. Washington, DC: Island Press, 1996.

Arnold, H. F. *Trees in Urban Design*. New York: Van Nostrand Reinhold Company, 1980.

Bainbridge, David A. *Sustainable Community—Village Homes, Davis, California*. March 21, 2004. San Diego, CA: United States International College of Business, Alliant International University. Accessed February 2007 <www.ecocomposite.org/building/villagehomes.htm>.

Barton, H. *Sustainable Communities: The Potential for Eco-Neighbourhoods*. London: Earthscan Publications, 2000.

Beatley, T. *Green Urbanism: Learning from European Cities*. Washington, DC: Island Press, 2000.

Beecher, J. *Charles Fourier: The Visionary and His World*. Berkeley: University of California Press, 1986.

Bemis, A. F., and J. Burchard. *The Evolving House: A History of the Home, Vol. 1*. Cambridge, MA: The Technology Press, 1933.

Boyer, C. "City of Collective Memory: Its Historical Imagery and Architectural Elements," in *Urban Design: Reshaping our Cities*. A. V. Moudon and W. Attoe, eds. Seattle: University of Washington Press, 1995. 82–83.

Boyle, G. *Renewable Energy: Power for a Sustainable Future*. Oxford, NY: Oxford University Press, 1996.

Brand, S. *How Buildings Learn: What Happens After They're Built.* New York: Viking, 1994.

Brown, G. Z. *Sun, Wind, and Light.* New York: John Wiley & Sons, 1985.

Brown, R. J., and R. R. Yanuck. *Introduction to Life Cycle Costing.* Upper Saddle River, NJ: Prentice Hall, 1985.

Browning, B., and K. Hamilton. "Village Homes: A model solar community proves its worth," in *In Context: Designing a Sustainable Future.* Spring 1993. Accessed February 2007 <www.context.org/ICLIB/IC35/Browning.htm>.

Brundtland Commission. *Our Common Future.* Oxford, NY: Oxford University Press, 1987.

Bryant, C., et al. "The City's Countryside," in *Canadian Cities in Transition: The Twenty-First Century.* 2nd Ed. T. Bunting and P. Filion, eds. Don Mills, Ontario: Oxford University Press, 2000. 333–356.

Buchholz, R. A. *Principles of Environmental Management: The Greening of Business.* Upper Saddle River, NJ: Prentice Hall Inc., 1993.

Burden, D. *Building Communities with Transportation.* Monday, January 8, 2001. Washington, DC: Distinguished Lecture Presentation, Transportation Research Board. Accessed February 2007 <www.walkable.org/trbpaper.pdf>.

Burenhult, G., ed. "The Megalith Builders of Western Europe," in *People of the Stone Age: Hunter-Gatherers and Early Farmers.* San Francisco: Harper San Francisco, 1993.

Burnham, R. *Housing Ourselves: Creating Affordable, Sustainable Shelter.* New York: McGraw-Hill, 1998.

Calthorpe, P. *The Next American Metropolis: Ecology, Community, and the American Dream.* New York: Princeton Architectural Press, 1993.

Campbell, S. *Let It Rot! The Gardener's Guide to Composting.* North Adams, MA: Storey Publishing, 1990.

Canada Mortgage and Housing Corporation (CMHC). *Residential Site Development Advisory Document.* Ottawa, Ontario: CMHC, 1981.

———. *Making a Molehill out of a Mountain II: Implementing the Three R's in Residential Construction.* Ottawa, Ontario: CMHC, 1991.

———. *Practice for Sustainable Communities.* Ottawa, Ontario: CMHC, 2000.

Canadian Heart and Stroke Foundation. *Heart and Stroke Foundation 2005 Report Card on Canadians' Health: Has the Suburban Dream Gone Sour?* Montreal, Quebec: 2005.

Canadian Home Builders' Association. *Canadian Home Builders' Association Builders' Manual.* Ottawa, Ontario: CHBA, 1989.

Carson, R. *Silent Spring.* Boston: Houghton Mifflin, 1962.

Cherry, G. E. *Town Planning in its Social Context.* London: Leonard Hill Books, 1970.

The City of Halifax Waste Management Task Force. *Review of Waste Management Systems Options.* Halifax, Nova Scotia: March 1992.

Cooper Marcus, C., and W. Sarkissian. *Housing as if People Mattered: Site Design Guidelines for the Planning of Medium-Density Family Housing.* Los Angeles: University of California Press, 1986.

Corbett, J., and M. Corbett. *Designing Sustainable Communities: Learning from Village Homes.* Washington DC: Island Press, 2000.

Courtaulds Fibres Canada. *Souvenir Book of the Courtaulds in Cornwall.* Cornwall, Ontario, 1993.

Dell'Isola, J. A., and J. S. Kirk. *Life Cycle Costing for Design Professionals.* New York: McGraw-Hill, 1981.

Duany, A., et al. *Suburban Nation: The Rise and the Decline of the American Dream.* New York: North Point Press, 2000.

Duly, C. *The Houses of Mankind.* London: Thames and Hudson, Ltd., 1979.

Earl, J. *Building Conservation Philosophy.* Reading, UK: The College of Estate Management, 1996.

El Bassam, N., and P. Maegaard. *Integrated Renewable Energy for Rural Communities: Planning Guidelines, Technologies and Applications.* Amsterdam: Elsevier, 2004.

Elsom, D. *Smog Alert: Managing Urban Air Quality.* London: Earthscan Publications, 1996.

Environment Canada. *A Primer on Water: Questions and Answers.* Ottawa, Ontario: Ministry of Supply and Services, 1991.

———. *Recycling in Canada.* Ottawa, Ontario: Ministry of Supply and Services, April, 1992a.

———. *Reduction and Reuse: The First 2Rs of Waste Management.* Ottawa, Ontario: Ministry of Supply and Services, April, 1992b.

Environmental News Network. *Research: Recycling buildings makes dollars and sense.* December 20, 1999. Accessed August 12, 2005 <http://archives.cnn.com/1999/NATURE/12/20/building.recycle.enn/index.html>.

Feilden, B. *Conservation of Historic Buildings.* Boston: Butterworth Scientific, 1982.

Ferguson, B. K. "Water Conservation Methods in Urban Landscape Irrigation: An Exploratory Overview." *Water Resources Bulletin,* Vol. 23(1) (1987): 147–152.

Ferguson, W. M. *The Anasazi of Mesa Verde and the Four Corners.* Niwot, Colorado: University of Colorado Press, 1996.

Fisette, P., and D. Ryan. *Preserving Trees During Construction.* Amherst, MA: Building Materials and Wood Technology Center, 2002.

Fourier, C. *The Utopian Vision of Charles Fourier: Selected Text on Work, Love and Passionate Attraction.* Trans. Jonathan Beecher and Richard Bienvenu, eds. Boston: Beacon Press, 1971.

Friedman, A. *The Adaptable House.* New York: McGraw-Hill, 2002.

————. "Innovation and the North American Homebuilding Industry." *Open House International,* Vol. 14, No. 3, (1989): 16–19. Reprinted in the Proceedings of Open House International Association Conference. July 1989. University of Newcastle, U.K. 137–140.

————. *Le Village: Retooling for the Next Century.* Cornwall, Ontario: Renaissance Waterfront Association, 1999.

————. "Prefabrication vs. Conventional Construction in Single-Family Wood-Frame Housing." *Building Research and Information*, Vol. 2, No. 4 (1992).

Gardiner, S. *Evolution of the House: An Introduction.* New York: Macmillan Publishing Co., 1974.

Girling, C. L., and K. I. Hepland. *Yard, Street, Park: The Design of Suburban Open Space.* Toronto, Ontario: John Wiley & Sons, Inc., 1994.

Goldbeck, D. *The Smart Kitchen: How to Design a Comfortable, Safe, Energy-Efficient and Environmentally-Friendly Workplace.* New York: Ceress Press, 1989.

Golton, B. L. "Illuminating the cumulative impact of small decisions—a case study of building demolition," in *Evaluation of the Built Environment for Sustainability.* P. S. Brandon, P. L. Lombardi, and V. Bentivegna, eds. London: E & FN Spon, 1997.

Greenroofs Projects Database. 2006. Accessed July 2006 <www.greenroofs.com/projects/>.

Hansen, M., and Y. Huang. "Road Supply and Traffic in California Urban Areas." *Transportation Research*, 31, No. 3 (1997): 205–218.

Hoffman, F., in "*Basquiat,* by Jean-Michel." Basquiat. F. Hoffman, K. Jones, M. Mayer, and F. Sirmans, comp. and eds. London: Merrell, 2006.

Holcomb, H. B., and R. A. Beauregard. *Revitalizing Cities.* Washington, DC: Resource Publications in Geography, 1981.

Hollister, W. C. *Medieval Europe: A Short History.* 7th Ed. New York: McGraw-Hill, 1994.

Howard, E. *Garden Cities of Tomorrow.* Reprint of *Tomorrow: A Peaceful Path to Real Reform.* 1898. London: Swan Sonnenschein & Co., 1902.

Humphrey, M. *Preservation Versus the People? Nature, Humanity, and Political Philosophy.* Oxford, NY: Oxford University Press, 2002.

Jackson, F. *Sir Raymond Unwin: Architect, Planner and Visionary.* London: Zwemmer, 1985.

Jacobs, J. *The Death and Life of Great American Cities.* New York: Vintage Books, 1961.

Jokilehto, J. *A History of Architectural Conservation.* Oxford: Butterworth-Heinemann, 1999.

Jones, P. B. "Ecolonia, Community Planning, Alphen-aan-den-Rijn, the Netherlands." *Architectural Review,* March 1992: 64–67.

Kain, R. "Introduction: Definitions, Attitudes and Debates," in *Planning for Conservation.* R. Kain, ed. London: Mansell, 1981. 1–16.

Kalman, H. *The Sensible Rehabilitation of Old Houses.* Ottawa, Canada: Mortgage and Housing Corporation, 1979.

Kibert, C. J. "The Promises and Limits of Sustainability," in *Reshaping the Built Environment: Ecology, Ethics and Economics.* Charles J. Kibert, ed. Washington, DC: Island Press, 1999. 9–38.

Knox, P. L., and S. A. Marston. *Places and Regions in Global Context: Human Geography.* 2nd Ed. New Jersey: Prentice Hall, 2001.

Kunstler, J. H. *The Geography of Nowhere: The Rise and Decline of America's Man-Made Landscape.* New York: Touchstone Books, 1994.

Kyte, E. *From Royal Township to Industrial City: Cornwall 1784–1984.* Belleville, Ontario: Mika Publishing, 1983.

Lamontagne, J., and D. Brazeau. *Entretien et taille des jeunes arbres au Québec.* Saint-Laurent, Québec: Éditions du Trécarré, 1996.

Landreville, M. *Toitures vertes a la montréalaise: rapport de recherché sur l'implantation de toits verts a Montréal.* Montréal, Quebec: Société de développement communautaire de Montréal, 2005.

Letchworth Garden City Heritage Foundation. *Letchworth Garden City Heritage Foundation.* 2001. Accessed February 1, 2001 <www.Letchworth.com>.

Logan, T. "The Americanization of German Zoning." *Journal of the American Institute of Planners.* 42.4 (1976): 377–385.

Low, N., B. Gleeson, R. Green, and D. Radovic. *The Green City-Sustainable Homes, Sustainable Suburbs.* Sydney, Australia: UNSW Press, 2005.

Lowry, R., "Defining the Fit Between User and Old Buildings: A 9 Step Procedure for Rehabilitiation," in *Conservation, Rehabiltiation, Recyclage.* L'école d'Architecture de Laval and L'ordre des Architects du Québec, Ed. Québec: Les Presses de L'Université Laval, 1981.

Lozier, B. *Sustainable High Density Housing on Burnaby Mountain.* Fall 2000. Accessed July 15, 2005 <www.university.ca/bmcp/geog4492000fall/pub_html/housing/sustain.html>.

Lynch, K. *A Theory of Good City Form.* Cambridge, MA: MIT Press, 1981.

Macfadyen, D. *Sir Ebenezer Howard and the Town Planning Movement.* Manchester, UK: Manchester University Press, 1933.

Macionis, J., and V. Parrillo. *Cities and Urban Life.* 2nd Ed. New Jersey: Prentice Hall, 2001.

Marbek Resource Consultants, Ltd. *Insulating Basements, Crawl Spaces and Slabs-on-Grade.* Ottawa, Ontario: Energy, Mines and Resources Canada, 1987.

May, M. J. *To Build the Compact Green City: Manifesto and Call to Re-Think Architecture and City Planning.* St. Petersburg, FL: Smart, 1993.

Mayer, P. W. and W. DeOreo et al. *Residential End Uses of Water.* Denver, CO: AWWA Research Foundation and American Water Works Association, 1999.

Mayerovitch, H. *Overstreet: An Urban Street Development System.* Montreal, Quebec: Harvest House, 1973.

McBride, J. R., and D. F. Jacobs. "Pre-Settlement Forest Structure as a Factor in Urban Forest Development." *Urban Ecology,* 9.3–4 (1986): 245–266.

McCullough, A. B. *The Primary Textile Industry in Canada: History and Heritage.* Ottawa, Ontario: Minster of Supply and Services, 1992.

McPherson, E. G., J. R. Simpson, and M. Livingston. "Effects of Three Landscape Treatments on Residential Energy and Water Use in Tucson, Arizona." *Energy and Buildings,* Vol. 13, 1989: 127–138.

Mendler, S., and W. Odell. *The HOK Guidebook to Sustainable Design.* New Jersey: John Wiley & Sons, 2000.

Miller, M. *Letchworth: The First Garden City.* Chichester, UK: Phillimore, 1989.

———. *Raymond Unwin: Garden Cities and Town Planning.* Leicester, UK: Leicester University Press, 1992.

Miller, R. W. *Urban Forestry: Planning and Managing Urban Greenspaces.* New Jersey: Prentice Hall, 1988.

Moughtin, C. *Urban Design: Street and Square.* Great Britain: Architectural Press, 2003.

Mumford, L. *The City in History: Its Origins, its Transformations, and its Prospect.* New York: Harcourt Brace, 1961.

Natural Resources Canada. *Energy Efficiency Trends in Canada, 1990 to 2003.* June 2005: 17.

Nebraska Energy Office. *Minimizing the Use of Lumber Products in Residential Construction.* Accessed February 2007 <www.neo.state.ne.us/home_const/factsheets/min_use_lumber.htm>.

Office of Energy Efficiency. *The State of Energy Efficiency in Canada, Report 2006.* Ottawa, Ontario: Energy Publications, Office of Energy Efficiency, 2006.

Organization for Economic Co-Operation and Development (OECD). *Motor Vehicle Pollution—Reduction Strategies Beyond 2010.* Paris, 1995.

Ouf, A. "Authenticity and the Sense of Place in Urban Design." *Journal of Urban Design,* 6.1 (2001): 73–86.

Palmqvist, L. "The Great Transition," in *People of the Stone Age: Hunter-Gatherers and Early Farmers.* Burenhult, Goran, ed. San Francisco: Harper San Francisco, 1993.

Parsons, K. C. *British and American Community Design: Clarence Stein's Manhattan Transfer Planning Perspectives.* Vol. 7. 1992. 191–210.

Perry, C. "The Neighborhood Unit," in *Regional Survey of New York and Its Environs.* Vol. 7. New York: State of New York, 1929.

Peterman, W. *Neighbourhood Planning and Community-Based Development: The Potential and Limits of Grassroots Action.* London: Sage, 2000.

Pickering Research. *Compost Management: A Field Examination of Cost Effectiveness, Waste Diversion Potential, and Homeowner Acceptance of Backyard Composting Units.* June 1992.

Pirenne, H. *Medieval Cities: Their Origins and the Revival of Trade.* Princeton: Princeton University Press, 1925.

Podmore, F. *Robert Owen: A Biography.* New York: Augustus M. Kelley, 1906.

Puma, J. *The Complete Urban Gardener.* New York: Harper and Row, 1985.

Ramage, J. *Energy: A Guidebook.* Oxford, NY: Oxford University Press, 1997.

Regional Municipalilty of Waterloo. *Healthy Lawns and Gardens with Less Water.* Waterloo, Ontario, 1990.

REIC Ltd. and Associates. *Residential Water Conservation: A Review of Products, Processes and Practices.* Ottawa, Ontario: Canadian Housing and Mortgage Corporation, 1991.

Reiner, L. E. *How to Recycle Buildings.* New York: McGraw-Hill, 1979.

Ritchie, A. *Prehistoric Orkney.* London: B.T. Batsford, Ltd/Historic Scotland, 1995.

Rocky Mountain Institute. *Village Homes, Davis, California.* 1999–2005. Accessed June 20, 2005 <www.rmi.org/sitepages/pid209.php>.

Rogers, Everett. *Diffusion of Innovations.* New York: Free Press, 1983.

Rudlin, D., and N. Falk. *Building a 21st Century Home: The Sustainable Urban Neighbourhood.* Oxford: Architectural Press, 1999.

Rudofsky, B. *Architecture without Architects.* New York: Doubleday & Company, 1965.

Scarlett, L. "The Seduction of Planning," in *Ecological Design Handbook: Sustainable Strategies for Architecture, Landscape Architecture, Interior Design, and Planning.* Stitt, F. A., ed. New York: McGraw-Hill, 1999. 329–337.

Schoenauer, N. *6,000 Years of Housing.* Montreal, Quebec: McGill University School of Architecture, 1992.

———. *6,000 Years of Housing.* Revised and expanded ed. New York: W.W. Norton, 2000.

Scholz-Barth, Katrin. "From Grey to Green," in *Green Roofs: Ecological Design and Construction.* Earth Pledge Foundation, ed. Atglen, PA: Schiffer Publishing, 2005. 18.

Schumacher, E. F. *Small Is Beautiful; Economics as if People Mattered.* New York: Harper & Row, 1973.

Schwela, D., and O. Zali. *Urban Traffic Pollution.* London: E & FN Spon, 1999.

Sharp, T. *Town and Countryside: Some Aspects of Urban and Rural Development.* London: Humphrey Milford, 1932.

Slater, T. R. "The Birmingham Jewellery Quarter: Cultural Continuity in Practice," in *Urban Design: Reshaping our Cities.* A. V. Moudon and W. Attoe, eds. Seattle: University of Washington Press, 1995. 67–75.

Southworth, M., and E. Ben-Joseph. *Streets and the Shaping of Towns and Cities.* New York: McGraw-Hill, 1997.

Statistics Canada. *Profile of Census Divisions and Subdivisions: 1996 Census of Canada.* Ottawa, Industries Canada, 1999.

Stein, C. S. *Toward New Towns for America.* New York: Reinhold, 1957.

Stitt, F. A. *Ecological Architecture: Excerpts from the Ecological Design Handbook.* Accessed June 20, 2005 <http://members.fortunecity.com/lwl1/env-ecoarchi.html>.

Stromberg, M. "Green is coming out on top: if hobbit holes come to mind when you think of a green roof, think again." *Planning.* Vol. 71, Issue 7 (July 2005): 22–23.

Tchobanoglous, G., H. Theisen, S. Vigil. *Integrated Solid Waste Management: Engineering Principles and Management Issues.* New York: McGraw-Hill, 1993.

Todd, K. W. *Site, Space, and Structure.* New York: Reinhold Company, 1985.

Unwin, R. *Town Planning in Practice: An Introduction to the Art of Designing Cities and Suburbs.* London: Adelphi Terrace, 1909.

U.S. Energy Information Administration. *Table 2.2 Residential Sector Energy Consumption.* January 26, 2007. Official Energy Statistics from the U.S. Government. Accessed 2006 <www.eia.doe.gov/emeu/mer/consump.html>.

U.S. Green Building Council. *Leadership in Energy and Environmental Design.* 2007a. Accessed February 2007 <www.usgbc.org/DisplayPage.aspx?CategoryID=19>.

———. *LEED for Homes.* 2007b. Accessed February 2007 <www.usgbc.org/DisplayPage.aspx?CMSPageID=147>.

———. *LEED for Neighborhood Development.* 2007c. Accessed February 2007 <www.usgbc.org/DisplayPage.aspx?CMSPageID=148>.

Van der Ryn, S., and P. Calthorpe. *Sustainable Communities: A New Design Synthesis for Cities, Suburbs, and Towns.* San Francisco: Sierra Club Books, 1986.

van Gerwen, P. *Ecolonia: English.* Accessed June 20, 2005 <http://home.hetnet .nl/~perronas/ecolonia.english.html>.

van Vliet, D., and A. Jones. *Case Study: Ecolonia, Netherlands.* June 2005. University of Manitoba. Accessed June 20, 2005 <www.umanitoba.ca/ academic/faculties/architecture/la/sustainable/cases/ecolonia/ecoindx.htm>.

Vital Signs Project. *Vital Signs Project: Siegel House Case Study.* April 23, 1996. UC Berkeley. Accessed June 20, 2005 <http://arch.ced.berkeley.edu/ vitalsigns/workup/siegel_house/sgl_home.html>.

Walker, L. *EcoVillage at Ithaca: Pioneering a Sustainable Culture.* Gabriola Island, British Columbia: New Society Publishers, 2005.

Wheeler, S. M. *Planning for Sustainability: Creating Livable, Equitable, and Ecological Communities.* Oxon, England: Routledge, 2004.

Whitehand, J. W. R., and C. M. H. Carr. *Twentieth-Century Suburbs: A Morphological Approach.* New York: Routledge, 2001.

Willet, W. C., W. H. Dietz, and G. A. Colditz. "Guidelines for Healthy Weight." *The New England Journal of Medicine.* Vol. 341, No. 6 (August 5, 1999): 427–434.

Wilson, R. W. "Suburban Parking Requirements." *Journal of the American Planning Association.* 61.1 (1995).

Wines, J. *Green Architecture.* Köln, Germany: Taschen, 2000.

Winter, S. *Market Potential for Structural Insulated Panels in Residential and Light Commercial Buildings.* Duluth, MN: Structural Insulated Panel Association, 1991.

Zelov, C., and P. Cousineau, eds. "Why is Architecture Oblivious to the Environment? An Interview with Ian Mcharg," in *Ecological Design Handbook: Sustainable Strategies for Architecture, Landscape Architecture, Interior Design, and Planning.* Stitt, F. A., ed. New York: McGraw-Hill, 1999. 17–21.

Zucker, P. *Town and Square: From the Agora to the Village Green.* New York: Columbia University Press, 1959.

Illustration Credits

Figures not listed here are in the public domain or have been conceived, drawn, or photographed by the author and members of his research and design teams. Their names are listed in the Acknowledgments or in the Research and Project Teams section. Every effort has been made to list all contributors and sources. In case of omission, the author and the publisher would be pleased to insert the appropriate acknowledgment in any subsequent edition of this book.

Chapter 2

Figure 2.1: Schoenauer (1992)
Figure 2.9: Radburn Association Archives (1929)

Chapter 3

Figure 3.9: Based on discussion with Jean Lamontagne of La Forêt de Marie-Victorin design team.

Chapter 4

Figure 4.1: Schoenauer (1992)
Figure 4.2: Schoenauer (1992)
Figure 4.7: Proposal by Yafeng Yu for the Daulphinn site, Fredericton, New Brunswick, Canada. Advisors: Avi Friedman, Louis Pretty, Miguel Escobar. With permission of Yafeng Yu.

Chapter 5

Figure 5.16: Drawings in the Canadian Home Builders' Association Builders' Manual (1989). Published with permission of the Canadian Home Builders' Association.
Figure 5.18: Drawings in the *Canadian Home Builders' Association Builders' Manual* (1989). Published with permission of the Canadian Home Builders' Association.

Figure 5.24: Drawings in the *Canadian Home Builders' Association Builders' Manual* (1989). Published with permission of the Canadian Home Builders' Association.

Figure 5.31: From a drawing by Jerold Weisburd, architect; Claudia Weisburd, planner; William Chamberlain, landscape consultant. Published with permission of Jerold Weisburd.

Figure 5.34: From a drawing by Jerold Weisburd, architect. Published with permission of Jerold Weisburd.

Figure 5.35: From a drawing by Jerold Weisburd, architect. Published with permission of Jerold Weisburd.

Chapter 6

Figure 6.34: Drawings by Beate Ioanide. Studio Director/Advisor: Avi Friedman
Figure 6.35: Drawings by Gustavo Corredor. Studio Director/Advisor: Avi Friedman

Chapter 7

Figure 7.5: Published with permission of the U.S. Green Building Council.
Figure 7.8: An axonometric sketch in the Ecolonia Route Map pamphlet. Published with permission of Atelier Lucien Kroll.
Figure 7.9: Sketch in the Ecolonia Route Map pamphlet. Design by BEAR Architecture, Architectural and Renovation Consultants, Gouda. Published with Permission of Tjerk Reijenga BEAR Architecten.
Figure 7.10: From *Designing Sustainable Communities* by Judy Corbett and Michael Corbett. Copyright 2000 by Island Press. Reproduced by permission of Island Press, Washington, D.C.
Figure 7.11: From *Designing Sustainable Communities* by Judy Corbett and Michael Corbett. Copyright 2000 by Island Press. Reproduced by permission of Island Press, Washington, D.C.

Research and Project Teams

Greening the Grow Home

Avi Friedman, Director
Vince Cammalleri
Jim Nicell
Francois Dufaux
Joanne Green
Susan Fisher, *Xeriscapes*
Aud Koht, *Environmental Comfort*
Kevin Lee, *Water Efficiency*
Aryan Lirange, *Water Efficiency*
Denis Palin, *Mechanical Systems*
Mark Somers, *Waste Disposal*
Nicola Bullock, *Recycling*
Michelle Takoff, *Recycling*
Client/Funding: Canada Mortgage and
    Housing Corporation
Project Manager: David D'Amour

Le Village: Retooling for the Next Century

Team I
Avi Friedman, Director
Latimer Hu
Manon Lanctôt
Carmen Lee
Richard Lu

Team II
Faculty:
Avi Friedman
Francois Dufaux
Richard Lu

Students:
Gustavo Corredor
Ray Culi
Beate Ioanide
Alejandro Perez
Qin Lin
Rohith Sringeri
Xu Feng
Client: Renaissance Waterfront Association,
    Cornwall, Ontario
Coordinator: Chuck Charlebois
Funding: Human Resources Development Canada

The Next Home

Architect: Avi Friedman
Design Team:
Jasmin S. Fréchette
Cyrus M. Bilimoria
David Krawitz
Doug Raphael
Consultants:
R. Kevin Lee
Julia Bourke
Richard Gingras
Vince Cammalleri
Contributors:
Maxwell Pau
Rosemary Olson
Shawn Lapointe
Hor Hooi Ping (Agnes)

281

Sponsors:
Matériaux Cascades
Canada Mortgage and Housing Corporation
Natural Resources Canada
Société d'habitation du Québec
Fermco Industries Ltd.
Ikea Canada

Quartier Jardins Project

Architects:
Avi Friedman
Jean-Pierre Lagace

Client: Immobiliere du Chemin du Golf Ltée

La Forêt de Marie-Victorin Project

Design:
Jean-Marie Lavoie
Paul Brassard
Avi Friedman
Jean Lamontagne

Clients:
Jean-Marie Lavoie
Paul Brassard

Vision 2020: Common Sense Communities for Montreal's West Island

Team I

Principal Investigator: Avi Friedman

Coordinator: Daniel Casey

Research Team:
Daniel Casey
Julie Giguère
Colin Hanley
Po Suen
Archana Vyas

Team II

Principal Investigator: Avi Friedman

Researcher: Martine B. Whitaker

Graphics: Fu Mingcheng

Funding: Woodcock Foundation, U.S.

Facilitators:
Jeremy Guth
Joyce Jenkins

Index